ArtScroll Series®

Rabbi Nosson Scherman / Rabbi Meir Zlotowitz

General Editors

RABBI AVIGDOR MILLER

Published by

Mesorah Publications, ltd

SPEAKS

Vol. I: Marriage, Children, Shabbos and Loving Hashem

COMPILED AND ANNOTATED BY
RABBI SIMCHA BUNIM COHEN

FIRST EDITION
First Impression ... December 2002
Second Impression ... November 2003
Third Impression ... November 2006

Published and Distributed by
MESORAH PUBLICATIONS, LTD.
4401 Second Avenue / Brooklyn, N.Y 11232

Distributed in Europe by
LEHMANNS
Unit E, Viking Industrial Park
Rolling Mill Road
Jarrow, Tyne & Wear, NE32 3DP
England

GOLDS WORLD OF JUDAICA
3-13 William Street
Balaclava, Melbourne 3183
Victoria Australia

Distributed in South Africa by
KOLLEL BOOKSHOP
Ivy Common
105 William Road
Norwood 2192, Johannesburg, South Africa

Distributed in Israel by
SIFRIATI / A. GITLER
6 Hayarkon Street
Bnei Brak 51127
Distributed in Australia and New Zealand by

ARTSCROLL SERIES®
RABBI AVIGDOR MILLER SPEAKS
© Copyright 2002, by MESORAH PUBLICATIONS, Ltd.
4401 Second Avenue / Brooklyn, N.Y. 11232 / (718) 921-9000 / www.artscroll.com

ISBN:
1-57819-716-3 (hard cover)

Typography by CompuScribe at ArtScroll Studios, Ltd.

Printed in the United States of America by Noble Book Press Corp.
Bound by Sefercraft, Quality Bookbinders, Ltd., Brooklyn N.Y. 11232

This *sefer* is dedicated
to the memory of our cousin

הרב ישראל מרדכי ז"ל
בן דודי הרב החשוב מאד
ר' אליעזר הכהן שליט"א
ואשתו החשובה מאד שתחי'

Yisroel Mordechai (Sruly) Miller זצ"ל

a close grandson of

הגה"צ מורי ורבי אביגדור הכהן מיללער זצ"ל

A young man who in his short life
touched the lives of so many.

He was called a "benefactor"
by a myriad of worthy organizations.

One who had a unique and special קשר
with his saintly Zeide.

His *simchas hachaim*
and his being ראש וראשון לכל דבר
are qualities that will never be forgotten.

May he be a מליץ יושר for for his entire family.

Dedicated by:
Rabbi and Rebetzin Shmuel Elchonon Brog
Rabbi and Mrs. Simcha Bunim Cohen

הסכמת אבי מורי הגאון שליט"א

אשרינו מה טוב חלקנו ...

"How fortunate are we and how pleasant is our lot." We were blessed in our times with a great gaon and tzaddik, a visionary, who although his thoughts and deeds rose to the heavens, yet his teaching and spiritual legacy are firmly planted on our earth.

HaRav HaGaon Rav Avigdor Miller זצ"ל touched the lives of tens of thousands of Jews during his lifetime with his shiurim, lectures and books, as well as with his concise responses to all sorts of questions on practical issues.

גדולים צדיקים במיתתם ...

Tzaddikim have an even greater influence upon the world after their passing. Everyday we witness a growing and intensifying interest in the timeless wisdom taught by this great tzaddik.

We are joyful and proud that our son, Rabbi Simcha Bunim Cohen, a grandson of Rabbi Miller and a foremost disseminator of his teachings, has compiled a book containing a broad spectrum of Rabbi Miller's thoughts. Much effort has been expended in making this work readable and useful. We are mispallel that the wonderful words contained herein will find their target and inpsire Jews everywhere to become students of Rabbi Miller and loyal servants of Hashem.

Moshe Cohen

הסכמת מורי חמי הגאון שליט"א

Braishis! What better description of the Creator! The Eternal Beginner Who constantly Recreates the universe *ex nihilo*.

Braishis! What better definition of Torah! The Guide to eternal growth!

Braishis! What better name for *Klal Yisrael*! The Children of Israel. The One Source of All Being compressed the story of the universe into one word — Begin. Our Master, our Rebbe our Father, HaRav HaGaon Avigdor HaCohen Miller זצוק"ל embraced that word with a passion, and as he grew the world grew with him. Entranced by the Talmud, The Book of Students, i.e. the Book of Growth, and the *Chovos Halevavos*, his guide to the inner world of man and his Creator, he searched endlessly for new ways to neutralize the material shell that obscures *Hashem*. And with the Almighty's blessing he found the vocabulary and the methods to reach and encourage thousands of fellow Jews both to begin and/or strengthen their commitment to Torah. He was one of the few *gedolim* who had a direct influence on all segments of the Jewish people, on men and women, *Chasidim* and *Misnagdim*, *Bnei Torah* and *Baalei Teshuvah*, *Ashkenazim* and *Sefardim*.

Our son-in-law, Harav Simcha Bunim Cohen שליט"א, himself a prominent מרביץ תורה and מחבר, and one of the closest תלמידים of the Zaidie זצוק"ל, has undertaken to perpetuate the Zaidies' word by exposing the broad Jewish public to a share of the inspirational gems to be found in the Zaidies' tapes and seforim.

May Hashem bless him in this and all his other undertakings להגדיל התורה ולהאדירה.

Shmuel Elchonon Brog

מכתב מהגאון ר' ארי מלכיאל קוטלר שליט"א
ראש ישיבה בית מדרש גבוה

כ"ו חשון תשס"ג

ברמב"ם פ"ב מסיוהד"ת הקל הנכבד והנורא הזה מצוה לאהבו
וליראה אותו שנאמר ואהבת את ה' אלקיך וכו'. והאיך היא
הדרך לאהבו ויראתו, בשעה שיתבונן האדם במעשיו וברואיו
הנפלאים הגדולים ויראה מהן חכמתו וכו'. מיד הוא אוהב
ומשבח ומפאר ומתאוה תאוה גדולה לידע השם הגדול וכו'
עכ"ל. ועיין בגמרא יומא דף פו מביא ברייתא ואהבת את
השם וגו' ע"כ. ומבואר שבכלל מצות האהבה להשפיע אהבתו
לאחרים וגם זה בכלל האהבה שרוצה שגם אחרים יאהבוהו ואם
אינו עושה לזה הרי יחסר באהבתו.

הנה הגאון הצדיק מגדולי מרביצי התורה ומשפיע היראה
בדורנו הג"ר אביגדור מיללער זצ"ל אשר בגדול אהבתו מתוך
התבוננות עמוקה במעשיו וברואים וגדלותו בתורה ליחד עצמו
להבין ולהשכיל בחכמות ותבונות המודיעים לו את קונו (כלשון
הרמב"ם סוף הלכות תשובה עיי"ש) והשפיע אהבת השם והעמיד
תלמידים הרבה לתורה ולתעודה בשיעוריו ובדרשותיו המופלאים.

אפריון נמטיה לידידי הרב הגאון ר' שמחה בונם קאהן, רב
ומרביץ תורה בקהילת עטרת ישעי, נכדו של הגאון ר' אביגדור
מיללער זצ"ל שהעתיק מדרשותיו של הגה"צ הנ"ל להמשיך
ולהשפיע גדול אהבה זו על אחרים. ומגלגלים זכות על ידי
זכאי הרב שמחה בונם שליט"א מחבר של כמה ספרי הלכה
חשובים והולך בעקבי זקנו זצ"ל בהשפעה על דרך זו לרבים.
ויה"ר שיתקבלו הדברים בבי מדרשא ויפוצו מעיינות אלו
לרבים להגדיל תורה ולהאדירה.

אריה מלכיאל קוטלר
באאמו"ר הגר"ש זצוק"ל

מכתב מהגאון ר ירוחם אלשין שליט"א
ראש ישיבה בית מדרש גבוה

יום ג׳ יד כסלו תשס"ג

שמחה גדולה היא לנו ולכל עולם התורה ההוצאה לאור עולם
את דבריו הקדושים של הגאון והצדיק המפורסם הרב אביגדור
מיללער זצ"ל. שיחות שנאמרו בשעתם לרבים ועכשיו נכתבו
ע"י נכדו הנעלה הרב הגאון ר׳ שמחה בונם קאהן שליט"א
שעמל ויגע יגיעה עצומה לברר וללבן שיחות אלו. ובודאי ראוי
הוא להחזקת טובה גדולה, שכידוע שדברי הגה"צ זצ"ל
השפיעו הרבה בחייו, ונתפשטו דבריו הק בכל תפוצות
ישראל. ואמרו חז"ל הקדושים גדולים צדיקים במיתתן יותר
מבחייהן, ואשר על כן בהפצת שיחות אלו יתרבה עוד יותר
השפעתו הנוראה בתוך בית ישראל. ובדורינו דור יתום, ובפרט
בזמן האחרון, שכל יום קללתו מרובה מחבירו, והצרות של
הכלל והפרט המה כנחל שוטף רח"ל, צריך כל אחד ואחד
התעוררות לשוב לאבינו שבשמים, ולעבדו ביתר שאת
וביתר עוז. וצריכין חיזוק הרבה בכל ענינים של עבודת השם הן
בלמוד התורה בתפלה ביר"ש ומדות טובות בהשקפת התורה
ובאמונה טהורה. ובעזרת השם יהי׳ לנו הספר הזה דברי צדיק
יסוד עולם לחיזוק ולהתעוררות לכל זה.

ב ע י ר נ ו וווהנני מברך את ידידי הנעלה הרב הגאון ר׳ שמחה בונם שליט"א
רב בקהלת עטרת ישעי שזכה להעמיד קהילה קדושה
עיר התורה דליקוואוד לשם ולתפארת. והוא הולך בדרך אבותיו
הקדושים מאורי הדורות, וממשיך את הדרך של זקנו הגה"צ
זצ"ל. והקב"ה יברכהו בהצלחה גדולה עוד יותר ויותר בעבודת
הקודש, בלימוד התורה ובהרבצת התורה והיראה בחיבוריו
החשובים מאד, ובשיעוריו ושיחותיו הנפלאים מתוך בריאות הגוף
מנוחת הנפש והרחבת הדעת ונחת ממשפחתו החשובה כל הימים.

הכותב והחותם לכבוד התורה ולמודי׳
בכבוד והוקרה
ירוחם אלשין

מכתב הסכמה מהגאון ר דוד צבי שוסטאל שליט"א
ראש ישיבה בית מדרש גבוה

הנני בזה לחזק ידי אהובי ש"ב הרה"ג ר שמחה בונם הכהן
קאהן שליט"א נכד ק"ז הגה"צ ממטרסדורף זצוק"ל ובן דודי
יבל"ח הרב הג הרב ר משה הכהן שליט"א. אשר זכה ברובי מפעליו
בעזרת השם יתברך לימנות בין גדולי מזכי הרבים, הן
בספריו החשובים והנעלים שחיבר בעניני הלכות שבת בשפה
המדוברת אשר נתקבלו בקרב בית ישראל בכבוד גדול והערצה
רבה, והן בהנהלת עדתו החשובה חברי ק"ק עטרת ישעי'
בעירינו עיר התורה ליקוואוד, בנועם מדותיו והליכותיו על אדני
חיזוקי התורה והיראה, ועתה איותה נפשו הטהורה — להוסיף
כהנה — ולהוציא לאור עולם ספר של שיחות שהוקלטו מפי
זקנו — מזקני גדולי התורה והיראה והעבודה ה"ה הגה"צ הג
ר' אביגדור הכהן מילער זצוק"ל דברי חיזוק והדרכה היוצאים
מלב טהור וקדוש אשר סגולתם רק ליכנס ללב מבקשי השם
השואפים ומשתוקקים לעלות בסולם העולה בית-קל — בקניית
מעלות היראה והעבודה — בהוספת ציון המקורות ומראי מקומות
למצוא עיקר הדרכה בספרי הגה"צ זצ"ל שכבר ראו אור הדפוס
— והנה כבר אמרו חז"ל הק מגלגלין זכות ע"י זכאי — ובכן
בטוחני שבעזרת השם בזכות אבוה"ק זי"ע יזכה לברך על
המוגמר ויעשו הדברים פרי תנובה להרבות תורה ועבודה ויראה
בקרב בית ישראל.

והנני בזה לברכו מקרב לב שאכן יצליחנו השי"ת להמשיך
דרכו ועבודתו בקודש ולהוסיף כהנה וכהנה מתוך מנוחת הנפש
ובריות גופא ונהורא מעליא יחד עם נו"ב החשובה העומדת
לימינו תמיד, לאורך ימים ושנים טובים לתפארת ולנחת הוריהם
הגדולים שליט"א, עד כי יבא שילה בב"א.

הכו"ח לכבוד התורה ומרביצי' בטהרה
דוד צבי שוסטאל
אור יד כסלו תשס"ג — פה לייקוואוד יצ"ו

מכתב הסכמה מהגאון ר ישראל ניומאן שליט"א
ראש ישיבה בית מדרש גבוה

מוצש"ק וישלח תשס"ג

שמחה גדולה וגם זכות הוא לנו לחזק ידי ידידנו הרב הגאון
ר' שמחה בונם קאהן שליט"א שנמה חלקו בין מזכי הרבים
בין ע"י חיבוריו בהלכה בפרט בהלכות שבת שמבאר הלכות
מסובכות בלשון צח ובשפה המדוברת שיהא דבר השוה לכל
נפש ובחסדי השי"ת זכה שדבריו הם לתועלת גדול לרבים מקטן
ועד גדול — ובין בתור רב ומרביץ תורה בקהילתו שזכה להקים
לשם ולתפארת קהל עטרת ישעי' שעומד כסדר על המשמר
לחזקים ולעודדם בכל פרט ופרט של עבודת ה' ויראתו.
בתור רב ר' שמחה בונם שליט"א הולך בעקבות זקני הגאון
הצדיק מגדולי מרביצי התורה ומשפיעי היראה בדורנו הרב
אביגדור מיללער זצ"ל שהי' מיוחד בזיכוי הרבים בין בקהילתו
ובין להמוני בני ישראל ע"י הדרשות שלו והקלטות (tapes)
שלהם בפרט להחדיר אהבת ה' בלב כל אחד מישראל
— ובפרט אחר הסתלקו זקנו הגה"צ זצ"ל ר' שמחה בונם
משתדל להמשיך השפעתו ולהפיץ מעינותיו ע"י שיעוריו
בחובת הלבבות.
ובנוסף לזה יגע ביגיעה עצומה לסדר וללבן משיחותיו שיוכל
להוציאם לאור עולם לתועלת הרבים ועכשיו שעומד לברך
על המוגמר ברכתנו נתונה לו מעומק הלב ומהכרת טובה שיזכה
להמשיך בדרך זו להשפיע מתורתו ויראתו מתוך מנוחת הנפש
הבריות הגוף לאורך ימים ושנים טובים עד כי יבא שילה.

הכו"ח לכב התורה ומרביצי
ישראל צבי ניומאן

PREFACE

T IS WITH GREAT TREPIDATION THAT I UNDERTOOK THE writing of this project. It is no simple matter to take the words and thoughts of a Gadol Hador and attempt to put them in print. However, it was the conviction that the words of my master and teacher, the Great Gaon Tzaddik HaRav Avigdor Miller *zt"l*, should be spread to all corners of the Jewish world. His teachings on the way we, as Jewish people, should live our lives has brought countless of individuals closer to Hashem. Both people who have tasted the sweetness of Torah from their youth and those who hadn't yet discovered it have had their lives enriched by HaRav Miller's wise and words.

This book is based on the famous Thursday-night lectures held in HaRav Miller's shul. Thousands of thirsty listeners from all walks of life have gathered there weekly, throughout the years, to drink from HaRav Miller's fountain of knowledge and be inspired.

A few tapes that discuss the sanctity and purpose of Shabbos, loving Hashem, raising children, and the entity of marriage were chosen to be transcribed and edited. All sources mentioned by Rabbi Miller were then researched and recorded. Further information found in other books by Rabbi Miller, regarding these topics, is also noted.

It is my fervent prayer that what I wished to accomplish with the writings of this book will be achieved. I hope that for his disciples it will be a review, and for newcomers it will be an introduction and welcome to the world of HaRav Miller.

ACKNOWLEDGMENTS

HERE ARE NO WORDS CAPABLE OF EXPRESSING THE DEEP *hakaras hatov* that I have for my dear parents, my father and mentor, HaRav HaGaon Rav Moshe Cohen שליט״א, and my mother, Rebbetzin Gitel Cohen שתחי׳. To grow up in such a home was to truly live in a *mikdash me'at* permeated with untold *hasmadah* in Torah, *kedushah,* and *gemilus chasadim.* Furthermore, I would like to extend my heartfelt appreciation to my father שליט״א for being so instrumental in tracking down the many sources quoted in HaRav Miller's lectures.

To my esteemed father-in-law, HaRav HaGaon Rav Shmuel Elchonon Brog שליט״א, and my mother-in-law Rebbetzin Sheina Brog שתחי׳, I would like to express my heartfelt appreciation for their constant input and encouragement which manifests itself in many ways. The chinuch they have instilled in their children is the most eloquent testimony to the timeless practicality of HaRav Miller's זצ״ל teaching.

May they always derive much nachas from their children and grand-children and great-grandchildren.

The void created by the passing of HaRav HaGaon Rav Avigdor Miller זצ״ל is one that cannot be filled. His numerous talks and lectures unfailingly brought to light countless insights and inspired many thousands to vibrant lives of Torah. His impact on me personally has left me humbly grateful to have had the opportunity to be his disciple.

May Hashem grant Rebbetzin Miller תחי׳, many more years of nachas and health with which to enjoy the dynasty they have built. She is the center of power from which we all draw inspiration and strength.

Once again I would like to thank the esteemed Rabbi Meir Zlotowitz שליט״א and Rabbi Nosson Scherman שליט״א for their support in this project. Their interest, devotion, and assistance have made this *sefer* into a reality. May Hashem bless them with many years of success in spreading the words of Torah.

I am deeply indebted to R' Avraham Biderman שליט״א whose advice, comments, and input have been extremely helpful in all aspects of this *sefer*.

I am very grateful to Menucha Mitnick and Tzini Hanover, who typeset the book; Mrs. Faigy Weinbaum who proofread, and Mrs. Hadassah Munk who offered valuable comments.

I would like to express my great appreciation to Mrs. Estie Dicker for her painstaking work in transcribing the tapes. She contributed her expertise to perfecting all aspects of the book and her dedication to this project was indispensable.

My heartfelt appreciation is extended to Mrs. Sara Chava Mizrachi who edited all of the tapes upon which this book is based. With great talent she was able to leave Rabbi Miller's indelible style untouched and unaffected by all the necessary editing.

Finally, I would like to take this opportunity to express my deep appreciation for the constant support and assistance I have always received from my wife, Basya Rivka תחי׳, who has had a major share in all aspects of the publication of this *sefer*. May Hashem grant us much nachas from our dear children and allow us to achieve ever-greater heights in His service.

Simcha Bunim Cohen

TABLE OF CONTENTS

FOREWORD:
A GLIMPSE INTO
THE GREATNESS OF
HARAV AVIGDOR MILLER זצ״ל

by Rabbi Avrohom Leshinsky and Rabbi Yehezkel Danziger

ORE THAN A YEAR HAS GONE BY SINCE THAT BITTER DAY when HaRav HaGaon Rav Avigdor Miller זצ״ל passed from this world to the next. Bitter in the sense described by the prophet (*Amos* 8:10) when he said, *And its end like a bitter day.* "No day is more bitter than the day of death," Rav Miller would say, for it marks the end of all possibility of further achievement. For Rav Miller himself, however, it was a day when a special radiance shone forth from his holy face, as he recalled and thanked his Master for all the great kindnesses He had bestowed upon him in the course of a long life.

This was the day for which Rav Miller had prepared all his life. As he often said, "A person should prepare himself to be able to say to Hakadosh Baruch Hu on his deathbed, 'I love You, and I thank You for the wonderful life You gave me, and for all the kindnesses You bestowed upon me.'" To see Rav Miller on that last day was to see someone "serving Hashem in joy" in the fullest sense.

To witness greatness is a rare privilege. But it carries with it a special challenge. The true tzaddik never reveals more than a fraction of his greatness. Even to those closest to him, he affords but passing glimpses into the sublime heights of his soul. How could it be otherwise, when we who are not great lack the very mental images by which to perceive what is beyond the range of ordinary human excellence. This was doubly true of HaRav Avigdor Miller זצ״ל, who made a concerted effort to conceal his greatness. He lived by the credo of הַצְנֵעַ לֶכֶת עִם אֱלֹקֶיךָ, which he translated as *walk secretly with your God* (Michah 6:8). "Perform the same everyday activities as everyone else — while cleaving in your mind to Hashem," he would say. To see Rav Miller in action was to see only the outermost manifestation of his extraordinarily radiant mind. To hear his words was to catch an echo — but only an echo — of the great roar of love of Hashem that welled up from the deepest parts of his soul.

No writer can truly portray that which he can only dimly perceive. But no witness to greatness can hold back his recollections of the tantalizing glimpses he caught. It is thus with full knowledge of our inadequacy that we undertake the irrepressible task of preserving for posterity a sketch of the most unusual personality we shall probably ever meet.

Rav Miller was born in the United States in 1909, at a time when yeshivos were almost non-existent and Torah observance was rare among the American-born youth. Despite his family's poverty, which drove so many others to think first and foremost of financial security, Rav Miller exhibited from his earliest youth a strong desire for truth and a love of Hashem and His Torah. He was the "Avraham Halvri," the "Avraham of the other side," of his time, for he stood on one side of the great river of American life, while the rest of his world stood on the other. It is almost impossible for the modern generation that has grown up in a world in which Torah, yeshivos, *Chassidus*, and *shemiras hamitzvos* flourish widely, to appreciate what it meant for a young person to be frum — let alone become a ben Torah — in those days of rampant Americanization and assimilation.

Rav Miller was blessed with an abundance of Heavenly assistance in overcoming the sea of religious indifference that flowed all around him. Whereas it is the nature of a person to be influenced by the standards of the society around him, Rav Miller from his earliest days was prepared to steer his own course. Early on he developed a strong yearning for truth and a fierce will to pursue it to its logical ends, regardless of the obstacles placed in his path or the difficulties encountered on the way.

Our Sages teach us that one who sets out to purify himself is helped by Heaven to attain that goal. In his old age he would recount a number of inspiring thoughts he heard as a child. He remembered a teacher telling him once that when he recited *Modeh Ani* in the morning, he should reflect on how fortunate he was to have been given another day of life — and how many people had not been so fortunate! This thought made such a lasting impression on him that he was still able to picture the face of that teacher eight decades later. As anyone familiar with his lectures and tapes can attest, it was a thought he repeated numerous times throughout his long life.

Once, as a young boy in Baltimore, he came out after Ma'ariv from shul and heard two old European Jews talking to each other. One said, "Ah! What a *geshmacke* Ma'ariv this was." The man rubbed his hands together in pleasure. Rav Miller would often tell what a deep impression it made upon him to discover that praying could be "*geshmack.*"

His first encounter with the classic mussar work, *Chovos Halevavos,* was as a teenager, in a *sefarim* store on the Lower East Side of New York. For the rest of his life, this *sefer* served as his constant companion and the foundation for so much of his thinking.

Rav Miller excelled in so many facets of Torah life, thought, and service to Hashem that a full-length biography would be needed to begin to do justice to his unique personality. Time and space do not allow us to do so. In the brief space available to us in this foreword, we will therefore offer just a brief description of some of his more extraordinary ways. The task of rounding out the picture will of necessity be left for future volumes, G-d willing.

Time

R AV MILLER TAUGHT HIS FAMILY AND FOLLOWERS THE PRECIOUS VALUE of time. He would often cite the verse: לִמְנוֹת יָמֵינוּ כֵּן הוֹדַע, *teach us to count our days* (Psalms 90:12). This, he would explain, was a request by Moshe Rabbeinu to Hakadosh Baruch Hu that He teach us to count our days *properly.* We should appreciate how valuable each day is, and utilize to the utmost *every* moment of it. "It pays to be born to live just one minute," he said. The notion of "killing time" was anathema to him. Wasting time, he would explain, is like suicide. Since a person's life span is fixed by Heaven, and a moment wasted can never be made up, wasting time is really no different than cutting one's life short.

Rav Miller epitomized the use of time to its fullest. His schedule of davening, learning, and teaching was tightly kept. Even his daily exercise routine of walking was precisely kept. People who wished to catch a few words with him knew exactly what time to meet him at which corner, and they would then walk along with him and converse briefly.

When attending a wedding, he would hold on to his coat. Once, when a grandchild offered to hold it for him, he declined, saying that it served to remind him that he must soon leave to return to his learning. On another occasion, when a bar mitzvah in the family required traveling a great distance, he politely refused to attend, saying that he had a great "*farher*" (exam) to prepare for, and could not afford the time.

One who values something as precious eventually develops a special appreciation for the finer aspects of its qualities. There grows in him a keen sense of how to extract the maximum benefit from that which he holds dear. Rav Miller was a connoisseur of time. Not only was time to be used to its utmost, but different periods of time were to be utilized in different ways, according to their special meanings. Shabbos was a time to contemplate the greatness of the Creator and His special relationship with His people. Rosh Chodesh was a time to recall and acknowledge the many kindnesses bestowed by Hashem in the just completed month, as well as a time to pray for all the good of the month just beginning. And each Yom Tov had its own unique meaning to which a thinking person ought devote himself, reflections to spur him on to ever-greater achievements in his career of serving Hashem.

Life is full of events both commonplace and rare. A Jew must surely participate in these events according to the prescribed actions of halachah. But to participate in these events with profound insights of Torah thought was a hallmark of Rav Miller's teaching. "When you dance at a wedding," he would remark, "don't dance with an empty head. You are putting in so much energy into this activity, isn't it a pity not to think about what you are really doing? By making happy the hearts of the chassan and kallah, you are emulating the ways of Hashem, for He too is engaged in gladdening the hearts of a chassan and kallah."

Every event of life has its lesson to teach. Every mundane task can be utilized to garner greater understanding and a greater love of Hashem. His lectures were full of practical advice on how to put the idle moments of life to great use. Lists of ideas to contemplate while sitting at a wedding waiting for the next course to be served or the next dance to begin. Reflections for a housewife standing beside her washing machine waiting for the laundry to be done. Considerations of Hashem's great kindnesses to brighten the dull moments of life. Noble thoughts with which to furnish the empty rooms of our minds.

"Teach us to count our days," Moshe Rabbeinu asked. Few have counted them more carefully or wisely than Rav Miller ל״צז.

Striving toward perfection

ONE OF THE MOST RECURRING THEMES OF RAV MILLER'S TEACHING WAS the need to work toward greater accomplishment. A person is put in this world to achieve, not merely to avoid sinning, he would say. He would offer a striking parable to illustrate this point. A trucker was sent to the west coast to pick up a load of valuable merchandise and return it to the east coast. The owner of the company, having had previous unpleasant experiences, called in the driver before his departure to warn him to drive carefully and not damage the truck or be involved in any road accidents. After three weeks the driver returned and reported to the owner that his trip had been a great success — there was not one scratch on the truck. "Fine," said the owner, "but where is the merchandise?" "Oh!" said the driver, "I was so focused on not damaging the truck that I forgot to pick up the merchandise." We too come into this world with strict warnings not to sin. But we are also expected to make something of ourselves, to return our souls to our Maker filled with accomplishments, not just with a clean but empty slate.

The main arena of accomplishment is internal, not external. To perfect one's character, to love Hashem and do His will. These are accomplishments anyone can attain. They require no special genius, wealth or opportunities. But they do require training and commitment.

Rav Miller would often repeat the words of the *Mesillas Yesharim* about letting a mitzvah slip away: "There is no danger so great as that danger." Consistency was his byword. There are no days off from the service of Hashem, and no vacations from the pursuit of success in the course He has laid out for us.

In his lexicon, vacation from work meant more time to learn. He arranged for numerous shiurim and *chaburos* to be given in his shul on the long Shabbos afternoons of the summer, and on Sundays throughout the year. "Learning on Sunday from early morning and throughout the day" was the motto of his shul. At his very last Thursday night lecture, someone asked how *"bein hazemanim"* [intersession in the yeshivos] was to be spent. "Learning all the time," was his response. "Why are you wasting your life?"

Consistency had another meaning for him as well. It meant paying attention to small things. Small things repeated often eventually add up to something big. When Rav Miller was mashgiach in Yeshivas Rav Chaim Berlin, he made it a practice each day to ponder one difficulty or oddity in the prayers as he walked to and from the yeshivah. He would jot down his thoughts every few days, and these eventually gave rise to his book on prayer, *Halleli Nafshi*.

His mussar *vaadim* (small seminars on ethics) were geared toward practical results. This meant focusing on one idea for weeks on end, during which time the participants were expected to work on internalizing the idea and implementing it in their personal lives. "Be consistent," he would say. Don't jump from one thing to another. Work on one improvement in character until you have attained some measure of it, before moving on to the next one. Greatness comes in increments, not in one giant leap.

His entire method of teaching flowed from this perspective. He did not believe in "fast results." True success comes through diligence. Although he completed teaching numerous *mesechtos* of Shas and a number of classic mussar *sefarim* many times, he would emphasize that each line of Gemara mastered was a success in its own right, and each insight of *emunah* and love of Hashem garnered was a worthy accomplishment. In his own life, it was the accumulation of thousands upon thousands of these individual successes and accomplishments that stands as one measure of his greatness. As anyone who listened to him can attest, he had a virtually inexhaustible fund of insights to impart to his listeners day after day.

Diligence and Love of Torah:

THE TRUE TALMID CHACHAM IS DISTINGUISHED BY HIS LOVE OF TORAH and his diligence in studying it. Rav Miller's diligence in this respect was truly remarkable. About him may be said without exaggeration that "his mouth never ceased speaking words of Torah." Even as a young boy his devotion to studying Torah was legendary. HaRav HaGaon R' Mordechai Gifter *zt"l*, who remembered Rav Miller from his boyhood, told how Rav Miller would study Torah so diligently that he would wear out the elbows of his sweaters.

Rav Miller would recollect with fondness the "good old days" when he studied in the famed yeshivah of Slabodka in Lithuania. Materially, conditions were difficult, especially for a boy raised in America. There was no running water in the yeshivah, and little to eat. Yet here was where he learned from early morning until late at night, without interruption, in the company of great talmidei chachamim. In this setting of physical want, Torah became the sweetness and pleasure of his life, and remained that way through all his long life.

A young man by nature approaches his Torah studies with a sense of freshness for his subject and a special ardor for his endeavor. Yet a passion for Torah knowledge and self-improvement, and a burning ambition for accomplishment, was especially palpable in the halls of the Slabodka yeshivah. Its atmosphere crackled with inspiration. It was a mark of Rav Miller's greatness that he somehow managed to maintain the youthful enthusiasm of his Slabodka years through all the twists and turns of his long and varied life. Every shiur, every lecture, every passing comment brimmed with ardor for Torah and mitzvos. The sense of freshness he brought to every topic was astonishing. The ideas were not new. They came from Tanach, from the Sages, from the *Chovos Halevavos,* the *Rambam, Rabbeinu Yonah,* and the *Mesillas Yesharim.* Yet somehow they emerged fresh and exciting when they came filtered through the prism of Rav Miller's mind.

Perhaps one secret of this special ability to bring new insight to eternal ideas was his extraordinary diligence in *chazarah,* reviewing his learning — often and regularly. Most of us think of review as simply an aid to memory. That it surely is. But to a serious and inquisitive mind it is also an eye-opener. As the basic facts of a Torah subject become more fully grasped with each review, secondary bits of data suddenly emerge from their shadow to cast a new light on the entire matter. And as these become more fully assimilated, still others come to the fore in an endless parade of revelation of profundity. The resulting understanding is truly panoramic and seems breathtakingly fresh to the audience of fortunate listeners.

Rav Miller emphasized over and over again the importance of *chazarah.* "Without review," he would say, "you can say good-bye to all you've learned." He himself constantly reviewed his learning. His personal *sefarim* were worn out from long and repeated use. Someone once asked him how he should express his gratitude to Hashem for the privilege of having completed the entire Shas. Rav Miller responded, "By reviewing it again. It will then become apparent to you that you have not yet finished Shas, for there are many sections that are still not clear to you, and entire *sugyos* whose very outlines you do not yet fully grasp."

Rav Miller felt the pressure not only to learn Torah, but to fully master it. He would often express this by saying that he had a major exam to prepare for, and he could therefore not afford to spend time on social occasions. His extraordinary knowledge of Torah was often underestimated. But to those who were around him constantly, it was abundantly evident from the numerous shiurim he gave each week on as many as ten different *mesechtos* (tractates) of the Talmud, *Rambam, Shulchan Aruch Orach Chaim, Yoreh Deah, Chosen Mishpat, Ketzos HaChoshen, Minchas Chinuch,* and Mussar *Sefarim,* in addition to the many lectures with which the larger world is more familiar. No one but a true *gadol baTorah* could possibly have taught so many difficult and diverse topics each week, with so little time to prepare.

Rav Miller's pleasure in learning Torah was manifest. Torah for Rav Miller was not just a holy obligation, but truly a labor of love and joy. He would always try to convey the sense of this to others. He once gave the following analogy. When someone learns through a complicated *sugya*, masters its details and various opinions, and then happens upon the difficulty raised by Rav Akiva Eiger in his *Gilyon HaShas* (printed in the margins of the standard *Vilna* Shas), he feels like someone who has finished a large dinner and who is then served a tantalizing and delicious dessert.

To live Torah, to love Torah, to sing the wonders and beauties of the Torah, to love Hashem with all one's heart and with all one's soul, this was the credo by which Rav Miller lived day in and day out, for many a long year. No one who heard his shiurim, his lectures, or his more than 2,000 tapes can fail to have been inspired by his great vision, the depth of his insight, and his overarching love of Hashem. The world was greatly enriched by his presence for ninety-plus years. We are poorer now that he has gone, much poorer. But we who were privileged to know him or hear him still carry within us the memories of his greatness. Indeed, with the slightest jog of our memories, we can still *hear* his unique voice resounding in our ears, calling out to us to grow as we live, to seek ever-greater heights of knowledge of Hashem and ever-greater passion in our love for Him. For those who remember him, this book will serve as a warm reminder of the splendors we once knew. To those who were not so privileged, this book, it is hoped, will serve to kindle anew the bonfire of spiritual and intellectual grandeur, and the boundless love of Hashem, that was HaRav HaGaon Rav Avigdor Miller z"tl. יהי זכרו ברוך.

TEN ASPECTS OF SHABBOS 1

E'U KI HASHEM NASAN LACHEM ES HASHABBOS,[1] THE Torah tells us. This unusual expression is not found in connection with any other mitzvah: "*Re'u* — see — that Hashem gave you the Shabbos" means that you must contemplate the Shabbos. In fact, *every* mitzvah must be done with *chochmah* and *da'as*. Nevertheless, since the Torah uses this expression in reference to Shabbos, it implies that we should utilize that day especially for contemplation, and the point we should contemplate is: What is the Shabbos all about?[2]

When you pass by a mezuzah you are wise if you think about its purpose

ALL MITZVOS MUST BE DONE WITH THE INTENTION FOR WHICH Hakadosh Baruch Hu gave them. In many places the reason is stated openly, and we are expected to keep that reason in mind and not mere-

---

1. *Shemos* 16:29
2. See *A Nation Is Born* p. 220 (16:29)

ly perform the mitzvah mechanically. A Jew must live with *machshavah*. When you pass by a mezuzah, for example, you are wise if you think, "Why do we need a mezuzah?" If you see children wearing tzitzis, you're intelligent if you stop to think about the purpose of tzitzis, as stated in the Torah: *Ur'isem oso*[3] — when you see them, *uzchartem* — you should remember, and there is a great deal to remember — *es kol mitzvos. ...*

On Shabbos, we're expressly commanded, *Re'u*, and so we should look into this more than into any other instance of serving Hashem. Let's contemplate ten points to ponder about Shabbos, although there are many more.

Hashem created the world from nothing

THE FIRST POINT IS: "*KI SHEISHES YAMIM ASAH HASHEM ES hashamayim ve'es ha'aretz.*[4] Before Hashem made the world, it had no existence — Hashem made a *beriyah yesh me'ayin*. There were no physical elements and no forces of nature — everything was imagined by Hashem into existence: "*Ki Hu amar vayehi*, He said, and it came into being."[5]

We must labor all our lives in order to gain even a little of the impact of this stunning idea. Whenever we see something in the world, we're actually seeing the Will of Hashem. One of the most important of all the purposes of Shabbos is to gain *emunah* that Hashem is the only Truth there is. Everything is in the world because He wishes it to be; nothing has any intrinsic existence. *Emes Malkeinu* — our King is true; *efes zulaso* — there's nothing other than Him. When I look at you, I see Hashem — you are a manifestation of His Will. Whatever we see is nothing but a sign of Hakadosh Baruch Hu's achievements.

Whenever we see something in the world we are seeing the will of Hashem

SHABBOS IS A TIME TO THINK ABOUT THAT POINT. IN FACT, THE GEMARA[6] says, when you say "*Vayechulu hashamayim*" on Friday night, two *malachim* come and put their hands on your head, and they say,

---

3. *Bamidbar* 15:39
4. *Shemos* 20:11
5. See *A Nation Is Born* p. 276, (20:11) *Sing You Righteous* p. 210 (470)
6. *Shabbos* 119a

"*Vesar avonecha vachatas'cha techupar*[7] — Your sins will depart and be forgiven." That moment is so important, it is like Yom Kippur. And even though you say it many times, each time is a priceless gem that you're adding to your intellect. Each time you are understanding more and more thoroughly, more and more deeply, and that is the achievement for which Hakadosh Baruch Hu made this world. The purpose of everything Hashem made is for people to recognize the Maker.[8]

Isn't it a pity that people who are *shomer Shabbos* don't think about this number one requirement? Let's keep in mind that Hakadosh Baruch Hu wants us to learn about His Presence and His greatness; about the fact that He is the One Who existed before anything else. Every moment that anything continues to exist, it is only because He continues to will its existence.

Reishis chochmah yiras Hashem[9] — awareness of Hashem is the first and most important form of knowledge. If people gain that from their mental attitude toward Shabbos, it is an atonement for their sins.

All of nature and all of science stems from the knowledge that the world was made by a super-Intelligence. Every object in nature is of endless wisdom; no matter how deeply you'll fathom the profundity of a natural object, you'll never be finished with the miracles of plan and purpose that unfold before your eyes. The deeper you delve into it, the more you see how little you know. Everything is so planned, so perfectly set out to serve a purpose, and the purpose is served with the minimum of expenditure of effort. There are millions upon millions of examples of Hashem's wisdom in the world, and each one is a miracle in itself.

When someone has a wound that causes a rupture in a blood vessel, in a few seconds he could lose enough blood to cause him to die. But this rarely happens, because as soon as the blood vessel experiences a trauma, certain movements are initiated along the vessel's wall, and these movements cause a spastic action that begins to close up the blood vessel automatically. Even some blood vessels that are as wide as three-eighths an inch in diameter can close up automatically, even before the blood begins to clot. If this did not happen, the injury could cause a person to perish within twenty seconds.[10]

---

7. Yeshaya 6:7
8. See *Sing You Righteous* p. 209 (468)
9. *Tehillim* 111:10
10. See *Awake My Glory* p. 18 (41)

We see immense purposefulness in reaction to a blow or a cut, which enables living creatures to sustain injuries and still continue to live. If not for this arrangement, no one could survive in this world.

A second point to remember about Shabbos is that a double portion of mann fell for Shabbos. Hakadosh Baruch Hu provided the people with sustenance every day in the midbar. A mysterious, nourishing substance fell; no other supplement was needed to provide the people with proteins or starches or vitamins.

Shabbos teaches us trust

SINCE HAKADOSH BARUCH HU DIDN'T WANT THEM TO GO OUT TO GET the mann on Shabbos, a double portion fell on erev Shabbos. The two challos you have on your table at every Shabbos meal are to remind you of the very important lesson that the Jew who is loyal to Hashem's mitzvos will not lose out by keeping them. We have to live with full trust that Hakadosh Baruch Hu is in charge, despite all the conditions and hardships imposed by the nations of the world and by those who oppose the Torah. The Jew who is loyal to the Torah will continue to prosper. The mann is the demonstration of *bitachon*, showing that Hakadosh Baruch Hu is in control.[11]

The Gemara[12] states that *pesi'ah gassah*, hurrying during the weekdays, takes away 1/500 of a person's eyesight. Anxiety, such as worrying that you will miss your bus, miss getting to your job on time, and all kinds of other worries — everyone has anxiety — has a physical effect on people. The Sages tell us it takes away part of your eyesight. David Hamelech said, "*Asheshah mika'as einai*[13] — My eye is worn out because of agitation." And the Gemara[14] asks, What's the remedy to this damage caused by the week's frantic efforts to make a living? "*Lehadreih bikedusha deveShimsha*" — to say Kiddush Friday night. *Vayechulu hashamayim veha'aretz* — Hakadosh Baruch Hu created everything and He is now conducting all the affairs of the world — nothing happens without His supervision. So why should we worry about anything? Sit back and enjoy life; Hakadosh Baruch Hu is in charge. On Friday night a Jew reminds himself not to be agitated in the week to come.[15]

---

11. See *A Nation Is Born* p. 216 (16:25)
12. *Berachos* 43b
13. *Tehillim* 6:8
14. *Berachos* 43b
15. See *Rejoice O Youth* page 370

Worrying is a waste of time

THERE IS A VERY IMPORTANT PRINCIPLE INVOLVED HERE: TRUST IN Hashem, and look back on your life and see how you wasted time worrying about so many things, and you're still here to tell the tale. When it comes to physical matters, Hakadosh Baruch Hu is in charge, and if something is destined to be, it is going to be, whether you worry about it or not.

Of course, a person must exercise caution. Hakadosh Baruch Hu wants you to do things to protect yourself. It's a good idea to take out insurance,[16] and don't put any toys on the steps. Make sure there is nothing that will cause you to fall, and take care of worn-out electric wires. When you cross the street, don't be reckless; don't touch your eyes or your mouth unless you've washed your hands with soap and water; and keep away from people who have colds. Certainly you have to do all of these things, but do not worry unnecessarily about things that are out of our control. "Cast your burden upon Me," Hakadosh Baruch Hu said; I'll take care of your worries. The mann was given as a double portion before Shabbos in order to reassure the Jew that the world is not a random, chaotic place.

Every Shabbos in the *Beis Hamikdash*, they took the *lechem hapanim* off the table and set out new *lechem*. The *lechem hapanim* tells us that Hakadosh Baruch Hu is *Nosen lechem lechol basar*[17] — He supplies all the living with their needs, and He will continue to support you, week after week. *Kol mezonosav shel adam kesuvim lo meirosh hashanah*[18] — all of a persons income is fixed (each year) from Rosh Hashanah. This is not a promise for luxuries; it doesn't mean you can waste your money, but when people live normally and rationally, they have the full right to expect Hakadosh Baruch Hu to provide for them, and he will continue to provide, forever and ever. Shabbos should remind you that Hashem is in charge.

The best thing in the world is to give thanks to Hashem

MIZMOR SHIR LEYOM HASHABBOS, A PSALM, A SONG FOR THE Shabbos day. We sing on the Shabbos day, "*Tov lehodos laShem.*"[19]

---

16. See *Responsa Igros Moshe O.C.* 2:111
17. *Tehillim* 136:25
18. *Beitzah* 16a
19. *Tehillim* 92:2

What is good? The best thing in the world is to give thanks to Hashem — that's our job, and Shabbos is the time.[20] Didn't He support you for six days before Shabbos, and don't you have something to eat on Shabbos? Don't worry about the rest of your days. And you have to say, "*Ki simachtani Hashem befa'olecha ...*"[21] — You've made me happy, Hashem, with Your handiwork; I sing at the deeds of Your hands." It's a wonderful world! A man stopped me in the street and asked me, "Isn't it hot to wear such a long coat today?"

I told him, "Look at the beautiful sky. Isn't it a wonderful day? Look at the bright sunshine ...." He smiled, and he shook my hand and thanked me. We have to teach ourselves the happiness of life. Life is happy, and Hashem wants us to enjoy this great gift of *olam hazeh*. *Olam chessed yibaneh*[22] — the world is built on kindness. We have a kindly Father. Instead of complaining, instead of ignoring all the blessings, let's utilize Shabbos and sing of the deeds of Hashem's Hands.[23]

Let's always be happy about Hashem's phenomena

SUMMER AND WINTER, SPRING AND FALL, LET'S ALWAYS BE HAPPY about Hashem's phenomena. Each one is a separate chorus in that great banquet that He serves us in this life. The weather is constantly providing different forms of enjoyment ... rain is wonderful. We ask for it, we pray for it. Winds are wonderful. Cold is very good — cold causes the grass to stop producing. Otherwise the earth would become arid. It would overproduce and lose all its fertility. And at the right time, the cold stops and the earth regains everything it needs in preparation for the coming spring. Cold is a great blessing. *Bisvunah meshaneh itim!* Hashem brings the darkness with wisdom. Don't think darkness is a simple thing. Darkness is a wonderful arrangement. Hakadosh Baruch Hu's world couldn't be beat for simplicity and accuracy and efficiency. Hakadosh Baruch Hu arranges the system of the seasons and of the days and nights in such a wonderful mechanism, and we don't begin to appreciate how great is the wisdom of the wonderful and efficient machinery of *olam hazeh*.

20. See *Awake My Glory* p. 375 (1184)
21. *Tehillim* 92:5
22. *Tehillim* 89:3
23. See *Sing You Righteous* p. 229 (503), *The Beginning* p. 50 (1:31), *Fortunate Nation* p. 64 (5:12)

Shabbos should make you happy and filled with *bitachon*, confidence, in the kindliness of Hashem. Try to appreciate that great gift — that's part of the purpose of Shabbos.

Shabbos demonstrates that Am Yisrael is the nation for whom the world was created

THE THIRD POINT TO PONDER ABOUT SHABBOS IS WHAT THE Torah says openly about Shabbos — that it is *zeicher litzi'as Mitzrayim*.[24] Shabbos commemorates the creation of Am Yisrael.[25] *Beini uvein Bnei Yisrael os hi le'olam*[26] — Shabbos is a sign of a covenant between Hashem and us. That's how great we are in His Eyes! Shabbos demonstrates that Am Yisrael is the nation for whom the world was created.[27] The entire Torah echoes with this amazing reality. *Meirosh mikedem nesuchah* — Shabbos was anointed from the beginning. Hashem was waiting for a nation to step forward, to volunteer to serve Him. Hakadosh Baruch Hu waited ten generations from Adam until Noach and was disappointed. Then He waited ten generations from Noach until Avraham and was disappointed. When Avraham came, Hakadosh Baruch Hu said, "This is the one I've been waiting for!"[28]

When Hakadosh Baruch Hu created the world, He was like a chassan who didn't have a kallah yet, who bought a very expensive diamond ring and was holding it for his future kallah. Hashem created Shabbos at the beginning, and was waiting with that diamond ring. Who would be the kallah worthy of this ring? When Bnei Yisrael stepped forward and said, "*Na'aseh venishma*, we will do whatever You tell us — we will give our lives for You, even before knowing what You want from us," then Hashem said, "I'm giving you this ring. *Harei at mekudeshes li*, I am making you an *am kadosh* for Me alone, forever and ever. *Yetzi'as Mitzrayim* is a demonstration of Hashem's choosing of Am Yisrael."[29]

Therefore, if a non-Jew wants to keep Shabbos, he is trespassing on holy ground, just like somebody who wants to practice medicine and never went to medical school or wasn't licensed by the state: He's committing a crime. *Akum sheshavas chayav misah*, says the

---

24. *Devarim* 5:15
25. See *Fortunate Nation* p. 66 (5:15); *A Nation Is Born* p. 276 (20:11), p. 426 (31:13)
26. *Shemos* 31:18
27. See *Awake My Glory* p. 304 (978)
28. *Avos* 5:2
29. See *Sing You Righteous* p. 259 (550)

Gemara — a gentile is not licensed to keep Shabbos, and he may not keep it even on Sunday or Tuesday or Friday. If he does, he's *chayav misah*, because he's stealing. Shabbos, this crown of glory, was kept only for Am Yisrael.[30]

The Gemara[31] tells that the gentiles saw that the Jews were enjoying the mann, so a gentile tried to taste it, but he found that it was a bitter mush; he couldn't take it. But when some deer fed on the mann, and the gentiles ate the deer, they tasted the taste of the mann in the deer's flesh, and they found it delicious. Why was the mann so bitter when a gentile ate it directly, but when they tasted it by means of the deer, it was delectable? The answer is that the mann is only for people who have the right to keep Shabbos and do it properly; Shabbos is a great blessing for the Jewish people.

Therefore, Hashem told the gentiles: Don't keep Shabbos. For them, it's a berachah to work all the time and not to keep any Shabbos. Long hours are a blessing for the gentiles[32] — they'll live longer. For a gentile, work is a blessing, while Shabbos is a curse for him. It's not for him to enter the sanctuary of the Shabbos.

"Idleness leads to immorality," the Gemara[33] says. Idleness leads to mental illness, and so it's a blessing for mankind that they're busy. On Shabbos, there are thirty-nine forms of work that we cannot do. How do we know that? We learn it from the Mishkan.

The Mishkan is the most unlikely way to learn. It was built in the midbar using thirty-nine forms of craftsmanship, and what was done to build the Mishkan should be avoided on Shabbos, in order to "build the Shabbos." What's the connection? Shabbos is also a *Beis Hamikdash*, a sanctuary. When Shabbos comes, we're entering a sanctuary, and a sanctuary is only for those who are permitted to come in. The Torah calls us "*Kohanei Hashem*" and "*mamleches Kohanim.*" We are a nation of *Kohanim*, and therefore we have a right to come into the sanctuary of Shabbos. But, the Torah says, "*hazar hakareiv yumas*,"[34] a stranger who comes into the sanctuary must be put to death. A gentile must not come into the sanctuary. There was a sign outside the *Beis Hamikdash*, written in Latin, stating that any gentile who enters shall be put to death, and the Roman government permitted it.

30. See *A Nation Is Born* p. 271 (20:8)
31. *Sanhedrin* 58b
32. See *Awake My Glory* p. 162 (553), *Sing You Righteous* p. 206 (464)
33. *Kesubos* 59b
34. *Bamidbar* 1:56

This is the great lesson of Shabbos — *beini uvein Bnei Yisrael os hi le'olam*[35] — it's a sign between Hashem and Bnei Yisrael! Utilize Shabbos to think about that. Think who you are — a *goy kadosh*, a holy nation chosen by Hashem.[36]

Shabbos should be utilized for learning Torah

A FOURTH POINT TO CONSIDER ABOUT SHABBOS IS, AS THE GEMARA[37] tells us, *BeShabbos nitenah Torah leYisrael*, the Torah was given on Shabbos. This was no accident; the purpose is for us to know that Shabbos shouldn't be wasted. Of course Shabbos should be used for eating and drinking, as well as for some sleep. But eventually, we must get up and utilize part of the day to contemplate that great gift that Hakadosh Baruch Hu gave our nation — the Torah. In ancient times, Shabbos was a day when the Jewish nation assembled in the "Shabbos houses." During the times of *Bayis Sheini*, a gentile who visited Eretz Yisrael wrote that on Shabbos, the Jews all gather in their Shabbos houses and spend the entire day meditating in their sacred Scriptures. These are a gentile's words, so we should surely understand that the Shabbos is a glorious opportunity to accomplish something in the knowledge of the great gift Hashem gave us when He gave us the Torah.[38]

A fifth aspect is that Shabbos is *"me'ein Olam Haba."* You enter *Olam Haba* only once you're ready for it — you have to prepare yourself! If, for example, you have to visit the king of England, you can't just walk in and stick out your hand! There are chamberlains with whom you make an appointment long in advance, and they help you rehearse: how you should walk in — so many steps, and you stop; how you bow down and stand up and keep quiet until you're addressed; how much you should talk; then, when you hear the signal, how you should back out. They tell you exactly how to prepare for that appointment.

And you have to rehearse for *Olam Haba*, too. What do you do to rehearse? Know that Gan Eden is the purpose of our existence. No matter how good this world is, no matter how fortunate you are, it will come to an end. There is death, there is a grave, and the body is destroyed in this world. To know the eternity of the soul is our great

---

35. *Shemos* 31:17
36. See *A Nation Is Born* p. 429 (31:17), *Awake My Glory* Chapter 12
37. *Shabbos* 86b
38. See *Sing You Righteous* p. 269 (582)

function here. Someone who doesn't believe in *Olam Haba* will not get *Olam Haba*.

You must strengthen your belief in Olam Haba

SO HOW DO YOU PREPARE FOR *OLAM HABA*? FIRST AND FOREMOST, BY learning how to believe in it — you must strengthen your *emunah* in the soul's eternity constantly. This is extremely important, because it's largely ignored. If we don't talk about *Olam Haba*, it becomes further and further away from our minds, and then people don't actually believe in it. This is such a great tragedy because these people will be very disappointed eventually. It's a *klal gadol*: if you don't believe in something, you won't get it. For instance, if you don't have *emunah sheleimah* that Yom Kippur atones for your sins, Yom Kippur will not atone.

Shabbos reminds us
to prepare for the next world

AND SO, *ME'EIN OLAM HABA* OF SHABBOS IS A VALUABLE OPPORTUNITY. Your table is spread with good things to eat; and you must realize that *Olam Haba* will be the same thing, only a million times better. Food for the mind is even more enjoyable than the food in your mouth. The food we eat takes work: you have to chew the food to grind it up, and then your tongue kneads the food, and swallowing is also a job, and so is digesting. At least it's enjoyable and nutritious, and we thank Hashem for it. But while you're enjoying your food, think of the great *seudah*, the banquet that lasts forever.

You'll never get tired of eating there. *Olam Haba* is joy following joy, pleasure after pleasure. We have to picture *Olam Haba*, and the more you picture, the more your *emunah* grows in you. So as you sit at your Shabbos table enjoying the delicacies of Shabbos, think about *Olam Haba*. If you don't, sitting at the table and eating is a real waste; nothing will remain of the good things you or your wife labored to prepare. At least there should be some gain — become a *ma'amin* in *Olam Haba* as a result of what you enjoyed today. In *Olam Haba* you'll enjoy only happiness, forever and ever.

It's not enough to just sign on the dotted line, "*Ani ma'amin* — I believe." You have to have *emunah* in your *hearts*, and that is not so easy to achieve, because what you see with your eyes contradicts emunah. *Resha'im* and *apikorsim* are all around. Hakadosh Baruch Hu put an ocean of foolishness in the world today, in order to let us know that they're actually crazy. In the olden days, there were those who looked more decent, so you might have deceived yourself into thinking that there was something worthwhile in them. Today you see an ocean of corruption, addictions, drunk drivers, terrorists ... and people's lives are being ruined. We have to work hard to counteract all this darkness, and bring as much light as possible into our worlds.

Talk about Olam Haba at your Shabbos table

EVERY SHABBOS SHOULD LEAVE OVER IN OUR HEARTS SOME RESIDUE of *emunah* in the World to Come. Talk about *Olam Haba* at your table. Sometimes your children won't want to listen to it; that very well might be a sign that they don't believe in it. Then you have to preach *Olam Haba* to them again and again. A person has to hear it a thousand times, and then maybe a little bit of *emunah* will come into his heart — that little bit is more precious than diamonds.[39]

A sixth point to contemplate about Shabbos is the Torah's injunction of "*lema'an yanuach shorcha vechamorecha*[40] — that your ox and donkey shall rest." What an amazing statement! This demonstrates the very important principle of Hashem's kindliness. David Hamelech examined the world and said, "*Ani amarti olam chessed yibaneh.*"[41] How much *chessed* can we find? To take just one of millions of examples, look at the three thousand enzymes in us — an enzyme is a miracle; it's a little bundle of proteins, processed to accomplish remarkable results. An enzyme is something wonderful and miraculous that we cannot make, and each of our three thousand different enzymes has a beneficial purpose — three thousand miracles of *chessed*. If we study the world we'll find millions of miracles of *chessed*.

"*Ki vo shavas vayinafash*"[42] — Hakadosh Baruch Hu rested then, and He wants our ox to rest, too. Hakadosh Baruch Hu told us about Himself only so that we should emulate Him. You find the word form of *vayinafash* in only one other place in the Torah: *veyinafeish ben*

---

39. See *Sing You Righteous* p. 254 (541-542), *Awake My Glory* p. 304 (980)
40. *Shemos* 23:12
41. *Tehillim* 89:2
42. *Shemos* 31:17

amasecha vehager...[43] — your slave boy should also rest. Hashem rested, and he wants us to do the same. Hakadosh Baruch Hu put these words in the first account of Shabbos, at the beginning of the Torah, to let us know that all of our creatures — our slaves as well as our animals — have a right to rest on Shabbos, and it's a Jew's obligation to see that they do. There's a prohibition and a positive commandment to this obligation; a Jew must not make his animal work on Shabbos, and even if an animal works by itself, a Jew has to stop it from working. An animal must rest.

Shabbos teaches us that Hashem desires kindliness

SINCE THE PRINCIPLE INVOLVED HERE IS HASHEM'S KINDLINESS, *"Vezacharta ki eved hayisa be'Eretz Mitzrayim"*[44] — on Shabbos we must remember that we were once slaves too. Therefore, we have to learn sympathy for the downtrodden; a Jew has the softest heart — *rachmanim bnei rachmanim*, the compassionate descendants of the compassionate Shabbos teaches us a model of kindliness, *ki chafetz chessed Hu*[45] — Hashem desires kindliness. Don't waste the opportunity; think of that great lesson on Shabbos.[46]

A seventh point to ponder is that on Shabbos we have three *seudos*. In ancient times they ate only two meals a day, but on Shabbos we are required to add a meal to our day. This is considered an extremely important achievement: *Kol hame'aneg es haShabbos*, anyone who causes joy to himself on Shabbos — this is the principle of *oneg* Shabbos. *Oneg* means pleasure; even if you're poor, no matter what you're eating, try to smack your lips and feel how delicious it is; feel the taste of Shabbos. Because of that, *nosenim lo nachalah beli metzarim*[47] — he's going to get an estate in *Olam Haba* that has no bounds. Hashem will give the tzaddikim — those who keep the Shabbos — so many worlds.

Shabbos is a day to enjoy in order to know how great is Hashem's kindness to us, and so we have to concentrate on enjoying the

---

43. *Shemos* 23:12
44. *Devarim* 5:15
45. *Michah* 7:18
46. See *A Nation Is Born* p. 332 (23:12), p. 430 (31:17)
47. *Shabbos* 118a

Shabbos in every way. Of course, don't do things that are dangerous to your health; even eating should be done with wholesome foods. But it's a very big mitzvah to prepare your table with every kind of delicacy you can afford, in order to honor the Shabbos.

The Sages[48] tell us that one's sustenance for the year is measured out on Rosh Hashanah, and if a person wastes too much money, he'll find himself short before the year is over — except for what he spends on Shabbos. That will not be deducted. *Kol hamosif, mosifin lo* — the more he adds for Shabbos, the more he's going to get for expenses during the year.

By honoring Shabbos one will be rescued from three great catastrophes

THE GEMARA[49] TELLS US THAT THROUGH *ONEG SHABBOS*, BY MAKING your joy of Shabbos, you will be rescued from three great catastrophes: from *chevlei Mashiach* — when Mashiach comes, there's going to be a very great disturbance in the world, and many people will be sorry they lived that long; from *milchemes Gog uMagog*, the terrible, cataclysmic war on a scale never before seen; and from *dino shel Gehinnom* — everyone has certain sins; maybe a person is trying to hide them from other people, but those sins will have to be atoned in Gehinnom unless he does a very great teshuvah in this world. But when a person is *me'aneg es haShabbos* and goes all out to enjoy Shabbos properly — because he wants to honor the Shabbos — then he will be rescued from these great disasters.

The *Mesillas Yesharim* speaks about varying degrees of greatness — *zehirus, zerizus*, and so on. Then he comes to a certain degree of perfection called *perishus*, a level involving abstinence and self-control. When the Alter of Slabodka was served food he especially liked, he would eat a small amount and then push it away, in order to practice self-control. Learning to control oneself applies not only to food but to every facet of life. Control yourself in words; count your words — don't say what you don't have to say. Control yourself in laughing; smile pleasantly, but don't burst out laughing like a drunkard in the saloon. *Perishus* means to do everything with temperance, under control.

Then he says there's a greater *middah*, and that is *kedushah* — not obstaining, but eating *leshem Shamayim*, even becoming fat

48. *Beitzah* 16a
49. *Shabbos* 118a

through *kedushah*, without any selfishness in one's actions. The Gemara tells us that there were three times when the courtyard of the *Beis Hamikdash* rang out with a *bas kol*, and one of those occasions was when a Heavenly voice rang out and said, *"Se'u she'arim rasheichem*, lift up your heads, O you gates, *veyikanes*, and let enter the Kohen Yochanan ben Narbai." What was so great about him? The Gemara tells us that he used to fill his belly with the *korbanos*. There's a mitzvah to eat *korbanos*, and Yochanan ben Narbai ate and ate. He didn't need it; he had plenty to eat at home. But he came to the *Beis Hamikdash* and got busy doing a mitzvah, and he became very portly because of that; this is called *kedushah*.

Eating leshem Shamayim on Shabbos can achieve you a great amount of kedushah

ON SHABBOS, WE GAIN *KEDUSHAH*. YOU MAY FAST ON THE WEEKDAYS if you choose, but Shabbos is a day when, the *Kuzari* says, eating accomplishes more for you than a number of fast days in the week. When you fast, you're a *kadosh*: "*Kol hayosheiv besa'anis nikra kadosh*[50] — whoever fasts is called a holy man." But if you eat *leshem Shamayim* on Shabbos, you achieve greater *kedushah* than you can achieve through fasting for a number of days. Isn't it a pity to let the *seudah* go by without thinking about that? When you are *mekayem oneg* Shabbos, keep that in mind. The more you enjoy the Shabbos, the greater will be your reward in the World to Come.

An eighth point to consider about Shabbos is that "*Shevus deShabbos takanas chachamim.*" The Sages added a number of decrees to our *shemiras Shabbos*. Rabbeinu Yonah (in *Sha'arei Teshuvah*) cites the *ma'amar Chazal* based on the pasuk, "*Ki tovim dodecha miyayin*[51] — Your love is better than wine." *Dodecha* means Your beloved ones, and refers to the Sages, and so, *Chazal* say, "*Chavivim divrei sofrim yoser miyeino shel Torah*[52] — The words of the *chachamim* are more beloved to Hashem than the wine of the Torah itself." When you fulfill the *takanos chachamim* — if for example, you don't pick up *muktzeh* — it's more precious to Hashem than the laws of the Torah. Why is this?

---

50. *Taanis* 11a
51. *Shir HaShirim* 1:12
52. *Yerushalmi Berachos* 1:4

He explains that when someone doesn't step into a garden because of the valuable plants growing there, that's a sensible thing. But if he builds a fence around the garden and makes it his business to ensure that nobody breaks down that fence, it shows much more consideration for the garden and the plants growing there. In the same way, we show greater love for Hashem when we do not merely keep the laws that He gave us but keep the fence around those laws. Keeping *takanos chachamim* shows real *yiras Shamayim*. Some people "flirt" with the halachah: "It's not Biblically forbidden, it's only forbidden by the Sages"; then one day they take a wrong step and find themselves walking in the garden and trampling on the beautiful plants. That is why *chavivim divrei chachamim*.

The decrees of the Sages are not burdens, they're all added jewelry on us

MANY ASPECTS OF SHABBOS SEEM BURDENSOME TO CHILDREN — THEY keep looking at the clock to see when Shabbos is over. But in fact, the longer Shabbos is, the better off you are. The *takanos chachamim* are not burdens, they're all added "jewelry" on us, every one an additional benefit for us. We should be happy and enjoy the decrees of the Sages.

Eiruvin is a very long and difficult *mesechta*, and nothing it contains is Biblically forbidden. The *mesechta* consists entirely of decrees of the Sages. That's the greatness of our nation. We are called "Chassidim" because we are especially devoted to Hashem. We don't limit ourselves to just what Hashem told us; we do much more. *Zocher chasdei avos* — Hashem remembers the *chessed* of our fathers Avraham, Yitzchak, and Yaakov, who did more than they were commanded to do, because they loved Hashem; and we emulate our Forefathers.

The *malachim* once asked Hakadosh Baruch Hu:[53] How can you say, *yisa Hashem panav eilecha* — that Hashem will be *nosei panim*, He'll be partial to the Jews? Isn't it said about Hashem, "*asher lo yisa panim* — He is not partial to anyone"?

Hashem answered them: Why shouldn't I be partial to them? They're partial to Me! I told them that when they eat bread and are satiated, they have to say *Birkas Hamazon*, but if they're not satiated, they don't have to say it. Yet they accepted the stringency that if

___
53. *Berachos* 20b

you eat *kazayis* or *kabeitzah* of bread, you say *Birkas Hamazon*. Am Yisrael accepted many things voluntarily, so because they do things for Me without being told, I'll do things for them without being asked.

Therefore, it's very important for us to realize what a great blessing it is to have the decree of the Sages.

The Jew has vacation one-sixth of his life

A NINTH POINT TO CONSIDER ABOUT SHABBOS IS THAT "*VAYEVARECH Elokim es yom hashevi'i*[54] — Hashem blessed the Shabbos day." What does this mean? You must realize that when you keep Shabbos, you're doing yourself the biggest favor. In terms of *gashmiyus*, the *Kuzari* says the Jew has vacation one-sixth of his life. Some people retire when they're old and sick; they are not able to enjoy their retirement, but when you are fully capable of living in every sense, you retire one day every week, and on Yom Tov, too. This is very significant in terms of health, longevity, and many other aspects of life. Think about family coherence: on Shabbos you spend time with your children, and you can talk to them; and they have a certain responsibility toward you — you can instruct them. And Shabbos is a day when you can associate with your friends in the *Beis Hakeneeses* and with your relatives. Shabbos is full of blessings.[55]

Until about one hundred and fifty years ago, Jews were never drafted into gentile armies. When gentiles would march out to the battlefields in wars all over Europe, no Jews were among them. In the times of the second *Beis Hamikdash* the Sanhedrin sent out emissaries to all the governments because the Jews were then scattered throughout the world, and they made treaties with all the gentile governments granting Jews exemptions from military service, since Jews cannot bear arms on Shabbos. Josephus brings a long list of the treaties that he copied from the books of these governments all around Asia Minor and around Eretz Yisrael.

When Alexander the Great came to Eretz Yisrael, in many instances Jews volunteered to join him. Still, when Alexander wanted to build a temple in a certain place, and he asked for the Jews' help, no Jew would lift a finger to help build a temple. And the order was given to punish them, until finally they saw that the Jews wouldn't give in, so they left them alone.

---

54. *Bereishis* 2:3
55. See *Rejoice O Youth* p. 359 (883)

While the gentiles were marching out to the battlefields, the Jew was sitting in his house enjoying his Shabbos and singing "*Yismechu bemalchusecha shomerei Shabbos vekorei oneg.*" Then, a hundred and fifty years ago, a certain Jewish *rasha* in Austria said: Why should Jews be deprived of the great *simchah* of being in the army? So he appealed to Franz Josef to do a favor and draft the Jews. Franz Josef did him that favor, and though the Jews of Austria and Hungary were fasting and praying, nothing helped. That's when they started drafting Jews into the army. Until then, the Shabbos protected them.

Shabbos transforms the Jew into a king

IF NOT FOR THE SHABBOS, GENERATIONS AND GENERATIONS OF JEWS who were poor would never change their garments. Yet even the wagon driver, when he would come home just before Shabbos, would take off his big, filthy boots and his clothing splashed with mud and would quickly take a bath and put on his Shabbos garments, and he was transformed from a hard-working servant into a king. And he marched to shul with his hands behind his back — slowly, with *kavod*, like a prince. The Shabbos transformed him and made the Jews a nation with dignity. Even the poorest dressed up on Shabbos and walked to the *Beis Hakenesses* with their families.

Shabbos was likewise a great blessing for people who wanted to accomplish something on Shabbos. It was a time when they could look in a *sefer*. Our nation was the only educated nation in the world. When most of the world was illiterate, almost every man among Am Yisrael could read. Shabbos was a time when everyone looked in a *sefer*. Some only said *Tehillim*; some learned *Ein Yaakov*; some learned Gemara. When I was in a small town in Europe I found an old *sefer*, and I asked an old melamed where this *sefer* was from. He explained that a chevrah of ba'alei battim learned *Choshen Mishpat* with *Shach* — Am Yisrael was an *am hasefer*, the people of the book.

And they gained a great deal of intelligence. They weren't materialistic or brutal like the peoples all around them. They didn't have to go to school — nobody went to school in those days; there were no schools. But on Shabbos, Am Yisrael went to school. The word shul means school. They went to shul on Shabbos, a school, and they — men and women alike — sat and learned. They would sit for hours on Shabbos and listen while *maggidim* spoke to them, and the *maggidim* made them laugh and made them weep, and the people were transformed as a result.

Shabbos is an opportunity to raise the level of intelligence of our nation

WHEN I WAS A BOY, IN EVERY SYNAGOGUE IN AMERICA THERE WAS A Rav speaking on Shabbos afternoon for at least an hour, sometimes for two hours, and people came en masse. A whole generation of *shomrei Shabbos* came. Unfortunately, there were many non-*shomer Shabbos* too — Communists and Socialists; but the *shomrei Shabbos* flocked to the shuls. It was the delight of the people to come and listen.[56] Shabbos was an opportunity to raise the level of intelligence in our nation, and so Shabbos was full of blessing. As Hakadosh Baruch Hu said to Moshe Rabbeinu: "*Matanah tovah yesh li beveis ginzai, veShabbos shemah* — I have a good gift in my treasury, and it's called Shabbos. *Leich vehodi'am* — go and let them know." Why let them know about Shabbos? The Gemara explains that it is because the reward of Shabbos is something that they won't know on their own. Shabbos is full of rewards, and we have to study that.

The most important thing in life is to gain true knowledge

THE TENTH POINT — THOUGH BY FAR NOT THE LAST — IS "*LADA'AS KI Ani Hashem mekadishchem.*"[57] The purpose of Shabbos is *da'as*, gaining understanding. It is a glorious opportunity to gain the most important thing in life — true knowledge. We accomplish many things in this life: we can do mitzvos; we can gain good character traits; we can learn Torah. Yet of all the things that are prized by Hakadosh Baruch Hu, "*gedolah da'as*" — achieving perfection of the mind — clarity and understanding — are prized most. "Know," says Hashem, "that I am making you holy."

When people utilize the Shabbos for thinking of all these things and of many other ideas and ideals of Shabbos, little by little their minds develop, and the development of the mind is the most important achievement of life. To develop your mind means to broaden your

---

56. See *Sing You Righteous* p. 271
57. See *Shemos* 31:13

understanding of all that Hakadosh Baruch Hu wants us to know about Himself, about His Torah, about Am Yisrael, about our function in history, about the way we have to behave in life, about our purpose in life, about *Olam Haba* ... Shabbos is the day when we gain *da'as*, and therefore we say, *Baruch Atah Hashem mekadeish haShabbos* — we thank You for having given us a day of *kedushah*, and *kedushah* includes everything that we have said and everything that could be said on the subject.

SHABBOS: THE SOURCE OF BLESSING

 AYIN WAS IN A CRISIS. HE WAS CRESTFALLEN AND DEPRESSED because his offering was not accepted, while Hevel's offering was accepted. Therefore, Hashem told him, "*Lapesach chatas rovetz*,[1] *chatas* crouches in ambush at the entrance" — know that there is such a thing as a *yetzer hara*, and it is trying to get hold of you. Be forewarned and do not succumb.

The *yetzer hara* has many names. Shlomo called it *sonei*. Others called it *ra*. The Gemara uses a number of names to identify it.[2] But here Hakadosh Baruch Hu calls it *chatas*. What is the meaning of that word?

Chatas means to lose out, to miss. Thus it refers not so much to the wrong things you did, but to the right things you failed to do. Hakadosh Baruch Hu is telling us that the greatest peril of the *yetzer hara* is not in what he can cause a person to *do*, but in what he can cause a person to *fail* to do.

---

1. *Bereishis* 4:7
2. *Succah* 52a

The greatest peril of the yetzer hara is what he can cause a person to fail to accomplish

THIS POINT IS CRUCIAL, BECAUSE WE ARE IN THIS WORLD TO accomplish. Of course, while we're accomplishing we should try to avoid any misstep. But to go through this world merely avoiding wrong deeds is not sufficient. If the yetzer hara has managed to persuade a person to refrain from doing things he could have done, that's the greatest achievement he could hope for in leading a person astray.

And so Hashem told Kayin, "Here's a golden opportunity. Your brother Hevel has triumphed over you, and you are so downcast. If you'll reinforce yourself — go shake hands with him and tell him, 'Congratulations' — you will gain the upper hand." That action would have made Kayin better than Hevel. Instead, not only was Kayin jealous, he was angry and vengeful, and he lost out on the greatest opportunity of his life. At that moment he could have gained a crown of glory.

The Gemara comments on the Torah's words, "Hashem blessed the seventh day," that Hakadosh Baruch Hu made Shabbos a day of berachah. To what berachah does the Gemara refer?

You might say that the greatest blessing a person could get is happiness in this world. Everybody wants it, but, of course, there's a higher success — there is happiness forever and ever, in the World to Come. And both are indicated in the berachah of Shabbos. When it's utilized properly, Shabbos is both olam hazeh (this world) and Olam Haba (World to Come). You may claim you don't care about happiness in this world, but Hashem does care; He wants you to be happy in this world as well. Most people are unaware of this purpose of Shabbos; they fulfill only the barest essentials of Shabbos observance by neglecting to do the wrong things — they do a few right things, too, but they miss the point.

Thinking that the world was created from nothing

WHAT IS THE POINT OF SHABBOS? ONE VERY IMPORTANT PRINCIPLE IS that Shabbos celebrates the fact that Hashem made the world ex nihilo — yesh me'ayin.[3] If you spend time on Shabbos thinking about that, it is certainly an achievement. Next Shabbos, make it your business to take out one minute to think that before Creation, there was ayin — nothing; and then Hakadosh Baruch Hu said, "Yehi" — that's

---

3. See The Beginning p.56 (2:3), Sing You Righteous p. 254 (541), Nation Is Born p. 276 (20:11)

why we call Him *Yud-Hei-Vav-Hei*: He said, "*Yehi*," and everything came into existence. That thought is a mitzvah, and you can know that this Shabbos, at least once in your life, you accomplished something on Shabbos! Many people say the words "*zecher lema'aseh bereishis*," a remembrance of Creation, but don't think about what they're saying — what a tragedy. If you are able to devote two minutes to this thought — a minute Friday night and a minute Shabbos morning — you've done so much more. At each *seudah* (meal), for example, spend one minute thinking that Hashem made the world out of nothing, *yesh me'ayin*, and you've fulfilled one of the great purposes of Shabbos. The more times you focus on that thought, the more you've accomplished; but that is not the whole lesson. That's still *chatas*, because there are other points that you're missing.

A crucial point of Shabbos is that the world was made for *ta'anug* — happiness. If you are not aware of that, you surely won't utilize the Shabbos for it. Many of us are so indoctrinated with the idea that this world is nothing that as we sit down and eat the cholent and the chicken, we may say nothing.

Hakadosh Baruch Hu says this is *chatas* — you're missing out. Shabbos comes to remind us of *ma'aseh bereishis*, at which time, "And Hashem saw all that He did and behold it was *tov me'od*." "*Tov me'od*" doesn't mean *very bad*; it means *very good*. In this statement Hakadosh Baruch Hu is giving us information we should never forget. He is referring here not to *Olam Haba* but to this world, as it says in *Chumash*, "Let the *earth* bring forth...." Hashem is speaking about plants, animals, fish, birds — they're all *tov me'od* — not just good, but *very good*. Of course it's good if He made it; but He said it to us because He wants us to say these same words all our lives: Ribbono shel Olam, we congratulate You. You did a great job — *tov me'od!*[4]

Most Jews are blind to this great truth that the world is a good place

THE *CHOVOS HALEVAVOS* COMMENTS ON THIS PASUK, "HASHEM IS good to all, but they are as blind people"; most people are blind to this. The *Chovos Halevavos* wasn't talking about nonreligious, liberal Jews. In his days, all Jews were frum Jews. Most Orthodox Jews are blind to this great truth: It's a good world! The Torah says it's a good world.

---

4. See *The Beginning* p. 47 (1:31)

And so we begin to understand one function of the Shabbos: It is for us to gain an attitude that this is a good world, a *very* good world. But let's take a look at a practical application of this principle.

Let's say you're a yeshivah bachur (student) and every day after Minchah (afternoon prayer) you walk out of the beis medrash and find a poor man standing there, stretching out his hand. You drop a nickel into his hand and others do the same. But one day you make a mistake and drop in a quarter. He looks at you and thinks, "Oh, there's a fine man!" The next day, in order to gain that look again, you drop another quarter into his hand. From then on, you drop in a quarter each day; you give him a quarter every day for a year. After a while, he starts complaining — "Only a quarter? How about a raise?"

So you see that even though a person is receiving benefits from you, if he keeps getting the same benefit, he gets tired of it and think it's nothing. He won't spend time congratulating you for giving him a quarter; he's spending time criticizing you for not giving more than a quarter!

So Hakadosh Baruch Hu gives us all the good things, and we're tired of it. "What are You giving us?" people ask.

"Why should I thank Hashem?" someone will ask me. He's a healthy man, well fed, living in a comfortable home — why should he thank Hashem? Perhaps he wants more excitement in life, thrills, entertainment. The Torah says, "*Im shamo'a tishma el mitzvosai,*[5] if you do everything that I've told you, *ve'achalta vesavata.*"

Do you hear that great promise? You'll have enough to eat!

Is that all? Tell an American Jew that as a reward for being frum he'll have enough to eat — what about a car? What about vacations? I know a man who took a vacation in the Catskills for two months, but he got bored, so he took another vacation in Switzerland.

When people are blind, they're never happy.

Hakadosh Baruch Hu wants us to stop and study what he's giving to us. *Ve'achalta vesavata* — you have enough to eat? You're very lucky! When I lived in Europe, a family next door told us that when they were younger they didn't have enough to eat. When a child asked his mother for another piece of bread, she'd say, "I'm sorry, I can't do it." You have all the bread you want! "*Chatas,*" Hakadosh Baruch Hu says: you're missing out — not only in your avodas Hashem, in understanding the truth, but even in *olam hazeh*; you're not enjoying life at all.

---

5. *Devarim* 11:13

In order to enjoy the full benefit of Hakadosh Baruch Hu's gifts, you must understand how great these gifts are; study them. Start with your piece of bread — see how good that piece of bread is. Forget about the chicken or the other foods; think about the piece of bread.

Bread is a pleasure

ONLY HUMAN BEINGS HAVE BREAD. ANIMALS DON'T HAVE IT. BREAD IS a manufactured thing; it doesn't grow. You have to grind up the grain, make a dough and bake it on the fire. Bread is an art; it's an expense. In the olden times, poor people couldn't bake — they didn't have stoves. The Gemara tells us that they would go to the bakery and ask for the use of the stove.

Bread is a confection, a pleasure. So now we have to get busy thinking. A yeshivah bachur from Boro Park was once telling me he doesn't care about *ta'anugei olam hazeh*, but he has a wristwatch; well, I also have a wristwatch. He drives a car; I never drove a car. He eats ice cream; I don't eat ice cream.

Rubam ivrim — they're blind! This blindness is a *cheit*. Everyone needs to learn how to put on Torah glasses. If you look at the world through rosy glasses, you see a rosy, beautiful world. If you look at the world through gloomy glasses, you'll have a gloomy world all your life. The life you have depends on how you look at the world. Hakadosh Baruch Hu gives you a pair of eyeglasses right at the beginning: He says "*tov me'od*," it's a very good world; start looking for the goodness of this world.

Mitzvah to have a good time in this world

THIS IS INCLUDED IN "*VAYEVARECH ELOKIM*" — HASHEM GAVE A berachah to the seventh day; on that day there is a special mitzvah to have a good time in this world. First of all, you don't work then. What a pleasure! And on Shabbos you eat special things during the *seudos*. People who eat more than they need on Wednesday and Thursday may not appreciate the *seudos* of Shabbos, so it's a mitzvah not to eat much on Friday, to work up an appetite so we'll feel a desire to eat on Shabbos.

When you sit down on Shabbos at the *seudah*, it's a time to get to work; that's the avodah of Shabbos. Get busy seeing how good everything is, how good the challah is. Compliment the baalebuste. (If she didn't bake it, praise other things.) Seeing the delightful foods of Shabbos is a *pesach*, an entrance to seeing the *tov*, the goodness of *olam hazeh*.

The Jew has always been more optimistic about this world than the other peoples of the world, because he's had Shabbos, a day of happiness. Together with his family, he's sat around the table and sung *zemiros* and eaten good foods; therefore his whole life is different. If once in six days you take a vacation and enjoy life, it's going to make the other six days much different. A Jew's life is punctuated with joy — with *oneg Shabbos* — every six days.

If you utilize this day of *berachah* as a way of replacing the glasses you use to view the world, it will give you the perspective to see the *tov me'od* of the world, and it will change everything in your life.

"*Kol hame'aneg es haShabbos, nosnim lo nachalah beli metzarim*," says the Gemara.[6] If someone causes pleasure on Shabbos, if he goes out of his way to do things that make Shabbos pleasurable, they're going to give him an estate that has no boundaries in *Olam Haba*. This is not a *mashal*. You're going to see great wealth that all belongs to you. You'll take a trip on a "space shuttle," and wherever you go, property belongs to you. Everything in this world has boundaries, but if you're *me'aneg es haShabbos*, your portion in *Olam Haba* will have no boundaries. From world to world, it's all yours — *beli metzarim*.

"*Lehanchil le'ohavai **yesh**,*"[7] Hashem said — I have the resources to give an estate to those who love Me; "*Ve'otzaroseihem amalei* — I'll fill their treasuries." The numerical value of *yesh* is 310, the Gemara explains (at the end of *Uktzin*); Hakadosh Baruch Hu will give the tzaddikim 310 worlds — not little worlds like this one we live in, but huge worlds.

Shabbos is a day when you can earn tremendous reward in Olam Haba

NOW WE BEGIN TO UNDERSTAND SOMETHING ABOUT SHABBOS. IT IS A day when you can earn tremendous reward in *Olam Haba*. Of course, if you learn Torah on Shabbos it is even better, but you must not take for granted this principle that Shabbos is meant to teach you about the great happiness that awaits you in this life, and about the infinite happiness of *Olam Haba*.

---

6. *Shabbos* 118a
7. *Mishlei* 8:21

Concentrate on learning how to enjoy life. Don't do it by running after pleasures. *Pas bamelach tocheil u'mayim bimesurah sishteh*[8] — eat bread and salt, and drink a little water; sleep on the ground and work hard in Torah. Then, "*ashrecha vetov lach — ashrecha ba'olam hazeh vetov lach ba'Olam Haba.*" I can understand that it's good for you in *Oham Haba*, but how does it bring you joy in *olam hazeh*?

This is the crucial point: If you learn how to utilize life, *ashrecha ba'olam hazeh* even if you eat nothing more than bread and salt and a cup of water — but you concentrate on what a pleasure bread is and how good salt is.

The miracle of bread

WHERE DOES BREAD COME FROM? ACTUALLY, IT COMES FROM THE wind. The wind blows carbon dioxide. If that carbon dioxide passes by the plant, the plant swallows it up, and there's no more carbon dioxide left. But then more carbon dioxide comes, and again the plant swallows it. The plant is swallowing carbon dioxide that the wind keeps blowing. "The world can't be without winds," the Gemara[9] says. Without winds we couldn't live. Did you ever thank Hashem for wind? Just once in your life, when you're walking in the street and a wind is blowing and you hold onto your hat, say with real thought, "Baruch Hashem *mashiv haru'ach*" — what a good thing wind is! If you do this once in your life, then in the next world you'll be able to say, "I said it once." It's not difficult — try saying it twice!

Without wind we'd have nothing to eat. The plants would die if the wind didn't keep bringing a new supply of carbon dioxide, constantly, like a conveyer belt. From the carbon dioxide the plant makes starch, and that starch becomes bread — bread is a miracle of *chessed*.[10]

When is the best time to think about this? Of course, we should think about it all week, but on Shabbos it's demanded of us that we think about it. That's why we eat even better bread on Shabbos — in order to emphasize the bread: bread with an exclamation point — challah. Taste that delicious bread and think where it comes from — it comes from the wind. Where does the wind come from? *Mashiv haru'ach* — Hashem makes the wind blow. The wind is a special mir-

8. *Avos* 6:4
9. *Taanis* 3b
10. See *Awake My Glory* p. 368 (1159), *Rejoice Of Youth* p. 100 (178)

acle, and its purpose is *mechalkel chayim bechessed* — to make sure that you have food.

The miracle of salt

SALT IS ANOTHER MIRACLE FOOD. EVERY CELL OF THE BODY NEEDS salt. People used to worry about not having enough salt. Nations used to go to war against one another because of salt. Salt — sodium chloride — is a miracle chemical. Sodium is a poisonous chemical; chlorine gas is a poisonous gas, but when they come together, they become life-giving, nutritious salt. Did you ever think about thanking Hashem for salt? But you couldn't live without salt! Animals sometimes travel great distances just to find rocks made of salt and to lick those rocks, because they need salt. Yet you may have spent your whole life not once having thought of thanking Hashem for salt. That's *chatas* — you're missing out on the purpose of living. Hashem gave us salt so that we can appreciate what He gave us.[11]

The Sages[12] tell us that one person who gives another a gift has to tell the other person about the gift, so that he should appreciate the gift and he should appreciate the giver. The Torah tells us that we must put salt on *every korban*. A Jewish table is like a *mizbei'ach*, and when a Jew eats it's like offering a *korban* to Hashem; and so he dips his challah in salt — but without giving it a moment's thought. He thinks he's doing Hakadosh Baruch Hu a favor, and the thought crosses his mind, "How frum I am!" He doesn't hear Hashem's Voice asking, "When will you thank Me for the salt?" So on Shabbos, in addition to thinking about the challah, think about the salt, too.

The miracle of water

AND THEN WE COME TO THE LITTLE BIT OF WATER. WATER IS ANOTHER *neis*, a great miracle. Without water a person will die. The atmosphere that surrounds us is full of the substances that make water — oxygen and hydrogen — but you can't drink them. Take the oxygen and hydrogen in the right proportions, put them in a little chamber and add an electric spark. That electric spark is the shadchan that brings together the unwilling chassan and kallah, which don't want to combine. The oxygen and hydrogen unite and there's water.

---

11. See *Sing You Righteous* p. 157 (351)
12. *Shabbos* 10b

If you take two gases, one filled with oxygen and one with hydrogen — neither of which can quench your thirst — and breathe all that you can, filling your lungs with them, you'll still be thirsty. And Hakadosh Baruch Hu brings them miraculously together and they become water — such an essential thing. Someone traveling in a desert without water, who sees a little spring, feels such a simchah. That water is better than anything in the world, and Hakadosh Baruch Hu asks, "Did you thank Me for the water?" You may mumble a berachah, but that's not thanking. Look at the glass in your hand and say *"tov me'od,"* even if you don't mean it. After saying it a few times, little by little you will internalize it. But if we fail to say it, we'll be judged for it — it's *chatas*; we're missing out.[13]

If a person utilizes Shabbos with a little thought, he begins to see the world as a good place. He begins to appreciate the glass of water. He gets into the habit of holding the glass of water in his hand and looking at it. How beautiful it is! If I had to buy water in the drugstore, I ought to pay $100 for a little bottle — we can't get along without it. Someone in the Sahara Desert looking for a little bit of water before he drops dead will gladly pay $1000 for it. We have to realize that every time we drink water we're being saved from extinction, and so we have to think of water as *happiness.*

When I was in Slabodka you couldn't drink the water. The water from the well always carried a danger of typhus, so you had to boil the water. People didn't bother boiling it, so there was no water to drink in the yeshivah — all day long not a drop of water to drink. There was a barrel that held water for washing your hands, but you couldn't drink that water. They hadn't washed out that barrel for fifty years! When you came home to your *shtanzia* and you wanted a drink, you had to ask the baalebuste to boil up some water for you; sometimes she did.

When I came back to America, I appreciated the water. Just open the faucet, and *mayim chayim!* What a blessing — water! And you can even drink it without boiling it.

If you don't recognize this blessing, it's *chatas* — you're missing out in life. Our purpose in life is to see how *mal'ah ha'aretz chessed Hashem* — Hashem's kindness fills the earth. This does not mean that someone who doesn't think these thoughts is not fulfilling his duty as a Jew. It is very good if he is *shomer Shabbos*, keeping all

---

13. See *Awake My Glory* p. 292 (941), *Rejoice O Youth* p. 312 (703)

the details of the mitzvos. But nevertheless, he is a failure; he hasn't lived properly. Don't allow yourself to be dragged along by the majority of people, because they have this fault of not thinking. "*Rachmana liba ba'ei*"[14] means He wants you thinking; He wants your *lev*, your thoughts. Shabbos is a day of berachah for that purpose: We should utilize the Shabbos to learn how to be happy in this world.[15]

Of course, it doesn't come all at once. Once you appreciate a glass of water, after having worked on it many times, then you start appreciating a piece of bread, by working on it. And your life is transformed: bread and water — you're a happy person!

Appreciating air

THEN START APPRECIATING THE AIR. AIR IS A SPECIAL MIXTURE — IT'S A cocktail when you breathe. If it were all oxygen, it would make you drunk; you would reel and you'd fall down dizzily. If it were all nitrogen, you wouldn't be able to survive for a minute. Nitrogen doesn't help you. Air is 20 percent oxygen and 80 percent nitrogen — those are exactly the right proportions for you. So it's made precisely to support life. No other location in the universe has air like we have here. Think about that; it's not an accident. It's a formula fit for us exactly. There's no air on Mars, no air on the moon, no air anywhere. Only this earth has air. Here the person has been breathing all his life, and did he ever once stop to say Baruch Hashem for air? It's a blind world.

"Well, everyone else is blind," you may say, "so I'll also remain blind." But that's why you came here. Open your eyes and get yourself a pair of Shabbos glasses, and through those glasses look at the world, and see the truth of Hashem's creation. "*Vayevarech*" — He blessed the Shabbos, in order that you should see how good it is to have air in the world.

Breathe deeply. Most people never fill their lungs completely. Fill your lungs all the way, until the bottom of your chest bulges out. And *think* the same way — most people think shallowly. The bottom of the brain is never used. Think deeply. Then you'll start enjoying the happiness of this world. Breathe deeply, and thank Hakadosh Baruch Hu for this cocktail. It's *tov me'od*!

---

14. *Sanhedrin* 106a
15. See *Rejoice O Youth* p. 314 (706)

Be careful in choosing your associates

IF YOU TELL THIS TO A *LETZ*, A SCORNER, AND HE RESPONDS DEADPAN, he discourages you. "*Be'oznei kesil al tedaber,*"[16] *Mishlei* tells us, "Don't talk in the ears of a fool, because he'll make the wisdom of your words into nothing." He'll do this in two ways. First, he's not excited about it, so your enthusiasm gets cooled off too (as the Torah tells us about Amalek, "... *asher koracho badarech*" — Amalek "cooled us off"). Second, he might tell you that you have to learn Torah. You have to keep the halachos of Shabbos; and that is all true. But you can do that and still be missing one of the most important parts of life, for Hakadosh Baruch Hu said we must recognize that the world is *tov me'od.*

Sefer Tehillim opens with the words "*Ashrei ha'ish,* happy is the man...*uvemoshav leitzim lo yashav* — who did not sit in the company of scorners. *Mishlei* is a *sefer* of advice, but *sefer Tehillim* is not; it's a *sefer* of praises to Hashem. The first *kapittel* of *Tehillim,* though, is entirely different; it fits into *Mishlei.* It warns us to keep away from *leitzim.* Why does it begin that way?

The tone of *Tehillim* is one of praising Hashem. But David Hamelech starts out with a warning against associating with the wrong people, for the simple reason that in order to be something in this world you must keep yourself separate from the *leitzim.* It's impossible to accomplish what you're supposed to in this world if you're going to think like others around you. And know that there are *leitzim* in the yeshivah and there are *leitzim* in the shul. Frum *leitzim* are also *leitzim.* Do'eg HaEdomi was a frum Jew, and so was Korach. This is why we are warned: Do not be influenced by your environment. You must have an independent mind and think only what the Torah wants you to think. We are in this world to gain a clear awareness of all the benefits Hashem is giving to us.

---

16. *Mishlei* 23:9

SHABBOS: DAY OF KNOWLEDGE 3

HE TORAH AND THE MITZVOS ARE TO BE VIEWED NOT merely as duties one must fulfill, but as opportunities. We thank Hakadosh Baruch Hu, *asher kideshanu bemitzvosav, Who has sanctified us with His com-mandments*. A mitzvah is a gift, but the chief value of the gift is the opportunity it offers to gain the right viewpoint, to gain a Torah mind, which is the greatest achievement of all. It is included in the principle of *talmud Torah keneged kulam*, and the study of the Torah is equivalent to them all, because in the learning of Torah the mind benefits most.[1]

Gaining a Torah mind

THE TRUTH IS THAT KEEPING THE MITZVOS WILL BENEFIT A PERSON IN many ways, including physically.[2] The Gemara gives us thousands of bits of advice to benefit our health and well-being, but that is just a by-product. There are greater benefits, which touch on relationships *bein*

---

1. See *Rejoice O Youth* p. 301 (673), p. 330 (747)
2. See *Sing You Righteous* p. 349 (799)

adam lachaveiro, instructions for how to live with others in harmony and how to have pleasure from your children.

Many forms of physical and emotional success result from the study of the Torah and the performance of the mitzvos. A kosher Jew will never get snail disease. If you keep Shabbos, one-seventh of the chances for automobile and plane accidents is ruled out. The Torah spares your money, your health, and your life. But among the benefits that we gain from Torah and mitzvos, the most important benefit is the acquisition of a Torah mind.[3] A Torah mind is a possession that endures forever — you take it with you. Your existence in the World to Come depends on the amount of clarity of your perceptions that you achieved in this world.

One of the great opportunities we have is Shabbos. Even those who are meticulous in their performance of this mitzvah are in most cases unaware of the wealth that it can bestow upon them if they will invest just a little bit of understanding and effort.

In one of the songs of Shabbos, we sing: *"De'ei chochmah lenaf-shecha*, know wisdom for yourself, *vihi keser leroshecha*, and it will be a crown upon your head; *Netzor mitzvas Kedoshecha*, guard the command of your Holy One, *shemor Shabbos kodshecha*, and keep your holy Shabbos.

The end of that stanza is an explanation of the opening words: *De'ei chochmah*, know wisdom for yourself, because by keeping Shabbos properly you are going to gain that crown upon your head, a crown that the tzaddik wears in the next world — *tzaddikim yoshvim ve'atroseihem berasheihem, venehenim miziv haShechinah*,[4] and they enjoy the splendor of the Shechinah. This means that the size and the nature of the crown determines how much a person is able to enjoy the sight and the splendor of the Shechinah. When you gain a Torah mind, then you are prepared for happiness in the World to Come. The more of a Torah mind we gain, the more happiness we will have.

De'ei chochmah lenafshecha, know wisdom for yourself, means *shemor Shabbos kodshecha*; it doesn't mean merely to keep Shabbos, which is, of course, extremely important and valuable. It means that Shabbos can be a gold mine of understanding that will transform your mind if every week you will utilize it to some extent.

---

3. See *Sing You Righteous* p. 207 (466)
4. *Berachos* 17a

When Shabbos is about to enter, we should acquire a frame of mind that prepares us for the great opportunity that comes once a week to attach to our thoughts permanent attitudes that accompany Shabbos. Then we can live all the days between the Shabbosos with a different mental attitude. When we say *bo'i kallah*, we must welcome Shabbos with the understanding that the Shabbos is going to change us if we are willing to cooperate.

Friday night we say *vayechulu hashamayim veha'aretz vechol tzeva'am* — everything has now become completed. This is such an important statement that, the Gemara[5] says, when you are saying these words, two *malachim* come and put their hands on your head and say *vesar avonecha vechatasecha techupar*,[6] your sin will depart and your iniquities will be forgiven. That moment is so great, it is like Yom Kippur. Of course, this requires as least the thought of repentance. Think of one incident, one wrong word you said, one wrong act you committed, one instance of carelessness in regard to *shemiras hamitzvos*; utilize that opportunity, because then it is going to be forgiven.[7]

When Shabbos enters, all of nature begins functioning like a well-oiled machine

THAT MOMENT OF SAYING *VAYECHULU* EFFECTS A CHANGE IN YOUR mind. You have already said these words many times, so if you look at them superficially there is no chiddush being added. But attempt to picture when you are saying these words that right at this moment, when Shabbos enters, all of nature begins functioning like a well-oiled machine; all the parts are cooperating. Until that moment, nothing worked by itself. Hakadosh Baruch Hu was controlling everything in an obvious manner: He said something should appear, and it appeared — *ki Hu amar vayehi*,[8] He said and it became. *Bidvar Hashem shamayim na'asu*,[9] everything came into being by the mere words of Hashem. What we have said week after week, until finally it begins to penetrate, is that the world was made out of nothing but the words of Hashem.[10]

The truth is, it is not so difficult to acquire such an attitude, because if you study the sciences, you will see almost the same approach.

5. *Shabbos* 119b
6. *Yeshaya* 6:7
7. See *Sing You Righteous* p. 209 (468)
8. *Tehillim* 33:9
9. *Tehillim* 33:6.
10. See *The Beginning* p. 54 (2:2)

The *apikorsim* don't say that every animal came from an animal, every plant from a plant — that would spoil all their theories, although they established the principle that there is no spontaneous generation of life. Life must come from life. Life is a very complicated business, so you have to go back to the theory that contradicts their own principles; they say that there was a time when there was no life — how life evolved from no life is a problem they have to solve. Even the non-life forms from which they say life developed were also extremely complicated. They say certain molecules were capable of combining in efficient chemistry. Where did molecules come from? Molecules are very complicated things; so we have to say that the molecules were once only atoms. Atoms bumped into each other and eventually became molecules. How did the atoms come into existence? An atom is extremely complicated. If you could split an atom it would release such an energy that could explode a huge building. How did the energy get there? They have to invent theories upon theories, but they also say it all began with energy that had no system of organization at all.[11]

So everyone agrees that the world began from scratch. What does that mean? *We* say "from scratch" means that *bidvar Hashem shamayim na'asu*[12] — it all began by the word of Hashem.

When you say *vayechulu*, you are declaring that until Friday night *bein hashemashos*, the world was in the process of coming into existence, step by step. At that point Hakadosh Baruch Hu was commandeering all the forces He created to organize and to become, in a complicated and purposeful manner, what would later be called nature. And when we turn to the door and greet the Shabbos, saying, "*Bo'i kallah bo'i kallah*, we should realize that at that moment the world began functioning — *la'asos* — like a machine. Plants came from roots and seeds; human beings came from parents; everything came from something else. From now on there is no such thing as "new" creation.[13]

Hashem made peace between everything and it all works together

WHEN WE SAY *VAYECHULU* ON FRIDAY NIGHT, WE SHOULD UTILIZE THE opportunity and try to picture a world that was not functioning, a world that depended only on *devar Hashem* to bring each detail into

---

11. See *Awake My Glory* Chapter 2
12. *Tehillim* 33:6
13. See *The Beginning* p. 56 (2:3), *A Nation Is Born* p. 270 (20:8)

being. Only when Friday night was ushered in did it become *la'asos*, and everything began functioning, because *vayechulu*, it was all finished, it was perfected and everything worked together in perfect harmony, as we say, *oseh shalom u'vorei es hakol*, Hashem makes peace, harmony, between everything, and it all works together. The sun works together with the soil, which works together with the earthworms — without any one of them you couldn't have food. The wind works together with the seeds, and the rain works together with the carbon dioxide in the atmosphere. The force of gravity works together with the sun; the sun brings the water up from the oceans, then the wind takes over and conveys the rain clouds to the continent and the force of gravity brings the water from the clouds down to the earth and it runs back down to the sea.[14]

Birds function together with a farmer, because birds eat the pests that attack the produce. We need snakes to destroy field mice. Nowadays, everyone realizes that there is an ecosystem in which all of nature cooperates. This system had to have a Designer Who made such perfect machinery. *Vayechulu*, it was perfected; *oseh shalom*, He makes peace between all the elements in the world, including those within your body. Your bloodstream conveys nutrients to every cell in your body, and different nutrients are needed for every different cell. All these nutrients are mixed together in the bloodstream, and one doesn't contaminate the other. At the same time, the bloodstream is carrying the wastes away from your cells. So here you have a big tube carrying a river of various materials, some elements that will give energy, others that will replenish used-up cells from your organs and tissues, and at the same time it is carrying waste. *Oseh shalom*, Hashem makes peace between all of them, so they don't interfere with one another's functions.[15]

Hashem is like an air traffic controller

HASHEM IS LIKE AN AIR TRAFFIC CONTROLLER. HE SENDS OUT messages about which airplane should take which route so they do not collide in the air. The sky is teeming with aircraft, but each one goes on a specific, mathematically calculated route that no other airplane follows, and since they are in touch with the director of navigation, each will arrive at its landing place safely. Of course, in man-made circumstances

---

14. See *Praise My Soul* p. 256 (748), *Rejoice O Youth* p. 30 (63)
15. See *Sing You Righteous* p. 150 (335), *Praise My Soul* p. 257 (748)

there are always tragic errors, but when Hashem directs the traffic of nature, it continues to function perfectly forever. That is *vayechulu*.

Before saying vayechulu, think that the world was made out of nothing

SUPPOSE THAT, BEFORE YOU ACTUALLY SAY THESE WORDS ON FRIDAY night, you stop and think: What am I about to say? I am going to declare that the world was made out of nothing but the word of Hashem, and now, at this moment when the Shabbos comes, it was *la'asos*, this is when the world began to function.

Do you know what an achievement that is? It is a complete change of attitude. You will be declaring that there is no such thing as "nature," only the principle of *bayom hahu yihyeh Hashem Echad*, [16]Hashem will be One, and there is nothing but the *devar Hashem*; everything is nothing but the various manifestations of Hashem's Will. That is the way to think when you say *vayechulu*.

Is it difficult? Just think of the reward that is waiting for you if you will only think every Shabbos, "Now the world began to function, the universe began, with its many millions of parts." Even you yourself are composed of millions of parts. This grand machine with millions of gears and wheels and cogs all began revolving, functioning, moving in perfect harmony at that moment, with one signal from Hashem.

That is what you will think when you turn around and say *bo'i beshalom ateres ba'alah*. You are welcoming the Shabbos, but you are also welcoming the great opportunity that Shabbos gives you. This is what the Chumash tells us.

Hakadosh Baruch Hu made clear in the Torah the connection between Shabbos and Am Yisrael: "*Ve'atah daber el Bnei Yisrael,*[17] speak to Bnei Yisrael; *ach es Shabesosai tishmoru*, you should keep My Shabbosos." This means that you must keep Shabbos despite the fact that I am commanding you to busy yourselves with erecting the Mishkan — which is a tremendous achievement, because that is where the Presence of Hashem is going to reside; it would seem that everything else should make way for the building of the Mishkan. What is more important than building the House of Hashem? But Shabbos is more important than the *Beis Hamikdash*, more important than the Mishkan.

---

16. *Zechariah* 14:9
17. *Shemos* 31:13

Ach means "but" — despite all the instructions I gave you, when it comes to Shabbos you have something else to build — you have to build a Shabbos. The Shabbos is a *mikdash* in itself, a separate sanctuary, and one that is in a sense more important, because it is a sanctuary of the mind. The purpose of the *Beis Hamikdash* is to make people aware that Hashem dwells among Bnei Yisrael — that is a very important principle! But the principle that follows is more important: *Ki os hi beini u'veineichem ledoroseichem,*[18] because Shabbos is a sign between Me and you for all your generations.

Note the next words: *lada'as ki Ani Hashem mekadishchem* — Shabbos is for you *lada'as* — to *know.* One principle of Shabbos is to learn that "I Hashem have made you holy." How can Shabbos demonstrate that Hashem made us holy? This pasuk tells us: keep the Shabbos, and that supersedes the building of the *Beis Hamikdash,* because it is a sign between Me and you. Shabbos is for knowing.[19]

The Torah continues: *beini u'vein Bnei Yisrael os hi le'olam,*[20] it is a sign forever between Me and Bnei Yisrael. Why do you need Bnei Yisrael? Yeshaya Hanavi declares: "*Atem eidai ne'um Hashem,*[21] you are My witnesses, says Hashem." You, Bnei Yisrael, have a purpose to fulfill — you are in this world to testify about Me. That is a Jew's job. Say *Shema Yisrael...Hashem Echad* several times every day. Before you leave this life you attempt to make them your last words. We try always to be aware of this pasuk, because all our days we are testifying to the great principle that *Hashem Echad.* With these words we are declaring not merely that there is only one G-d, but that Hashem is everything and there is nothing but Hashem, nothing but His words — that is what Shabbos says: the whole world is only a result of His Will, and Shabbos is the sign between Me and you. I have chosen you as My testimony, so all your lives you should declare this to the world and to yourself. By keeping Shabbos, you are testifying.[22]

And so it is important, when Shabbos begins, to have in mind that you want to begin testifying. That is why Jews stand up and say together *vayechulu,* like witnesses. *Ve'amdu shnei ha'anashim lifnei Hashem,*[23] the two witnesses stand up and deliver testimony, *vayechu-*

---

18. *Shemos* 31:13
19. See *A Nation Is Born* p. 486 (35:2)
20. *Shemos* 31:17
21. *Yeshaya* 43:10
22. See *A Nation Is Born* p. 276 (20:11), *Praise My Soul* p. 307 (896)
23. *Devarim* 19:17

lu, that Hashem made everything out of nothing, and that *Hashem Echad*, He is One. The more you think it, the more the *malachim* will be happy to put their hands on your head and the more enthusiastically they will declare that your sins are forgiven. If a person accomplishes what Hashem wants of him, then certainly his sins will be forgiven.

Once you understand that your function in keeping Shabbos is to be a witness, you must appear properly in court to testify. A witness doesn't just walk down the street and say his testimony — he comes to the court. So on Shabbos you come to a place where the Jewish people gather, and you make a declaration. One of the ways of making this declaration is through Kiddush. You stand at your table clothed in your *bigdei Shabbos*, and you lift up the cup. In Torah culture, a cup is always a sign of declaring something important. *Vayechulu!* You are testifying, but at least you should know for yourself what you are saying. What are you thinking when you say these words? You are thinking of that principle that the world doesn't have any existence of its own, that it is only the words of Hashem that we see all around us. Even we ourselves are only manifestations of Hashem's words. The more frequently you say *vayechulu* with *kavanah*, the greater is the crown you are gaining, the crown of *de'ei chochmah lenafshecha vihi keser leroshecha*. Its wisdom is a transformation of your mind.

Everyone is aware of these ideas to some extent, but these words are telling tell us how to celebrate the Shabbos in order to gain the great benefit of Shabbos, which is a Torah mind.

Shabbos is a great gift

HAKADOSH BARUCH HU TOLD MOSHE RABBEINU THAT HE *MUST* GO and tell the Jewish people, "*Re'u* — see — *ki Hashem nasan lachem es haShabbos*[24] —that Hashem gave you the Shabbos." That is a remarkable introduction to any mitzvah. The Torah doesn't say that Hashem gave us *korbanos*, kashrus or Pesach; only Shabbos. The Gemara[25] explains the meaning of this unusual statement: *Amar Hakadosh Baruch Hu: matanah tovah yesh li beveis ginzai*, I have a precious gift in my treasure house, *veShabbos shemah*, it's called Shabbos, and I want to give it to Bnei Yisrael; *leich vehodi'am*, go and let them know.

Hashem wants Moshe Rabbeinu to let them know what they are getting. We will never appreciate Shabbos unless we let ourselves

---

24. *Shemos* 16:29
25. *Shabbos* 10

know what Shabbos is going to do for us. The Gemara says *matan secharah lo havi legilui*,[26] the rewards of Shabbos will never be revealed — that is how endless the benefits of Shabbos are. All our lives we must try to understand that Shabbos is giving us more and more reward. All mitzvos are paid out forever and ever, but here we have Shabbos singled out. *Re'u* — see; look into it. Appreciate how great is the value of what Shabbos will bring to you.[27]

The most important is the creation of a Torah mind. That is the *matanah tovah*, the wonderful gift that Hashem wants to give us. He chose from all of His possessions that which He considered one of the most desirable, and gave it to Am Yisrael.

When you spend Friday preparing for Shabbos think about Shabbos

IN ORDER FOR US TO APPRECIATE THE VALUE OF THE GIFT, OUR SAGES instituted a specific aspect of Shabbos preparation. When you spend all day Thursday and Friday preparing for Shabbos, you should do it with intention; think about Shabbos as you prepare. If you would leave out, let's say, the onions, the food will lack taste. But if you leave out the correct intent, everything lacks taste. As you prepare, think: This is for the great gift of Shabbos. That is the important *hachanah* for Shabbos. When you take a shower or bath *lechavod Shabbos*, keep in mind you are going to do something extremely important, and you want to be presentable in the best way possible in honor of the occasion, bathing and putting on *bigdei Shabbos*. As you march to the synagogue, you are coming to receive that gift. How fortunate you are that you survived for one more Shabbos, one more opportunity to gain that gift, week after week.

There are many principles that Shabbos can teach us.

When you sit down at the table Friday night, you have two challos before you on the table. They are a *zecher lamann*. The mann and the Shabbos are connected in a very important way. When the mann first came down, Hakadosh Baruch Hu admonished Bnei Yisrael that they should not go out on Shabbos expecting to find the mann. *Vayomer*[28] *Moshe ichluhu hayom*,[29] Moshe told them: Eat it today, on Shabbos, for you won't find it in the field. *Sheishes yamim tilke-*

---

26. *Shabbos* 10a
27. See *A Nation Is Born* p. 220 (16:29)
28. *Shemos* 16:25
29. *Shemos* 16:26

tuhu, every day for six days you should gather the mann, *u'vayom hashevi'i Shabbos, lo yihyeh bo*, but on Shabbos you won't find any.

What is the connection between mann and Shabbos? Mann is a very great lesson of *bitachon*. *Bitachon* means to know that Hakadosh Baruch Hu is managing your affairs. Because you keep Shabbos, you will have enough income to make up for the loss of that workday. The *shomer Shabbos* never loses out from his income because of Shabbos.

The great problem of mankind is earning a livelihood. In the beginning, Adam Harishon was created not for working. His purpose was to utilize his great mind to make progress in thinking. But subsequently, Hakadosh Baruch Hu said: You are better off if you work. Working means that most of your life is wasted, but a great part of that waste is caused by the worries that accompany our efforts for parnasah. How much better would it be for us if we could go through our daily chores calmly, with an assurance that everything will turn out right in the end because Hakadosh Baruch Hu manages everything. That is the great principle of *bitachon*.

Bitachon means in your mind there should be no turmoil

BITACHON DOESN'T MEAN TO RETIRE FROM YOUR JOB AND SIT AT HOME waiting for checks to come from the sky. You should continue to do whatever you are doing, but inwardly, in your mind, there should be no turmoil. Peace of mind is one of the great gifts that the Torah can bestow upon you. Anxiety causes a host of illnesses and spoils the happiness of life. Hakadosh Baruch Hu wants you to live normally, in what we call a natural mode of existence, but the results will depend solely on His Will. When a man knows that Hakadosh Baruch Hu is managing his life, he does his work with calmness and is reassured that whatever happens is intended for the best eventually.

That is what the mann says. When they went out to gather the mann, if someone was ambitious and gathered a double portion, and he came home and measured it, he found that it had shrunken down to a single portion. If he tried to store up the mann to last for a week, by the next day it had become wormy and was spoiled. Everyone could gather only enough for himself and his family. (Note that the Torah says you have to gather for your family. Man had to hustle and make a living for his family. That is included in the mann; you have to make a living for your family.)

This is the lesson of the mann: don't be in anxiety; everything is under control; you will succeed; Hakadosh Baruch Hu is in charge; whatever happens is for the best, and the best is what Hashem considers the best.[30]

Excitement affects the eyes

THE GEMARA SAYS:[31] *PESI'AH GASSAH* — STEPPING HASTILY — TAKES AWAY ⅟500 of a man's eyesight. When you are anxious and worried, running here and there, your eyesight is affected. Eye specialists will tell you that excitement often affects the eyes. David Hamelech said, "*Asheshah mika'as eini,*[32] My eye became worn out from *ka'as,* anger." So be careful of *ka'as;* it could ruin your eyes. I once lived with a man who was blind as a result of *ka'as.* Emotions, fright, and anxiety can upset the function of your eye nerves. The hasty footstep of *pesi'ah gassah,* the anxiety that plagues us all week, takes away ⅟500 of a man's eyesight.

Mai takanato, what is the remedy, the Gemara asks, that will restore his eyesight? Drink from the Kiddush he makes Friday night. How does that happen? You were so tired and so worried, but you've finally made it. Now you are standing dressed in *bigdei Shabbos,* with the wine in your hand, and it is all behind you. You are declaring that it was all a waste of worries, a waste of anxiety. *Vayechulu hashamayim veha'aretz* — everything was done by Hashem until now, and He is still in charge, conducting our affairs. Shabbos is a great consolation. Hashem says, "Don't worry. I'll take care of everything. You keep on doing what you are supposed to be doing, and leave everything to Me. I'll worry for you." That is what Shabbos tells us, and that is the way to restore your eyesight.[33]

Shabbos tells us not to worry

YOU ALSO LOSE YOUR EYESIGHT WHEN YOU LOSE SIGHT OF THE GREAT principles of truth; you can lose your mental eyesight during the week. You become materialistic; you think everything depends on your efforts to make a living — if you think your efforts will give you success,

---

30. See *A Nation Is Born* p. 216 (16:25)
31. *Berachos* 43b
32. *Tehillim* 6:8
33. See *Rejoice O Youth* p. 370 (869)

you might be disappointed. And so on Friday night your spiritual eye-sight is restored.

That is the lesson that our forefathers learned in the midbar when they ate the mann. Every Shabbos as they sat at their tables in their tents in the midbar and enjoyed the mann, they were thinking about the great principle of it being no use even trying to get more in the midbar; no use saving up in the midbar. Every day Hakadosh Baruch Hu sends you your allotted portion — there is nothing to worry about. And they were thinking, what will be when we get to Eretz Yisrael? We will have to plow the land and plant and reap. We will have to grind the wheat, knead it, bake it, and make bread. We will have to exert effort. But in those days we should keep in mind the lesson of the mann, even though once we start trying to make a liv-ing for ourselves, we should know that we are not the ones accom-plishing it. *Baruch Ata Hashem hazan es hakol*, You Hashem are the One Who feeds everyone.

Hashem, not the baker, gives you the bread

WHEN THEY WERE SITTING IN THE MIDBAR EATING THE MANN, THEY were preparing themselves and telling their children, "Children, we may not live to enter Eretz Yisrael, but when you come there, don't forget the mann. Everything you ever get will be nothing but mann. Even when you go to a store and buy canned goods, it is mann. It is not the food factory and it is not the people who made these products who are feeding you. *Nosen lechem lechol basar* — Hashem gives you bread, not the baker! As the baker stretches out his hand to give you a loaf of bread, it is the Hand of Hashem. *Posei'ach es yadecha*[34] — you should look at his hand as the Hand of Hashem. And as you pay him for the bread, you too are Hashem's Hand, supporting the baker."[35]

That is how they studied in the midbar. Moshe Rabbeinu explained it to them and it was interpreted by means of all those who helped him, the *zekeinim*, who taught the people these principles: Shabbos and *bitachon* and mann all show that Hakadosh Baruch Hu cares for us lovingly. Do away with all anxiety! You should live your whole life with confidence that it will all turn out well in the end. The most important part of your success is not just in living a happy life, but in succeeding in gaining a Torah mind. Shabbos is to gain *da'as*. *Vihi*

---

34. *Tehillim* 145:16
35. See *Praise My Soul* p. 141 (396)

keser leroshecha, there is a crown on your head, the crown of knowledge that everything is under control.

Shabbos means "Slow down, I'll take care of everything. You do what you can, and it will be well in the end."

Hashem is in control. The lessons of the Shabbos are intended to permeate the entire week. When the pasuk says *zachor es yom haShabbos*,[36] remember the Shabbos, it means to remember the Shabbos principles all week long.

When you come to the Shabbos table you see two challos with one cloth covering them and another cloth underneath, exactly like the mann, which rested between two layers of pure dew. Don't go to the table without thinking of this symbolism. And there are two challos, *lechem mishneh*, at every Shabbos meal, to remind you that Shabbos and mann — *bitachon*, trust in Hashem — are all one. All our lives, even when we are being persecuted and harassed, when we are worried or frightened, we must keep in mind that Hakadosh Baruch Hu is in charge.

Another opportunity that Shabbos offers us is the awareness that it is *mei'ein Olam Haba*, a premonition of the World to Come. As you sit at the Shabbos table you should think, "This is a rehearsal for *Olam Haba*." Teach that to your children, too. They won't understand it, but in forty years they will. Tell them, "*Mi shetarach be'erev Shabbos ...,*"[37] if your mother hadn't gone shopping and cooked on erev Shabbos, there wouldn't be any Shabbos. If I hadn't worked six days, there wouldn't be any Shabbos. You have to prepare for Shabbos. Now that we've prepared, we have Shabbos. And if you want to prepare for the World to Come, you have to do some shopping; you have to work, to make preparations. If a man was loafing all week and his wife was taking it easy all week, then there is nothing to eat and they sit at a desolate table on Shabbos. The same thing will happen in the World to Come. You must prepare for the World to Come.

"*Ogeir bakayitz ben maskil*,"[38] the wise son is busy collecting the harvest in the summertime, as long as the produce is available. When you enter the funeral home, the winter begins. Whatever you prepared to take along during the summertime, you will have. That is what you should think Friday night at the table — it is a rehearsal.[39]

---

36. *Shemos* 20:8
37. *Avodah Zarah* 3a
38. *Mishlei* 10:5
39. See *A Nation Is Born* p. 277 (20:11), *Sing You Righteous* p. 253 (540)

Shabbos reminds us of the World to Come

THINK, TOO, HOW MUCH YOU ARE GOING TO ENJOY SHABBOS, AND know that *Olam Haba* is going to be a million times more enjoyable. You will be together with your family, there will be children and grandchildren and great-grandchildren there, all together. In the scenario Hakadosh Baruch Hu will make, you will all enjoy the *yom shekulo Shabbos* forever and ever. *Zemiros* will resound at your Shabbos table forever, and you will never tire of eating there. They will serve one fine dish after the other, beyond the ability of the best chef in this world to conjure up in his mind. There will be happiness without end. That is what you are supposed to think about on Shabbos.

The more you enjoy the Shabbos, the more happiness you will enjoy in *Olam Haba*. Even if all you can afford is a piece of challah and herring, think what a mitzvah it is to enjoy that food, and as you eat it, trying to get the fullest delight out of it. Eventually this happiness will multiply infinitely. *Kol hamisangim ba yizku lerov simchah.*

It is important to utilize the opportunity of Shabbos. As you sit and look at the light of the candles burning, think about light. How do candles in combustion cause light? It has never been explained. Light is a form of energy. This energy is produced when the wick burns and melts the paraffin. That energy could have been sound or all heat, but it is transformed into a particular form of energy called light. Light is a miracle, but our nerves and senses are desensitized to this miraculous phenomenon. As you look at this light you are seeing a creation of Hashem. *Vayomer Elokim yehi ohr,*[40] let there be light!

Everything in the world demonstrates mysteries of Hashem's management. We can't explain these things. They are so complicated, they are beyond understanding! The entire world is a mystery. Why is it that when you drop a spoon from your table on Shabbos, it doesn't fall onto the ceiling but only onto the floor? You explain this mystery with the concept of gravity: the earth is a bigger body than the spoon, so the earth attracts the spoon. A bigger body attracts a smaller body. Can you see the attraction? If you wave your hand between the spoon and the floor, will you feel the attraction? *Ki hu amar,* Hashem commanded the forces of nature to come into being.

Gravity, light, and sound are all miracles. How do sound waves travel? Nobody knows. Their impulses travel between us, and a

---

40. *Bereishis* 1:3

machine can capture the impulses and show them as pictures. These pictures are themselves miracles; the whole world is a miracle. People who think they understand are greatly mistaken. They never even think about the root causes of the miracles. There is only one root cause — *Hashem Echad*. That is what Shabbos says: Hashem with His words caused everything to come into being.

Shabbos reminds us that we are Hashem's armies

THE TORAH STATES THAT SHABBOS IS *ZECHER LITZI'AS MITZRAYIM*; the Gemara[41] tells us that if you don't mention *yetzi'as Mitzrayim* on Shabbos you have not fulfilled the mitzvah of Kiddush. What is the connection? The purpose of *yetzi'as Mitzrayim* was, as the Torah states openly, *asher hotzeisi eschem mei'eretz Mitzrayim lih'yos lachem leilokim*,[42] "so that I should be your *Elokim*," which means that I, Hashem, am now hiring you and engaging you in My service, as it says, "*yatzu kol tzivos* Hashem,[43] all the armies of Hashem went out of Mitzrayim." We are Hashem's armies! Iyov says, "*halo tzava la'enosh al ha'aretz*,[44] a man has military service in this world." We are drafted by Hashem, for the service of "*atem eidai*, you are My witnesses, says Hashem."[45]

We went out of Mitzrayim in order to demonstrate and declare all our lives, all throughout our history, that *Hashem Echad*. Shabbos is a great opportunity for this, because this is exactly what Shabbos says. Shabbos and *yetzi'as Mitzrayim* are one. *Ki os hi veini u'veinecha*,[46] it is a sign between you and Me: I took you out of Mitzrayim, so you be My witnesses. It is a sign that Hashem created the world out of nothing in six days, and you have to present that to the world.

Our main method is to preach to ourselves and to our families, and Shabbos is a glorious opportunity for that. It is for this purpose that we were taken out of Mitzrayim and made into a nation. Our purpose is to keep Shabbos; that is why Shabbos is of the utmost importance. To profane Shabbos is a capital crime, punishable by *sekilah*. A per-

41. *Pesachim* 117a
42. *Bamidbar* 15:41
43. *Shemos* 12:41
44. *Iyov* 7:1
45. See *Fortunate Nation* p. 66 (5:15), *Praise My Soul* p. 334 (992), *A Nation Is Born* p. 276 (20:11)
46. *Shemos* 31:13

son who profanes Shabbos loses his right to exist, because the whole purpose of his existence is to proclaim these great principles to the world and to himself.

The Torah also states that Hashem gave the Shabbos *lema'an yanu'ach shorcha*,[47] that your ox should be able to rest, *veyinafeish ben amasecha*,[48] your slave boy should have a rest. When the slave boy sees Shabbos is coming, he tells his boss, "It's Shabbos; I'm stopping," and the boss doesn't say a word. On the contrary, the boss should tell him to stop. He stops because he has to imitate Hashem. *Ki vo shavas vayinafash*,[49] because Hashem stopped and He "rested."

Shabbos teaches us compassion

HASHEM USED THE WORD "*VAYINAFASH*, AND HASHEM RESTED," AND your servant has to rest, too — the Torah says "*Veyinafeish ben amasecha*," using the exact same words. We emulate Hashem. Hashem doesn't have to rest; He wants us to rest, and even about our slave boys Hashem said: Don't drive him to despair. Give him a chance to rest![50]

Sheinah beShabbos ta'anug, the Sages[51] tell us, sleeping on Shabbos is one of the pleasures of the Shabbos. So when you lie down on Shabbos to take a nap, have in mind that you are doing what Hashem did. Hashem didn't sleep; He "acted" like He was sleeping, because He wanted you to do the same. You shouldn't be ashamed of sleeping on Shabbos, thinking, "How could I sleep on such a holy day? It is a shame to sleep on Shabbos, such a glorious day." This is not the correct attitude. Hashem rested on Shabbos, so you rest also. Hashem was willing to use that expression, saying that He was resting, although it doesn't apply to Hashem. But Hashem wants to help you. He sacrifices some of His *kavod* by saying He rested, and so you should rest. Hashem has compassion on us. He wants us to rest. It is an opportunity for us to come to recognize the great teachings that Hashem wants to bestow upon us. That is why resting on Shabbos is a blessing.

Hakadosh Baruch Hu announced that Shabbos is for compassion too, so on Shabbos people get together and think about doing good things for others. Shabbos is a time when people would put their

---

47. *Shemos* 23:12
48. *Shemos* 23:12
49. *Shemos* 31:17
50. See *A Nation Is Born* p. 275 (20:11), See *The Beginning* p. 54 (2:2)
51. *Yalkut Reuveni, Parashas Va'eschanan*

heads together and put forth their best efforts for the welfare of their fellow man. Most of the good organizations that Jews have begun started on Shabbos, *Ki hi mekor haberachah*, because it is a fountain of blessing. All week people are too busy to think about each other. Their minds are occupied with parnasah. On Shabbos the kehillah comes together and people notice what is needed and raise money for good causes. So Shabbos is the source of all good things.

Vayevarech Elokim es yom hashevi'i,[52] Hashem blesses the Shabbos day. From Shabbos comes forth all good things. When does the father have the opportunity to examine his children to see whether they are learning well? You have to do that yourself — don't rely on the yeshivah or even on a private tutor. You must check up on your child. Is he becoming discouraged? You must continually supervise his learning.

All the blessings come from Shabbos. *Matan secharah lo havi legilui*, the reward of Shabbos will never be discovered. Although you will never discover the reward for any mitzvah — *Ein atah yodei'a matan secharan shel mitzvos* — Shabbos has so many by-products, so many different results, that you can't know where they come from. Many times people's lives are saved because of Shabbos; yeshivos are funded by appeals on Shabbos. Shabbos has so many different facets to it that bring in blessings. This is why Hakadosh Baruch Hu said of Shabbos "*re'u* — see," look into it, tell the people about it. They should realize what a great gift it is, for they will never understand fully how profound is the benefit of Shabbos.

These are only the beginnings of the thoughts you could utilize on Shabbos. So *de'ei chochmah lenafshecha*, know wisdom for yourself — for your own sake; *vihi keser leroshecha*, it will be a crown on top of your head, a crown of gold studded with diamonds. *Netzor mitzvas Kedoshecha, shemor Shabbos kodshecha*, keep Shabbos — not only by not working on Shabbos, but keep the Shabbos with all the possibilities that Shabbos can give you, so that you can gain the crown on your head.

---

52. *Bereishis* 2:3

BRINGING UP CHILDREN 4

Of all the children you have, the best one is yourself

F ALL THE CHILDREN YOU HAVE OR EVER WILL HAVE, THE best one is yourself, and so, whenever you learn something on the subject of teaching children, remember that it applies equally to teaching oneself. "*Eileh toldos Noach, Noach...*[1] — The children of Noach were Noach." So if you want to have nachas, get busy on yourself!

Yirmiyahu Hanavi said, "*Ve'ayir pere adam yivaled,*[2] a man is born a young wild donkey." Even when a donkey is tame, it is still a donkey; but when a man is born he is compared to a wild donkey, and a young one at that. An old wild donkey has, at least, learned something from experience, but a young one has no experience behind it.

---

1. *Bereishis* 6:9
2. *Iyov* 11:12

A one-day-old ox is already an ox, but a one-day-old human being is entirely independent

THE *NAVI* TELLS US THIS BIT OF INFORMATION TO LET US KNOW THAT there is work to be done. By the time a young wild donkey grows old, he gains the experience of the wild, but if a human being is not taught, he will remain "young" all his life — he'll always be immature, with all the faults of his youth. And so Hakadosh Baruch Hu gave human beings a big job to do; He designed their career, their lifestyle, altogether different from that of an animal. "*Shor ben yomo karui shor*," [3] the Sages tell us — a one-day-old ox is already an ox. It can already stand and walk, but a one-day-old human being is weak, defenseless, and entirely dependent. This is Hashem's plan, and we have to study it.

Living is a glorious career, but if you never prepare for it you can ruin it

HAKADOSH BARUCH HU MADE HUMANS DEPENDENT ON THEIR PARENTS for so long so that they should have a long apprenticeship with their parents and learn the art of being a man. This doesn't come naturally; being an *adam*, a human being, is something we have to learn through much instruction, and instruction is most effective when the one who gives it is someone on whom we are physically dependent. Living is a glorious career, but if you never prepare for it you can ruin it, either partially or entirely.

You have to learn how to do everything in life. What if you never learned to eat and were too lazy to chew? You'd have to learn to predigest the food in your mouth. You'd need someone standing over you demanding that you chew; if you chew properly, the saliva acts on the food and begins the process of digestion and makes it easier for your intestinal tract to do its job. The stomach is not supposed to be teeth; you need both. There are many things that animals know through instincts that are created precisely for their needs, since they cannot talk and they cannot teach. We don't have most of the useful instincts that other creatures possess, so we have to gain those skills and that understanding through instruction.

---

3. *Bava Kamma* 65b

You must be taught how to live
with your brothers and sisters

YOU MUST BE TAUGHT HOW TO LIVE WITH YOUR BROTHERS AND
sisters, because mastering the art of getting along with others is
the first requirement for living in the world. A human being is a social
creature, not a lone creature like an eagle living alone on a mountain
or tall pine. That is why there are brothers and sisters in the house.
When an animal matures a bit, it goes off to live on its own and loses
contact with the family. A human family stays together for many years
before its members separate, because they have to be trained to get
along; then they can go out and get married, deal with an employer, a
neighbor, a landlord.

And children must be taught the important lesson of not wasting
anything, otherwise they will not have what they need. If you don't
save, you don't have! It is in the home that children are prepared for
living successfully and happily in this world.[4]

But the truth is, the home is a preparation for the World to Come,
because "*Olam hazeh domeh laprozdor bifnei Olam Haba*[5] — this world
is a vestibule before the World to Come." What do you do in a vestibule?
"*Haskein atzmecha ...*" — ready yourself in order to enter the great banquet hall. But even before we enter this world — before we go into the
lobby where they are handing out just the knishes — we also have to be
prepared, and it is in the home that we prepare ourselves to go out into
this world with happiness, where we prepare ourselves for *Olam Haba*.

Where the Torah describes how Hakadosh Baruch Hu completed
everything, it uses the words "... *es melachto asher asah*[6] — the work
that He did." If it was Hakadosh Baruch Hu's work, we know that He
did it! Why the extra words, *asher asah*? Soon afterward, the Torah
repeats these "superfluous" words again, describing how Hashem
rested *mikol melachto asher asah*. And so we know that something
important is being pointed out to us here.

Human beings have to be polished

THE TORAH IS TELLING US THAT THE WORK THAT *HE DID* WAS FINISHED,
but there is other work to be done, besides that which Hashem did.

4. See *Awake My Glory* p. 351 (1117)
5. *Avos* 4:16
6. *Bereishis* 2:2

We pick up where Hashem left off: we have to make human beings, to fashion and polish them, to sand them; to instruct them and prepare them for the career of being what they have to be. The Yerushalmi states, "*Afilu ha'adam tzarich asiyah* — even man needs to be 'made.'" As the Gemara explains on the words "*va'asisem osam* — you should *do* — or *make* — them," the word *osam* appears without a *vav*, so it can be read as *atem*, yourselves — "You should make yourselves."[7]

Talking to yourself for a purpose is invaluable.

WE USE THE WORD *CHINUCH* TO DESCRIBE THIS JOB. "*CHANOCH lana'ar al pi darko*[8] — train a youth according to his way," according to the way that he will need to go in life, because he is embarking on a great journey. What if a person's parents didn't teach him? David Hamelech was in that position, as he says, "*Ki avi ve'imi azavuni*[9] — my parents forsook me," because he had to run away to save his life and couldn't remain to listen to his parents' instruction; then *Hashem ya'asfeini* — Hashem will take me in. As Rav Yisrael Salanter said, you should take Hashem's words and say them to yourself in lieu of what your parents should do for you, and so he instituted the practice of learning mussar. Talking to yourself *for a purpose* is invaluable.

The Hebrew word *omein* denotes training a child. The Megillah tells us that Mordecai was *omein es Haddasah*.[10] When her parents died, he took her in and trained her. *Omein* sounds like *amen*, which is like *emunah*. *Emunah* means to be steadfast, to stick to the path you chose, through thick and thin. Even when other religions reigned supreme, and the Jew was pressured and threatened from all sides, harassed and sometimes slaughtered, he kept his *emunah*, he was steadfast. The Torah says about Moshe Rabbeinu, "*vayehi yadav emunah*[11] — his hands were steadfast"; Moshe didn't lower his hands. This is the meaning of *emunah* — to stick to the place where you chose to be. *Amen* means "That is how it is going to be." With *amen*, we declare that the words of a berachah will be that way — it means to be steadfast.[12]

---

7. See *The Beginning* p. 57 (2:3)
8. *Mishlei* 22:6
9. *Tehillim* 27:6
10. *Esther* 2:7
11. *Shemos* 17:12
12. See *A Nation Is Born* p. 226 (17:12)

A mother makes a child
into what he will be forever

BUT WE CAN LOOK AT *AMEN* AS A TWO-LETTER ROOT WORD, SINCE *amen* is associated with *emes*, truth; the *nun* then changes to a *saf*, so *emunah* and *emes* are one word. So the *nun* is not part of the root of the word *amen*. We are left with *alef-mem* — *eim*, mother! So Mordechai was *omein es Hadassah*, he "mothered" Esther. A mother makes a child into what he will be forever; and if she doesn't do it correctly, it will still be forever. If she allows her child to be lazy or selfish or mean, she is also *omein*, and that is how he will remain as an adult. That is *emunah* — it will be steadfast, forever. Before the child even enters pre-1A, she already did the job. When someone asked Rav Simchah Zissel Ziv, "How old should my child be when I start training him?" Reb Simchah Zissel answered, "From this second, while he is an infant!"

It is never too late to change, but a person is made in his earliest years. "*Halomed yeled lemah hu domeh...*[13] — if he learns when he is young, what is he like? Like ink written on fresh paper." The ink sinks in and makes an impression that lasts. What you accomplish early is of the utmost importance.

There are various other forms of the word. The word *omer*, to talk, means mother-talk. In many words in *lashon hakodesh*, a *reish* is added to the root of a word but isn't really part of it, such as *dibbeir*, from the word *dibbah*; *chakor* from *chok* or *cheik*; *hadar*, which is related to *hod*; *gozer* from *goz*; *kavar*, which is related to *kov* and *kubah*; *ozer*, which is related to *oz*, and many others. In the same way, *amar*, talk, comes from *em*; *amar* means what a mother says to a child. That is the first talk a child hears, and it is the real talk. Of course, you can learn elegant language later on in life, but your basic thinking is based on what was put in your head when you were a child.

When you speak to a person
you are engraving ideas forever on his heart

AND SO WE CAN BEGIN TO UNDERSTAND WHY THE TORAH STRESSES so often "*Dabbeir el Bnei Yisrael*,[14] Speak to the Jewish people." That is a big job of Moshe Rabbeinu's, as it is of all of us. *Dabbeir*

---

13. *Avos* 4:20
14. *Bamidbar* 15:38

means more than speak. It means to lead — when you talk to someone, you are leading him in a certain direction. Do you realize what a responsibility you have when you open your mouth? When you speak to a person, you are actually engraving ideas forever on his heart, and you'll never be able to erase what you told him. Even if you forget, your words sink down into his subconscious and remain there forever, and they affect all of his thoughts and emotions.

A fool will have an effect on you forever

THIS IS WHY SHLOMO HAMELECH SAID, "*PAGOSH DOV SHAKUL BE'ISH* ..."[15] — Let a man meet an enraged bear, a mother bear that has lost her cubs, rather than to encounter a fool in his foolishness. A bear that has lost her cubs is the worst kind of animal to meet, because she is looking for someone on whom to vent her anger. But that is better than running into a fool who will buttonhole you and say, "Oh, Chaim, do you know what I heard today ...?" and fill your ears with foolishness. The bear endangers your life, but the fool will have an effect on you forever. In the same way, people who watch television are injecting garbage into their brains and into their souls, and it will remain there forever. You'll never be able to get rid of it. And so *dabbeir*, speaking to people, means leading them. When you talk to anyone, you are guiding him.

If only we could eavesdrop on a conversation between Shlomo Hamelech and his mother, we would learn so much, we wouldn't need any lectures! We can find just such a conversation in Chapter 31 of *Mishlei*, which speaks of *divrei Lemu'el melech* — the words of the king Lemuel. Lemuel is a nickname, which means "for G-d." Shlomo Hamelech was brought up to be for Hashem. David had promised Batsheva that her son would sit on the throne, so she was preparing him from the start. What she told him applies to all of us, because *Kol Yisrael bnei melachim heim* — every Jew is a king, and we have to learn that right away, or we won't understand anything about Judaism. Hashem first sent Moshe Rabbeinu to Pharaoh to make a declaration that reverberated this day: "*Beni bechori Yisrael*[16]— Yisrael is My firstborn son," so we are certainly *bnei melachim*, children of kings. We must all prepare for a career of kings, and so all that Batsheva said to her son applies fully to us.[17]

---

15. *Mishlei* 17:12
16. *Shemos* 4:22
17. See *A Nation Is Born* p. 60 (4:22)

Shlomo tells us *masa asher yiserato imo*[18] — a lecture, which his mother chastised him. It wasn't just a simple conversation; she wasn't pampering him or "smoothing his fur." She was ruffling his feathers! The Gemara tells us that she told him to bend over, and she dealt him blows! And each time the slipper went down, she would say a pasuk. And Shlomo was not thinking about the indignity or the pain; he was thinking about what she was saying, and he was trying to memorize the words. And when it was all over, he went off and reviewed it all, and then he recorded it in writing.

In those sessions, his mother addressed him in three ways: "*Mah bri* — what is this, my son; *u'mah bar bitni* — and what is this, son of my belly; *u'meh bar nedarai* — and what is this, son of my vows?"

Shlomo's mother was planning and dreaming for his future long before he entered the world

BRI, MY SON, IS AN ARAMAIC TERM. IN ANCIENT HEBREW, SLIPPING IN some Aramaic was a way of saying something poetic. *Bri* is a special expression of affection, not just a matter-of-fact expression, Rav Saadia Gaon explains. *Bri* says: You are my beloved child; my heart is in you, and so your behavior is hurting and distressing me very much. And *mah bar bitni*, in addition to the fact that you are my son, I carried you around in my belly, and all that time I was thinking and hoping that you would turn out to be the very best. When Shlomo's mother was expecting a child, she did not think only of how she should conduct herself to make sure her child would be healthy; she was planning and dreaming for his future long before he entered the world.

And she said *u'meh bar nedarai*, what is this, son of my vows? Even before you were conceived, I was praying to Hakadosh Baruch Hu for you, and I made vows for you. I told Hashem: Give me a child and I will fast; I will bring offerings; I will give tzedakah, and so on. She made many vows, and that son was a gift from *Shamayim* in response to her prayers. And so, she told her son, is this what I wanted?

Shlomo's mother told him many things that are listed in that chapter of *Mishlei*, enough to make up many lectures, and we can be sure that her words had an effect, because Shlomo repeats in *Mishlei*, "*Shema beni mussar avicha ve'al titosh Toras imecha*[19] — Hear,

18. *Mishlei* 31:1
19. *Mishlei* 1:8

my son, the instruction of your father, and forsake not the Torah of your mother."

The job of a parent continues forever

THE JOB OF BEING A PARENT CONTINUES FOREVER; YOU'LL NEVER complete the function of influencing your children as long as you live. Don't lean back and relax when you are older, because the watchful eye of the father and grandfather, of the mother and grandmother should continue to train the family, and not just to teach them *derech eretz*, but "*Dor ledor yeshabach ma'asecha*[20] — generation to generation should praise Your deeds, Hashem." You will never learn on your own to appreciate Hakadosh Baruch Hu or his Torah, to have *emunah*, unless you have a tradition handed down. A person's parents and grandparents stand behind him.

Today, many people do not have the good, Torah influence of their parents and grandparents, so they have to find "foster parents" — teachers to influence and guide them. "*Veshinantam levanecha*[21] — You should teach them to your children," says the Torah. Who are the children? The Gemara says "*Eileh hatalmidim*[22] — these are one's disciples."

In times of old, the Gemara tells us, there were no schools for children. Such schools were begun only in the time of the second *Beis Hamikdash*. That was the first instance of compulsory education, whereas among other nations, even as late as the late 19th century, there was no compulsory education. In 1870, when the Germans were holding French army officers captive in the war, the French had to sign a document promising that if they were released they would not participate in any warfare against Germany; the French officers were unable to sign their names! It is a great triumph for us that compulsory education existed over 2,000 years before this time!

In the olden times every home was a school

YET WE CAN ASK THE QUESTION: WHY DIDN'T MOSHE RABBEINU himself institute schools? The simple answer is that compulsory education was not necessary after the Torah was given — every home was a school where the father taught Torah to his sons, as the Torah says, "*Veshinantam levanecha*," at all times, in every spare moment —

---

20. *Tehillim* 145:4
21. *Devarim* 6:7
22. *Sifrei, Parashas Va'eschanan*

"beshivtecha beveisecha u'v'lechtecha vaderech, u'v'shochbecha u'v'kumecha"[23] — whether you are at home or on the road, before you go to sleep and when you get up in the morning, before you go to work. Nor did girls need schools. The mother was teaching them all day; she would teach them *emunah* and *yiras Hashem* along with all the other skills they would need to live in the world.

The best Bais Yaakov education does not help if there is no training in the house

EVEN WHEN THERE IS COMPULSORY EDUCATION FOR CHILDREN, IF parents raise a child without training him to be a mensch, the compulsory education he receives is of no benefit to him. It was a tremendous achievement of Sara Schenirer's, may her memory be blessed, to have raised a generation of proud and knowledgeable Jewish girls and women. But the best Bais Yaakov education does not help if a girl never learned to get along with other people during those years. In the ancient Bais Yaakov, they didn't learn Chumash with Malbim, Abarbanel, Or HaChaim and all the other *mefarshim*, but they learned Chumash with *derech eretz*, with the arts of proper living. When a girl in Russia, Hungary, Spain or Bavel moved on to her husband's home, she was a finished product, well trained in the career of living.

A Bais Yaakov wife may know a lot — Jewish history, *dinim* — sometimes more than a boy knows — and she might even know all about cooking; but there still may be a lot of things she hasn't yet learned. She may never have learned what topics not to discuss, and she may never have learned to keep herself appealing to her husband. Of course, idealism is very important and very necessary, but the basic, practical lessons of marriage are crucial. The old, home-based "Bais Yaakovs" would teach their girls these things, and the girls came out finished products — painted, varnished, shiny, and smooth!

Being a mensch is an integral part of Judaism.

PARENTS' OBLIGATION TO TEACH THEIR BOYS IS NO LESS DEMANDING. A boy may come out of yeshivah as a tzaddik, ready to get married — he may be everything, but not always a mensch! His mother must participate in his training, so that he learns to get along with people and so that he learns all the arts of living in the line of Torah. Being a mensch is an

---

23. *Devarim* 6:7

integral part of Judaism. This is *Torah Sheba'al Peh*; without it, you cannot know how to execute *Torah Shebichsav*. If you learn only *Torah Shebichsav*, you won't have any idea how to slaughter an animal — as the Gemara[24] asks, maybe you should slaughter it from the tail? *Torah Shebichsav* tells us about Rosh Hashanah, "*Yom teru'ah yihyeh lachem*,"[25] it is the day of blowing; but blowing what? How? Hakadosh Baruch Hu gave the Torah in such a way that it is impossible to understand it from the written Torah alone, because *He wanted you to go to a live teacher to learn!* Even though they finally gave permission to write down the *Torah Sheba'al Peh*, people must go to learn from living teachers. And while you are learning Torah from these teachers, they will teach you how to be a human being, too, and how to *practice* Torah, because the theory and the practice are two different things.

A young man may be learning *perek Merubah*, for example, learning how bad it is to steal — if you steal you have to pay double; he is learning it well, with Gemara, Rashi, and Tosafos. But the fact is, he stole the Gemara he is learning in from a nearby synagogue — stealing a *sefer* is called stealing. You can't use a *sefer* you found in a synagogue without permission.

So it is not enough to learn the theory of Torah; you need a rebbe to guide you; you need a mother and a father to train you all your life. When a mother begins her job, she is never finished; as long as she lives, she has to stand guard. And what she put into her children's heads in their earliest years was what they got first, and it will continue to influence them forever.

Whatever you say to a child registers in his brain

AND SO, WHEN PARENTS ARE TALKING IN THE PRESENCE OF THEIR children, they shouldn't think that the children don't hear; everything they say is being recorded. If parents are talking to their children and the children seem to be uninterested, don't be discouraged. A tzaddik once said, "*Kol ta'alumah einah chozeres reikam*— no propaganda is wasted." Whatever you say to the child registers in his brain, even though he doesn't seem to care about it. It is etched in his mind.

Always remember, of course, that the voice of the Jewish people is *Shema Yisrael* — Listen, Yisrael! And to Whom do you listen? To your Father in Heaven — *Hashem Elokeinu, Hashem echad*. He is the *only*

24. *Chullin* 27a
25. *Bamidbar* 29:1

one you should listen to. And when a mother and a father both talk His words and we listen, that is *Hashem echad*. But if a parent speaks things that Hakadosh Baruch Hu doesn't want him to say, if a parent speaks of wealth, ambition, good times, *olam hazeh*, liberalism, and so on, then it is up to the child to exercise his option of not listening.

What happens if you have a good child and you have done a good job on him? When does a parent have the right to lean back and relax? The Gemara explains the pasuk in *sefer Zechariah*, "*Velayotzei u'va ein shalom*[26] — for the one who goes out and comes there is no shalom": Rav comments, "*Keivan sheyotzei adam midevar halachah lidevar mikra*,[27] when a man forsakes Gemara and instead learns Tanach, *ein lo shalom*, he has no shalom." There is a major principle involved here. What is so bad about a man learning Tanach diligently? Aren't we happy to see that? No, explains Rashi, you can't learn any halachos from the Tanach, "*shehamishnah mefaresh sitmas haTorah*, the Mishnah explains the Torah's mysteries." So if you "go out" of Mishnah or Gemara and go to Tanach, *ein shalom*.

Hakadosh Baruch Hu is not satisfied with a minimum

IF SOMEONE COMES IN FROM THE STREET, AND UNTIL NOW ALL HE HAS learned were African studies, and now he is beginning to learn Tanach or siddur — we greet him, we help him and teach him, we teach him alef-bais and siddur, and we teach him how to be a Jew. But if there is a person who could have been better, if he came from a strong Torah background but chose an easier career of learning only Tanach instead of Mishnah and Gemara, then *ein shalom*. A person should never be satisfied with a minimum, because Hakadosh Baruch Hu is not satisfied with a minimum. No matter how good you are, if you could have been better, then you are blamed for not being better!

The Gemara[28] states, "*Botzei'a beirach ni'etz* Hashem[29] — If you bless a robber, you make Hashem angry." Rav Meir says that this statement is referring to Yehudah — Yehudah is the *botzei'a*, the robber. When Yehudah saw that his brothers had sentenced Yosef to death because they considered him to be a *navi sheker*, he stepped in and

---

26. *Zechariah* 8:10
27. *Chagigah* 10a
28. *Sanhedrin* 6b
29. *Tehillim* 10:3

said, "*Mah betza ki naharog es achinu?* What benefit is there in killing him? Let's sell him instead." Yehudah is the hero who saved Yosef's life, but Rav Meir says he is a *botzei'a*, because he left off half the job. Why didn't he say, "Let's bring him back to his father"? He failed to go all the way, and Hashem is displeased with someone who does half a job.

Of course, half a job is a great achievement. We love someone who achieves that much; it is a glorious thing to learn half a *masechta*, but it is not a full job, and Hashem is displeased.

And so parents must make sure they do the full job with their children! Choose the very best school for your daughter. Don't send your son to a yeshivah on a lower level. Send him to a place where the atmosphere is Torah-true. And don't encourage your child to interrupt his learning at a certain point to pursue a career. It's wonderful that we have frum professionals we can be proud of, but why not make your children talmidei chachamim we can be proud of?

A woman can believe in Hakadosh Baruch Hu and think about him all day long

EVERYONE SHOULD DO *HIS* BEST. YOU MAY BE A FRUM, IDEALISTIC young man who keeps all the mitzvos, but are you doing all that you really could do? Are you learning and making progress toward becoming a big *lamdan*, a *ben Torah,* and a *yarei Shamayim*? As a frum woman, are you doing all you can? There are happy, busy, sociable women who are *mekayem shemiras halashon* — it's not impossible! And a woman can believe in Hakadosh Baruch Hu and think about Him all day long. A woman can climb the ladder of Yaakov Avinu, *sulam mutzav artzah verosho magi'a hashamaymah.*[30] She can pray to Hakadosh Baruch Hu constantly; pray to him that the oatmeal turn out well, that the challos turn out well .... She can climb the ladder all day, so why should she remain standing in the middle?

It is the parents' responsibility, as long as they have the opportunity, to look forward always to their children's future, like Shlomo Hamelech's mother did. Even before her son was born, she prayed and she dreamed; she wanted the very best that she could produce. This very same opportunity is given to all parents, and in the earliest years they can lay the foundations that will last forever.

---

30. *Bereishis* 28:12

BRINGING UP CHILDREN — GAINING KNOWLEDGE 5

 ABBEINU YONAH STATES IN *SHAAREI TESHUVAH:*[1] "*TZADDIKIM misgabrim biziknasam* — tzaddikim become stronger as they grow older; *Veya'azru chayil* — and they gain new energy; *veyachalifu koach la'avodas Hashem*, and they exchange the old attitudes and gain stronger attitudes in avodas Hashem. *Kemo she'amru rabboseinu zichronam liverachah ....*" And he quotes a Gemara in Shabbos: *Talmidei chachamim, kol zeman shemazkinim, chochmah misvasefes bahem*, the older talmidei chachamim get, the more they gain in *chochmah*. Note that at first he speaks about *koach, chayil,* and *gevurah,* and then he cites a source that states that they are gaining *chochmah*, so we understand that Rabbeinu Yonah has explained this *ma'amer Chazal*, which states that they gain in *chochmah*, to mean that they are gaining in energy and enthusiasm as well.

Then he cites another pasuk that can refer to energy: "*Od yenuvun beseivah*[2] — they will continue to produce in their old age, *Desheinim vera'ananim yihyu* — they will be 'fat and juicy' in their old age." But

1. *Shaarei Teshuvah* 2:9
2. *Tehillim* 92:15

Rabbeinu Yonah makes this conditional: It is mentioned above, he says, that *"Tzaddik katamar yifrach,"*[3] the tzaddik will blossom like a date palm." When? *"Shesulim beveis Hashem"*[4] — because in their youth they were planted in the House of Hashem, *bechatzros Elokeinu yafrichu*, which means that since they spent their youth in the right environment, in *mekomos haTorah*, then in old age, *od yenuvun*.

Based on the Gemara he quoted, *od yenuvun* implies not only that they will *continue* to produce, but that they will give forth *more* fruits in old age. So, he explains, since the tzaddikim were planted in the *beis Hashem* from their youth, then the tzaddik is *katamar*, like a date palm that blossoms, and *ke'erez*, like a cedar tree that grows great. Planting them in the *beis Hashem* when they are little children is the very best portent for their future as successful servants of Hashem in their old age.

It's a tzaddik's spirit that causes him to have strength

RABBEINU YONAH SPEAKS OF ENERGY IN AVODAS HASHEM, BUT YOU cannot have energy in avodas Hashem if you are not full of energy in general. He is telling us that the tzaddikim are energetic — they are *gibborim* — in their old age. It is a tzaddik's spirit that causes him to have *gevurah*. Elsewhere it states, if a man has a *ruach nechei'ah*, a broken spirit, who can uphold him? As *Mishlei* says, a good spirit holds you up. The spirit of a person's character and mind gives him most of his energy. There are young people who are despondent, broken in spirit and discouraged, and some go so far as to commit suicide, although nothing is physically wrong with them — but their mentality does not supply them with enough energy to function. But people who have trained themselves in their youth — in good yeshivos that train them properly in the *chochmah* of the Torah — in their old age only increase and multiply their spiritual energy, which gives them so much happiness that they are full of *koach* physically.

Harav Aharon Kotler and the Satmar Rav zt"l were full of energy

HARAV AHARON KOTLER, *ZT"L*, WAS SO FULL OF ENERGY IT WAS remarkable; he was bubbling with energy. The previous Satmar

---

3. *Tehillim* 92:13
4. *Tehillim* 92:14

Rav, *zt"l*, too, even when he was much older, was full of energy — the most enthusiastic person in the whole congregation. It was a fire of *chochmah* that they gained in their youth that gave them a spirit that burned more brightly in their old age.

Hashem did a kindness to weaken people in their old age

OF COURSE, HAKADOSH BARUCH HU WEAKENS PEOPLE IN THEIR OLD age, in preparation for the Next World, because if they would be full of the same enthusiasm to their last minute on earth, they wouldn't want to depart from this world. Hakadosh Baruch Hu made people like a candle that starts to go out slowly as it nears its end, and so when the time comes it is not a very difficult matter to say goodbye to this world; this is the plan of Hashem. But in general, when other people are sitting on park benches and staring into the gloom waiting for the grave, these tzaddikim are full of *gevurah*, and they are accomplishing.[5]

Chochmah changes their nature and their character. If you see that *chochmah* is not changing your character, you must realize that you are not absorbing the *chochmah*. About a hundred years ago, there was a physician from Holland who was serving in the army in Jaban, which belonged to Holland at that time, and he noticed that the people there who lived on rice were suffering from a certain unusual illness. He decided that their ailment might be due to their diet. He looked outside in the yard where they threw the husks from the rice, and he saw that the chickens that fed on the husks were in the best of health. What was it about the rice that was making them sick, while the chickens were flourishing on it? He realized that there must be something in the husks they were throwing out that gives energy and prevents illness. He discovered vitamins in rice.

Wheat too has ingredients that keep you well nourished and healthy. But suppose you take out the bran from the wheat, take out the vitamins and eat only the white flour — after a while people will feel a big difference; they are missing something in their diets. You can't be too wise against the plan of Hashem. *Al tischacham yoser*; Hakadosh Baruch Hu made bran together with the wheat because they are supposed to be together.

---

5. See *Rejoice O Youth* p. 109 (196)

If Torah doesn't make you happier in this world, your Torah is missing something

IN THE SAME WAY, HE MADE GEMARA TOGETHER WITH MUSSAR AND *yiras Shamayim* — the Gemara is full of *yiras Shamayim*, which is the "vitamins" and which helps you digest the halachos in the proper manner. It is not right to learn only the halachos; the *inyanim* of *derech eretz, emunah,* and other things that have to do with the building of the character are the vitamins. Sometimes you see that deficiencies show themselves in people's behavior, and they do not even fulfill the halachos properly. For instance, a man may be learning the laws of *nezikim,* not to injure other people. He may know *Bava Kamma* well enough to say shiurim, and he may go early in the morning to his *beis medrash* with his talmidim and repeat the shiur in a loud voice — and people are trying to sleep in the house next door and he is waking them up. He is a robber. Rav Yisrael Salanter, *zt"l,* said these are robbers and there is no *hashavah* — you can't make it up to people; you can't give them back their sleep.

When people learn the *yiras Shamayim* of the Gemara together with the halachos of the Gemara, together it has an effect. The halachos become effective by means of the *yiras Shamayim.* Just like the wheat's flour is effective because of the bran, and the rice is even more valuable because of the rice polishings that you didn't throw away, so Hakadosh Baruch Hu made the Torah with halachos and *yiras Shamayim.* You cannot live on white flour alone; a person will become ill if he doesn't have the elements necessary to keep him healthy, which means the whole wheat, the whole rice, and the whole Gemara, *lehavdil.* If you skip the *aggadata,* for instance, you are skipping the vitamins in the bran.

The *chochmah* that Rabbeinu Yonah is talking about, however, requires a definition. "*Chochmah misvasefes bahem* — chochmah is added to them." If he means that they learned more, it is obvious that when you continue learning, the older you get the more you will know, so this is not his intent. *Chochmah* here means what *Mishlei* calls *chochmah* — it means translating the Torah into personality — when you learn something it becomes part of you, part of your worldview. While a person learns and acquires the attitudes of the Gemara, he changes and he gains *chochmah.* The Torah that he has made part of himself becomes part of his personality; he lives and thinks that way, and the Torah is going to make him happy in this world, *ashrecha ba'olam hazeh*, and certainly in the Next World — *vetov lach la'Olam Haba*. But if Torah doesn't make you happier in this world, you are missing something from your Torah.

In *sefer Ohr Yisrael*, Rav Yisrael Salanter discusses the idea of *lefum tza'ara agra*,[6] the reward is according to the difficulty. When you are young, you find so many temptations for your *yetzer hara*, since you don't have experience in *chochmah*, and you have to fight against all the falsehood of this world; it is not easy when you are young, and so you get more reward. But when you are older and more experienced, you are full of *chochmas haTorah*, and you are already accustomed to restraining your appetites; you have more self-control, so you should get less reward in your old age, since fighting the *yetzer hara* is less difficult. So the longer you live and the wiser you become, the less reward you should get — life is easier for an old talmid chacham, who learns and knows that all the lewd and corrupt ideas of the world are foolishness and *tumah*. Then it is much easier for a person to live successfully. But at the same time, he is lacking *lefum tza'ara agra*. Perhaps he doesn't get a reward anymore?

Rav Yisrael Salanter tells us that nothing will be deducted from the tzaddik, even though he may have no difficulty in keeping the Torah, "*ki lo ya'eh sechar* — he deserves to get reward," because he has accustomed himself to *derech haTorah*, *vena'aseh kala*, and it became easy for him. This is an important principle: A man in his old age receives no less reward, although it is much easier for him to live well because he already knows the driving rules on the highway of life. He knows what to do and what not to do. He understands what is true and what is false. This man continues to reap *sechar* until the last minute.

Learning Torah is like plowing the earth

L EARNING TORAH IS LIKE PLOWING THE EARTH. WHEN YOU BEGIN learning Gemara it is not easy, and the more you learn the more deeply you try to plow into the earth. When you being learning you are learning superficially, and as you progress, you try to learn more deeply. The deeper you try to dig into the ground the harder it is. You are always making progress, and it is always difficult. Nevertheless, when you are young you don't yet feel the *geshmakeit*, the sweetness

---

6. *Avos* 5:26

of the Torah, and so we pray to Hashem, "*Veha'arev na ... es divrei Sorasecha befinu* — Make your Torah sweet in our mouths."

But as you become accustomed to the ideas of the Gemara and you know many of its principles, your mind begins to adjust to its systems of thought and you think along with the Gemara. Once you get a Torah mind, it becomes much easier to understand the general run of the Gemara's arguments. Then, when you ask questions you enjoy yourself. You are at home; you are no longer a *ger* in a strange country, looking around without knowing what to say. The Gemara is your country and you know all the addresses, only sometimes you will ask questions that you didn't think of before.

When you are learning Gemara in your old age, it is Gemara that you learned many times in your youth. You may say, "What reward will I get now? When I was young I had to work hard to understand a difficult piece of Gemara, but by now I've learned it fifty times already." Rav Yisrael Salanter is assuring us that we are not getting less reward. The fact that it is easy is because you made it easy and you deserve reward, "*ki lo ya'eh sechar*," the reward is fitting for him, because it is his efforts that made it easy. And so when you review something in your old age that you learned when you were young, it is not a waste of time. Of course, you could learn more and more deeply, but even when it is easy you are being rewarded.

In order to prepare for a successful old age, it is important to understand some things about learning in your youth: Some people came to the world of Torah and began learning late in life. They should know that they also have a youth and an old age. If you came into a world of Torah at age 50, for example, that is your youth; but don't postpone your learning until you are 51. The earlier you start, the sooner you start gaining these ideas, and that is the best thing for you. Of course, when you have children, don't wait until they are 50; start right away with them.

Everyone knows the story of Abaye: Abaye once heard a statement from Rabbi Yirmiya, and he didn't accept it. Some time later he heard it again, and he accepted it, and he said, "*Halevai* that I would have accepted it the first time."

They responded to him, "What do you care? You accepted it now."

"The difference is in the *girsa deyankusa*,[7] the difference in the learning you do when you are younger." Yet when Abaye rejected Rav

---

7. *Shabbos* 21b

Yirmiya's statement, he wasn't a boy. Rabbi Yirmiya's was a valid opinion, a *man de'amar*, but when Abaye rejected Rabbi Yirmiya's statement, he was also a *man de'amar*. Nevertheless, even if you are a *gavra rabba*, a great man, if you learn something now, it is much more effective than learning it tomorrow.

Learning must become part of your personality

WITH EVERY ADDITIONAL DAY THAT PASSES, YOUR LEARNING RIPENS in your mind, and it is *od yenuvum beseivah*. You put something in your mind now and you don't even feel it — it's like a green apple; you put it in your mind and it will ripen there, and you will be surprised later. It becomes more luscious and delicious fruit and it will give you energy. The thoughts you put in your mind now may seem alien to you, and at times you won't accept them fully. Learn them anyway! As the years go by, they become part of your personality and start affecting your behavior, and they become so clear to you that it seems that they were always part of your knowledge and were never something new to you.

The tzaddikim used to come sing at the *Simchas Beis Hasho'eivah*, and they would sing "*Ashrei yalduseinu shelo biyeshah es ziknuseinu*[8] — how fortunate was our childhood that didn't put our old age to shame." Their childhood was actually the cause of their success in their old age.

Rav Simchah Zissel Ziv, *zt"l*, explains this command to get busy when you are young, as the *pasuk* in *Mishlei* says, "*Chanoch lana'ar al pi darko*,"[9] train a youth for his way in life — that is a big thing. Don't just tell them things; train them. If you are a melamed, take out a minute or two from the *sugya* and explain to them things that will train their minds to think the way those in the Torah world have to think.

Sixty-five years ago, a rebbi of mine who was a Volozhiner talmid was teaching us *Nedarim*, and we came to the mishnah that began "*Derech talmidei chachamim*." He explained, *Derech talmidei chachamim* — you should know that talmidei chachamim have a different *derech* in life than the other people, and a talmid chacham should become different from other people. When you know you are going to be a talmid chacham, your ambitions are different; your

---

8. *Sukkah* 53a
9. *Mishlei* 21:6

behavior and middos have to be different. This rebbi planted something in my mind sixty-five years ago.

Tell your children all that Hashem does for us

MELAMDIM MUST UNDERSTAND THE IMPORTANCE OF CHANOCH lana'ar, and so must fathers and mothers. It is very important to plant ideas in your children's minds right now. Don't wait! Your children won't understand, it's true, but plant ideas all the same: Tell your child all that Hakadosh Baruch Hu does for us; tell them that He gives us such a beautiful gift. When they ask what it is, tell them, "See the sun, it is a big gift!"[10]

The child won't see it that way; to him, something that costs a quarter is a gift. Even adults don't understand that the sun is a gift, because they never learned the idea. But we say, "Le'oseh orim gedolim, ki le'olam chasdo," and you have to train your child's mind to think that way. The seed you place in his mind won't grow right now, but later — shesulim beveis Hashem bechatzros Elokeinu yafrichu — he'll start thinking about it.

Tell your child the sun is very good

IF YOU ARE WALKING IN THE STREET WHERE THE SUN IS SHINING YOU ought to be thinking, "Baruch Atah Hashem, yotzer hame'oros," because if you don't think about that, you are missing one of the fundamental principles of tefillah and of avodas Hashem: Hodu laHashem ki tov, ki le'olam chasdo; le'osei orim gedolim, ki le'olam chasdo. There are older people who don't even think about thanking Hashem for the sun! For so many years they have said, "Baruch Atah Hashem, yotzer hame'oros," and they have no idea what they were saying. Chanoch lana'ar — put into a child's head that the sun is a very good thing, even if he won't listen to you. It will have an effect sooner or later.

A piece of bread is magic

THERE ARE MANY THINGS THAT YOU HAVE TO PLANT IN A CHILD'S head. When you get a piece of bread, tell the child, "This bread comes from Hashem." The child knows that is not true — bread comes from his mother, the kitchen or the baker, but tell it to him anyway. "Look what Hashem is giving us!" Plant in his head again and again.

---

10. See Career of Happiness p. 72

Chanoch lana'ar — don't wait until he says it by himself, because he never will! He says *hamotzi lechem min ha'aretz* without thinking what he is saying. Appreciating Hashem's gifts is the *chochmah* that you have to gain through *chinuch*, and age causes that appreciation to ripen in your mind.

[11]Hashem doesn't give small presents; a piece of bread is magic. If you give a child an electronic toy one morning, he will go wild with simchah. But a piece of bread is so much more exciting; it has locked in it the energy of sunlight that traveled from 83 million miles away. As he eats and digests it, that energy goes into his body, and he is an electronic toy that runs around; and he talks and he plays and he thinks with the energy that the sunlight sent to him through the bread. It is a *neis*, a miracle. You have to teach him that. Plant the idea and you will be surprised; in a very short time he will look back and say, "My father told me that bread is a *neis*," and he will be grateful to you forever.

Reb Simchah Zissel Ziv explains in a different light that "*chanoch lana'ar*" is a statement to the child: You, *na'ar* — *chanoch lana'ar*! Don't wait for people to tell you, because people have their own business to worry about. Even the best rebbis are worried mostly about themselves, so get busy worrying about yourself! This is the meaning of the mishnah, "*Im ein ani li mi li*[12] — If I am not for myself, then who is for me?" I have teachers and parents — but their interest in me is nothing compared to my interest in myself. Therefore, David Hamelech made it his business to speak to himself. "I am a little boy," he said. "Someday I want to be a gadol, someone important, so I have to get busy and train this little boy to become a gadol. I am responsible for the future gadol, and no one worries about me except myself."

So David said to himself, "*Halleli nafshi es Hashem*"[13] — praise Hashem. Imagine David walking in the fields and watching the sheep; he is a *shomer ne'eman*. But as he is walking he tells himself, "*Halleli nafshi* — Let my soul praise Hashem." And Devorah said, "*Uri uri Devorah*[14] — Wake up, Devorah." She wasn't asleep, but she told herself: Wake up; stir yourself.

"*Barchi nafshi es Hashem*,"[15] David said; he spoke to himself all the time. *Chanoch lana'ar* — you, *na'ar*, have to be busy training

---

11. See *Rejoice O' Youth*, p. 317 (715)
12. *Avos* 1:14
13. *Tehillim* 146:1
14. *Shoftim* 5:12
15. *Tehillim* 104:1

yourself. And the truth is that you have to train yourself in order to live happily even in this world, not only in *Olam Haba*.

I gave a whistle toy to someone recently, and I gave him the instructions: "Don't just hand your child the toy — he won't enjoy it. First put water in the whistle and then if you blow it, it will sound like a bird. If you don't put water in, it won't make a sound. And tell the child not to put his mouth over the hole, because that doesn't let the sound come out." I gave strict instructions, because without them the person is wasting his time.

Hashem wants us to enjoy this world

HASHEM GIVES US THIS WORLD AS A TOY AND SAYS: ENJOY THIS world. And Hashem gives us instructions how to enjoy this world: *Vaya'ar Elokim es kol asher asah vehinei tov me'od*[16] — the first instruction of the world is: "*very good.*" If you don't know that the world is very good, you'll never enjoy it. These are His instructions written on the back of the toy for how to use it. It is a very new world. When you teach a child that everything is "*tov me'od*," he becomes *samei'ach bechelko*. So teach yourself that; in case your parents didn't do the job, do it yourself, and don't wait another day to start saying it is *tov me'od*.

Teach your child to enjoy water

SO MANY THINGS ARE *TOV ME'OD*. WATER, FOR EXAMPLE, IS THE most important liquid, the best drink in the world.[17] Teach your child to enjoy a glass of water. *Tov me'od* — this world is very good! Teach him that a piece of bread is very good; he should be happy with that and enjoy it. When you put it into your mouth and start chewing it, it becomes sweeter and sweeter every second. This is the principle of starches. When a starch comes in contact with saliva, it changes to sugar. Hashem made it that way, and you should enjoy it and start digesting it before you swallow it.[18]

When you give someone a gift, *tzarich lehodi'o*, you have to let him know how good the gift is, otherwise he won't enjoy the gift. Hashem gave us a gift and is telling us how to enjoy the gift: It is a very good

16. *Bereishis* 1:31
17. See *Rejoice O Youth*, p. 312 (70), *Awake My Glory* p. 290 (933)
18. *Shabbos* 10b

gift I am giving you. This world is very good. And the results of seeing things this way are felt both in this world and in the Next World.

Have you ever heard of a man being happy with a belt?

"ASHRECHA BA'OLAM HAZEH[19] — YOU WILL BE HAPPIER IN THIS world"; you are an *ashir, samei'ach bechelko*. Have you ever heard of a man being happy with a belt? Everyday, when we say *ozer Yisrael bigvurah* — You gird Yisrael with *gevurah* — it is not just a *mashal* — it is talking about a belt. How lucky I am to have a belt! It is a simchah! The belt has an iron buckle and good leather and it is adjustable. A belt is a man's happiness. A man trains himself to enjoy his belt, and to enjoy his socks and to be happy with his shoes. He will look at his shoes when he says *Baruch Atah Hashem … she'asah li kol tzorki*. It is very important to learn to enjoy your shoes. That is how a man gains in his youth the wisdom that causes him to be more energetic and full of joy in his old age.

This boy has to understand that a very great responsibility rests on him, a responsibility for his whole life in *olam hazeh* and for the future, in *Olam Haba*. Everything depends on this child. If the child takes himself in hand right now, he can realize all that Hashem wants him to do. A child can ruin himself, *chalilah*, and ruin the future gadol. If the child does something reckless and dangerous he can even kill himself, and he is held responsible for that great man he could have become. And so, *Chanoch lana'ar*, teach the child — whether it is yourself you teach, or whether you teach the child who is a talmid in your class, or a child who is in your home. *Chanoch lana'ar* — take time out! Don't say he is too young.

Once a man asked Reb Simchah Zissel, "When should I start training my little daughter in chinuch?" He asked how old she was and the man told him that she was 3 years old.

"Run home fast!" Reb Simchah Zissel said. "It is late already."

You have to train a child as soon as possible

YOU HAVE TO START AS SOON AS A CHILD HAS ANY SENSE AT ALL, AND a child has sense from the first day. A child looks you in the eye. A young animal, *lehavdil*, doesn't look you in the eye, but a little baby is a human being, with *sechel*. So as soon as possible a child should hear good middos in the house. People should talk "*divrei chachamim*

---

19. *Berachos* 8a

benachas nishma'im."[20] And as soon as he understands what you are saying, start talking to him about the *yesodos ha'emunah*. Don't think it's a waste of time. It is the best investment for his future, and we should make that investment for ourselves, too, telling ourselves, *barchi nafshi, halleli nafshi.*

Those who wish to be *mechanech* themselves should concentrate on a number of principles. It states, "*Tashes choshech viyhi laylah*[21] — You, Hashem, made darkness and it becomes night. The Gemara[22] says, "*Zeh ha'olam hazeh domeh lelaylah* — This world is like night." This means that it is a world of darkness and *ta'us*, a world of error. Hashem made it a world of error; it is not an accident.

The Gemara analyzes the alef-beis, and the Sages saw that the words *emes* is scattered throughout the alef-beis: *alef* in the beginning, *mem* in the middle and *taf* at the end. This shows us that if you want to see the *emes*, you won't see it right away — you have to keep looking until you have seen everything.

If you want, you will see the truth

THE LETTERS OF THE WORD *SHEKER*, ON THE OTHER HAND, ARE ALL found in one place, which tells us that "*Sheker mekorvan milei*[23] — *Sheker* is easy to see." Alef-beis is *miSinai*. Hakadosh Baruch Hu is teaching us that the first thing you see when you are young is the *sheker*. You don't see the *emes*. You have to be *mesunim badin* — you have to be deliberate, to take time. *Mesunim* is related to the word *hamtein*, to wait. If you wait, you will see the *emes.*

But there is another lesson here: *Sheker* is *mekorvan milei* — it is close together, all in one little spot, but *emes* fills the whole world. *Emes* goes through the whole alef-beis, which means *sheker* is only in isolated spots, but when it comes to *emes*, "*melo chol ha'aretz kevodo*"[24] — the glory of Hashem fills the whole world with *emes*, and wherever you look you can see the *emes*. It is the single natural object in the world that is so full of complicated, structured planning and wisdom, which demonstrates the Hand of a great Designer.

---

20. *Koheles* 9:17
21. *Tehillim* 104:20
22. *Pesachim* 2b
23. *Shabbos* 104a
24. *Yeshaya* 6:7

If you don't recognize Hashem all around you, you are a blind man

IF YOU DON'T RECOGNIZE THE *BOREI* ALL AROUND YOU, YOU ARE A BLIND man. There are so many things people are blind to and never stop and think about. When I walked in the street the other day, I saw a little bird picking up a piece of paper. Why does he need that paper? Does he have notes to write? He wants to make a nest. Who taught that bird how to make a nest? That is a *kasha* that would knock over all the scientists if they were honest with themselves. Did that bird learn from his mother how to make a nest? No! When that bird was born, it came out of an egg that was already in a nest. It never saw the nest being made. How did he acquire the ability to make a nest? Some people say it happened by accident, through a process of evolution. It was an accidental change in the genes, in the cells, and by accident this wisdom happened to come. And those birds that learned how to make a nest by accident, they are the ones that survived. The other ones that didn't have a nest didn't survive. How could an accident have taught a bird how to make a nest?[25]

The human brain is the best computer

LET'S LOOK FURTHER, AT A BEEHIVE. A BEEHIVE IS A FEAT OF ENGINEERING. Bees have a place where they put their youth to incubate them. They have a special army of workers to fly out and get honey and pollen, and they have a queen bee. They have a whole organization. How did the organization happen? Was it by accident? And did an eye happen by accident? Can a camera happen by accident? It is so obvious — if people would only look at the truth, they would see the evidence on all sides. The human brain is a "computer," and even the best computers are considered nothing in comparison. How did a computer come into existence? There are people who built up a whole world of *sheker* to support their theories. They are spending millions of tax dollars to further their investigations into *sheker*. The whole thing is nothing but an attempt to keep denying the Presence of the *Borei*, which any person with plain common sense can see.

Hakadosh Baruch Hu made *sheker* in the world in order to test us. The world is "*ta'aseh choshech*," it is made with darkness, and our job is to see through the darkness and recognize all the *sheker bekorvan milei*. People who don't think are taken in by the foolishness promot-

---

25. See *Rejoice O Youth* p. 91 (172)

ed by the media, and many people, even *shomrei mitzvos*, have fallen into their trap. But when people use their eyes and their senses, then they see that *melo chol ha'aretz kevodo*, there isn't a single object in the world that doesn't demonstrate the Presence of Hashem.

Why is a rose red?

WHY IS IT THAT A ROSE IS RED? WHERE DOES THE BEAUTIFUL ROSE color come from? There is no redness in the mud at the bottom of the rose. Where does the beautiful fragrance come from? What of the engineering of the rose — the arrangement of the petals, with a stem and pistol with pollen on them — a whole factory to reproduce? Is reproduction an accident? Is a child a result of an accident? The whole world speaks openly about the *Borei*. Hakadosh Baruch Hu is waiting for us to use our eyes and see that the world is full of *emes*.

If we train ourselves when we are young to recognize this great truth, then the older we get, the more convinced we become. If you never heard it before, then you will grow up without *emunah*. But when a man trained himself *mine'urav*, as the *Chovos Halevavos* in *Sha'ar Habechirah* teaches us, to recognize the *Borei* on all sides, then he has *emunah*. He said: Why is it when you pass by a Bais Yaakov and you see the girls coming out, not one of the girls has a moustache? Is it an accident? It is *Yad Hashem* — a miracle! And why is it that women's voices are different from men's voices? And why aren't all men's voices the same? Every man among thousands and thousands has a different voice. A person stopped me in the street and asked me for directions to get to a certain place. When I started to tell him, he said, "You are Rav Miller — I recognize you from your tapes." There are thousands of voices, and you can recognize them. It is a *neis*!

The angels are excited over the physical creation of light

THE *MALACHIM* SPEND THEIR TIME *TAMID MESAPRIM KEVOD EL*. THEY are doing their job: *tamid*, always, they speak of *kevod El*. What are they saying? They say *Kadosh, melo chol ha'aretz kevodo*. People who don't know *peshat* think that *kevodo* means something invisible that fills the whole world, a certain *kedushah*. Certainly this is also true, but what they are talking about is the *ohr* — "*al me'orei ohr she'asisa*." They are praising Hashem for the light, and they see that the light fills the whole world. Wherever you look there is light. The *malachim* are excited over the physical creation of light! The *kevod Hashem* shows itself in the *beriyah*, in the form of *ohr*, light.[26]

Light is a miracle. Light is energy and it travels with a tremendous speed. There is a lot to talk about when it comes to light. There is a "*machlokes*" among physicists regarding what exactly light is. Whatever it is, it is a miracle of miracles, it is *kevod Hashem*, like everything that Hashem made in this world. *Hashamayim mesaprim kevod Kel uma'asei yadav maggid harakiya.*[27] Everything is talking, and it all speaks *lichvod Hashem.*[28]

If you're a rebbi, you have to teach your talmidim this idea when they are young. If they didn't hear it when they were young, tell them when they are older. And you have to tell it to yourself all your life. As you grow older, *od yenuvun beseivah*, you will have more energy in your old age. You will see that the whole world is full of *gevurah*, simcha, *chessed Hashem*, *chochmas Hashem*. And you will have more *koach*. You will be walking on solid ground and you will be able to get more *sechar*. It will be easier for you because you have worked in your youth and prepared yourself for old age. But there are those who didn't prepare themselves. Even those who are *shomrei mitzvos*, who learned Gemara, some shiurim, halachos, may never have worked to get the *bren* of the Torah, the ideals of the Torah. How much time did they spend on *Mesillas Yesharim*, on *Sha'arei Teshuvah*, on *Chovos Halevavos*, or on the *aggadata* of *Bava Kamma*? Aggadata is jewels and diamonds! Where the *bren* is missing, the white flour doesn't help a person much. *Kol zeman shemizdaknin da'atan mitarefes;*[29] he becomes more and more confused the older he gets. An old lamdan who has no *yiras Shamayim* becomes discouraged and despondent. He expected to have wealth, more *kavod*. He is despondent, and if you don't the energy of simchah, your health suffers. But it's all his own fault, because *chanoch lana'ar* — you young men should train yourselves. Don't wait for people to give it to you. It is up to you to learn these things, to prepare yourselves when you are young.

Every act of Hakadosh Baruch Hu's outlined in *parashas Bereishis* is a miracle: "*Totzei ha'aretz nefesh chayah leminah*,"[30] the earth

---

26. See *Praise My Soul* pp. 256-292
27. *Tehillim* 19:2
28. See *Praise My Soul* pp. 258, 291 *The Beginning* p. 20 (1:4)
29. *Kinnim* 6:3
30. *Bereishis* 1:24

produced animals. Imagine seeing an ox coming out of the earth! If you saw that, you would have absolute *emunah*, but it would be a great pity, because you would lose the *sechar*. Hakadosh Baruch Hu didn't let Adam see it. If Adam could have seen all this taking place, he could have told his children, "I saw the *bri'ah* with my own eyes." But Hashem didn't want that. After everything else was created, then Hashem created Adam. Now Adam has to look at the *bri'ah*, and with his own efforts he has to recognize Hashem's works. That is man's purpose in this world. He gets reward for recognizing Hashem.

That is why the seventh day is called Shabbos. Shabbos means to stop, and our whole *zechus* of being in this world comes from the fact that Hashem stopped. If He didn't stop, we would be out of luck — if He showed openly that He is the *Borei*, we couldn't get any reward. Hakadosh Baruch Hu stopped everything, so Adam didn't see anything. And now we have to work on our own to recognize the *Borei mitoch haberiyah*.[31]

Our purpose in this world
is to learn to recognize Hashem

OUR PURPOSE IN THIS WORLD IS TO LEARN TO RECOGNIZE HASHEM — the *emes, alef-mem-taf* — and not be trapped in *sheker* — that *kuf-reish-shin* that is all in one place. Those who pass through this world without learning are trapped by all the falsehood that they see around them. But the person who learns the truth of the world knows that *sheker* is nothing. Look at the whole world, *mimizrach shemesh ad mevo'o mehulal shem Hashem*[32] — look at everything, from the sun's rising to the sunset and all that is happening in between, and in the whole *beriah* you see the *Shem Hashem*. It is open for us to see.

Did you ever say to Hashem
in English or Yiddish that you love Him?

IN *MISHLEI* IT STATES, "*ATZLAH TAPIL TARDEIMAH*[33] — LAZINESS CAUSES A deep sleep to descend." People tend to be lazy and don't want to utilize their lives to achieve *yiras Hashem, emunah*, good middos, *ahavas Hashem*. *Ahavas Hashem* is such a far-off idea that people don't even think about it. Did you ever say to Hashem — in English or Yiddish —

31. See *The Beginning* p. 56 (2:3)
32. *Tehillim* 113:3
33. *Mishlei* 19:15

that you love Him? Have you said it once in your life — "I love You, Hashem"? *Ahavas Hashem* is a *chiyuv*. We say every day, "*ve'ahavta es Hashem*." It is a *mitzvas asei*. What are you doing about it? You have to learn. We are all unconscious; we walk around with our eyes closed. We think we see, but "*venefesh remiah sir'av*," a soul that deceived itself, a dishonest soul, will remain hungry, and hungry means you will never be satisfied in this world, you won't get what you are looking for. It will be an unhappy world.

This is our great test: When you are young and you have the opportunity to start your career, start investing in yourself. There are many things you should do when you are young. Among the things we have mentioned is to learn how to understand the *chessed* of this world, how good this world is. It is very important to study that. Another thing is the *chochmah* of this world, to see the cunning in everything, the plan and purpose; how complicated every little thing is and how much wisdom it shows.

Thank Hashem for your nose

THINK ABOUT YOUR NOSE. WHEN YOU BREATHE IN, THERE ARE LITTLE hairs in your nose, so in case a bug wants to fly in, it finds hairs and changes its mind and goes out. When you are sleeping, a bug might want to creep in. As you breathe in dust, the hairs take out some of the bigger particles of dust. Why is your nose always damp inside? In order to keep wet the interior of your nasal passages, so as you breathe it catches the dust there, like flypaper, and the air becomes purified as it passes through to your lungs. Why is it that these sinus passages are all twisted? The twisting gives the air a long time to get to your lungs. The flypaper action of the mucus on the walls of these passages catches all the particles of dust. In addition, the liquids add moisture to the air. As it passes through these sinus passages, the air gets wetter and wetter, so that by the time it enters your lungs it is pure and wet, which is what the body needs.

The fact that apples turn red is enough for everyone to know there is a Creator

WHENEVER YOU LOOK INTO THE WHOLE PURPOSE OF THE UNIVERSE, there is not a thing that doesn't show plan and purpose. Apples turn red when they are ripe to show that they are ripe and fit to eat. When they are not the right color, they are hard and sour. They are not healthy that way, and you could get a stomachache if you eat them. The fact that apples turn red is enough proof for everyone to know that there is a *Borei*. And peaches turn pink and red, and pears turn red if you keep them long enough. Oranges turn orange and bananas turn yellow and Granny Smith apples turn green, as if Hashem signed His name on them — "Hashem is here." Everything proclaims Hashem's Presence. I take yeshivah bachurim into fruit stores and tell them I see the *Yad Hashem* there. You see Hashem's handiwork everywhere. When a banana is ripe to eat, it is remarkable thing. Not only does it turn yellow, but it is easy to peel. An unripe banana is hard to peel. When bananas are ripe, they beg, "Please peel me!"[34]

Have you ever seen a horse chestnut that grows in a tree, in a box that has spikes on it? When the chestnut is ripe, the outside shell breaks in half, the two spiked halves fall off and inside is a beautiful, shiny round ball, which is the chestnut. Why is it covered with spikes when it is unfit to eat? Why do the spikes fall off when it is fit to eat? Is it an accident? It is so simple; everyone can recognize the *Yad Hashem*. And so we should begin this great function of "*Shesulim beveis Hashem, bechatzros Elokeinu yafrichu*," in the courtyard of Hashem we should start blossoming in our youth. Whether you are 50 or 5, start as early as you can. "*Od yenuvun beseivah*," you will continue to produce in your old age — you will be amazed at your happiness and your energy in your old age; you will live longer. "*Yiras Hashem tosif yamim*,"[35] *Yiras Hashem* will give you length of days, *u'shenos resha'im tiktzornah*. The *reshaim* are dying young. (Sometimes Hashem makes an exception, because once a *rasha* gave a quarter to an old man for tzedakah, so Hashem says, "I will give you *olam hazeh*, but don't bother me in the Next World. You may live to be 90 in this world for the quarter you once gave to tzedakah.")

When people have sense when they are young, they tell themselves: "I am responsible for my old age; I am responsible for my career not only in this world but also in the World to Come. Let me do the best I can with myself. Let me train myself." *Chanoch lana'ar* — Train a child, putting into him all you can, and the results will be happiness, *Ashrecha ba'olam hazeh vetov lach la'Olam Haba*.

---

34. See *Sing You Righteous* p. 132 (275)
35. *Mishlei* 14:27

NACHAS FROM CHILDREN — HONORING SOMEONE AFTER THEY PASS AWAY 6

Even after a person has passed away there is still an opportunity for him to gain atonement for his sins

HE PASUK STATES, *KAPER LE'AMECHA YISRAEL ASHER padisa Hashem.*[1] As the Medrash explains it, *"Kaper le'amecha Yisrael — eilu hachaim,* these are the living ones." We pray to Hashem that He forgive the living Jewish nation — all Bnei Yisrael should be favored by Hashem, and He should give them *kaparah,* atonement. *"Asher padisa Hashem — eilu hameisim,* the ones that You redeemed are the *meisim."* One thing we see from this statement is that even after a person has passed away, there is still an opportunity for him to gain atonement for his sins.

We know that the great gift of *bechirah,* free will, exists only in this life. As the *Rambam* states in his introduction to *Shemonah Perakim,* the way a man is when he leaves this world, *kach yisha'er le'olam,* that is how he will remain forever. You cannot change once

---

1. *Devarim* 21:8

you leave this world, even in the time of *techiyas hameisim*. That is why life is so precious. Every second is a glorious opportunity that you will never have again.

But now we are hearing that even after a person has passed away there is an opportunity to wipe out his sins, to be *mechaper*, and this is a very big chiddush. He himself, of course, cannot do anything. Once he leaves this world, the opportunity is finished. But there is a function that the living can accomplish, a tremendous *chessed* that they can do for those who have passed away.

When Naomi spoke to Rus, she thanked Hashem, "*Asher lo azav chasdo es hachaim v'es hameisim*[2] — Hashem didn't stop doing *chessed* with the living and with the dead." This means that her family that passed away, her husband and her sons, were now going to have a remembrance, through all that was about to happen. Rus, who was left, was going to be taken in the course of time by Boaz, and she would have a son. That was going to be a *zechus*, a merit, for both the *chaim* and the *meisim*.

If it is possible to help a person so much after he passes away, why is it that "*Nishkachti kemeis mileiv*,[3] I have been forgotten like a dead person is forgotten from people's minds"? The Gemara[4] explains that after twelve months a *meis* is forgotten; people who were mourning for him, who were brokenhearted because of him, have now forgotten him. The reason for this is that Hakadosh Baruch Hu has pity on mankind — *Baruch Merachem al haberiyos*. This forgetfulness is a miracle.

Our minds hold millions of facts; no computer is a comparison

IMAGINE A COMPUTER THAT IS ABLE TO REMEMBER MILLIONS OF FACTS and that had a mechanism whereby certain facts that were not helpful would be erased automatically. Hakadosh Baruch Hu gave us minds that are marvels — computers are nothing in comparison. Our minds hold millions of facts; all the faces that you ever saw are stored in a gallery in your mind. You can meet someone you haven't seen in years and recognize him — you take that picture out of your mind and compare it to this man standing before you right now.

---

2. *Ruth* 2:20
3. *Tehillim* 31:13
4. *Berachos* 58b

There are millions of experiences inscribed in the mind. If you pass a pickle factory and smell the pickles, you may remind yourself, "Fifty years ago I passed a pickle factory and it had the same smell." Everything is inscribed — and you take it with you. That is why it is so important to load your mind with necessary and valuable merchandise. If you load your mind with unnecessary things, you are not going to be happy when you reach the Next World, and they say, "Let's see what you have in your pockets," and you empty out a collection of garbage, and they will ask, "Is that all you have to show here?"

And so, the pasuk says, "*U'veda'as chadarim yemalu kol hon yakar vena'im*,"[5] with *da'as* — if a person's mind is busy collecting *important* information in this world — then he has filled his chambers with the most wonderful of treasures. The chambers of the mind are like the many rooms of a mansion. There are people who collect all kinds of unimportant things and pile them up here and there, and they leave the house full of garbage when they die. But with *da'as*, all the chambers of your mansion will be filled with *kol hon yakar vena'im*, all precious — and pleasant — wealth. When we gain the right ideas, which we learn in this world from the right places — learn the right *sefarim*, associate with the right people — then our minds become full of ideas. These ideas are wealth of all kinds of precious, valuable things that fill all the rooms of the mind, all the chambers of your mansion.

Our business in this world is to fill our minds with values

Loving the wind

OUR BUSINESS IN THIS WORLD IS TO FILL OUR MINDS WITH VALUES. *Hon yakar vena'im* means a very pleasant kind of wealth. If you learn the right things, you are actually enjoying them. Sometimes you don't even know you have them, but in your subconscious mind they are making you happy. You may learn, say, that wind is a good thing — it is a Gemara;[6] *vechi efshar la'olam beli ruchos?* — the world cannot be without winds. And we daven, *Mashiv haruach... mechalkel chaim bechessed* — the wind causes us to eat! The wind makes seeds travel; it makes carbon dioxide travel; without the wind we wouldn't

5. *Mishlei* 24:4
6. *Taanis* 3b

eat. You've forgotten all about that; you were a little boy when your rebbi told you that in cheder. But you didn't lose that information! It's stored away inside you. When you feel a wind you will feel that it's a good thing, a *chessed*. The more you think about it the more you will enjoy it. Automatically, with your subconscious mind, you learn to enjoy the wind.

Suppose you were never told that — all you heard is that it is a nasty day and the wind is blowing, so now all your life you will think the wind is unpleasant, and all your life you won't enjoy the wind.[7]

Fill your mind with da'as.

IF YOU FILL YOUR MIND WITH *DA'AS*, YOU WILL ENJOY THINGS MORE, EVEN in *olam hazeh*; you will see that *vehinei tov me'od*. If you learn how everything is very good, then all your life is going to be a very good life. It is important to understand how good the wind is, how good rain is, how good air is, how good a piece of bread is ... Everything becomes good to you — *kol asher asah*, everything is *tov me'od*, very good. But it will help you even more in *Olam Haba*, because you will arrive with a mind full of wealth, and they will ask you, "What did you bring from downstairs?" and you will start unloading all your wealth, and Hakadosh Baruch Hu says, "That is a rich man. We want him here!"

If you fill your mind, for example, with *Bava Kamma, Bava Metzia,* and *Bava Basra,* with Chumash, Mishnah, *Tehillim,* and *Mishlei,* then when you come to the Next World, all that is wealth and you are welcome there — *Ashrei mi sheba lechan vetalmudo beyado.*[8]

The Miracle of Forgetting

HOWEVER, SOMETIMES IT DOESN'T PAY TO KEEP CERTAIN THINGS IN your mind. Sometimes, *chalilah*, when a beloved one passed away, the experience was heartbreaking, and you feel you cannot go on living. Then Hakadosh Baruch Hu sets up a certain mechanism — a miracle — called *shichechah*, forgetting. And little by little He starts erasing certain things from your mind. It is not erased entirely, but the pain and anguish that you felt at the moment, the feeling that you cannot carry on in life, is erased over the course of time, and your feelings normalize and you are able to function properly.

---

7. See *Carrier of Happiness* p. 79, *Awake My Glory* p. 368 (1159), *Rejoice O Youth* p. 99 (178)
8. *Pesachim* 50a

There are many people who have accomplished very great things in life, but if such a person didn't use that *shichechah* when his wife died, he broke down entirely. He couldn't function anymore because he had nothing else in life. A person who lives with *da'as*, though, has great purposes in life. The loss of his wife was a terrible blow, but still, when the time came, Hakadosh Baruch Hu started that broom sweeping at the memory, and *nishkachti kemeis mileiv*. Hakadosh Baruch Hu made that *neis* that we should forget.

Hashem makes us forget many worries. You can go to sleep at night feeling terribly worried, and when you wake up in the morning you are back to normal. What happened to yesterday's worries? Overnight your mind was mending itself, and even though the problem is still there, you've already forgotten the worry. *Shichechah* is a *neis*, and we have to thank Hakadosh Baruch Hu for that miracle that we forget unpleasant experiences.

That is why, with the passage of time, we forget about those people to whom we owe a great debt. If our parents have passed away, forgetting them seems like ingratitude, but it is natural for us to forget them.

Nevertheless, *Kabeid es avicha ve'es imecha*,[9] you have to honor your father and your mother, and the Gemara says,[10] "*mechabedo bechayav u'mechabedo bemoso*," you have to honor your parents even after they pass away. Some people think this means that if someone mentions your parents, you should say some good word about them to honor them; but that is not enough. *Mechabedo* means you have to *do* something, and there are many things you can do.

If you drop a nickel into a tzedakah box for a deceased person you are benefiting him tremendously

THERE ARE SIMPLE THINGS YOU CAN DO TO HONOR THEM, AND LIKEWISE to honor anyone who has passed away. Perhaps you had a family doctor you used for years and you wanted to pay him, but he wouldn't take any money from you — he knew you were a poor yeshivah man and didn't have a lot of money. If when he passed away he had no one to say Kaddish for him, what can you do for him?

---

9. *Shemos* 20:12
10. *Kiddushin* 31b

If you will drop a nickel into a tzedakah box every day for him, you are benefiting him tremendously. Moshe Rabbeinu would give almost anything to be able to come back into this world to drop a penny into a tzedakah box, to be able to use that most precious gift of *bechirah*! But you can do it for him; and you can do it for your father or your mother. This is one of many ways to be *mechabedam bemosam*. Not only is it a *kavod*, it is a *kaparah* for your parents, because tzedakah rescues people from Gehinnom (not that you are suspecting that a parent is in Gehinnom, but tzedakah always helps).

The Gemara[11] tells of a famous non-Jew who once asked a Tanna: Jews say *Elokeichem oheiv aniyim*, your G-d loves the poor people — if this is true, then why doesn't He make them rich? The Tanna's answer is, *Kedei shenitzol anu bahem midinah shel Gehinnom* — when we give tzedakah to an *ani hagun*, a worthy poor man, he is doing us a big favor by taking our money; he is rescuing us from the judgment of Gehinnom.

Poor people have a very great merit in the next world

THIS IS A VERY GREAT *ZECHUS* FOR THE POOR MAN. EVENTUALLY, WHEN the poor man will come to the Next World and say, "Ribbono Shel Olam, I served You: I lived in poverty to save so many people from Gehinnom," then Hashem will respond, "Yes, I will reward you for serving Me so faithfully." It makes no difference that he didn't want to be poor. He was a *shaliach* for such an important purpose that he deserves a reward. So the people who give tzedakah to the poor are saving themselves from Gehinnom, and the poor man, by accepting it, is rescuing them from Gehinnom, and both are going to be rewarded.

When parents pass away, Hashem does us a great chessed that we should be able to live normally without them

WHEN ONE'S PARENTS HAVE PASSED AWAY, HAKADOSH BARUCH HU did a great *chessed* and caused his anguish to depart so that now he is able to live normally — but he must not forget about his parents. *Mechabedo bemoso* — he drops a nickel in the tzedakah box and says,

---

11. *Bava Basra* 10a

"This nickel is for the *zechus* of so-an-so *ben* so-and-so, my father." That is a very great — and effective — thing to do.

Doing chessed for those who passed away.

ANOTHER, MORE GENERAL PRINCIPLE RELATING TO DOING *CHESSED* for those who have passed away is the mitzvah of *yibum*. *Ki yeishevu achim yachdav*,[12] when brothers were alive at the same time, and one of them died without children, the Torah commands the remaining brother to marry his widowed sister-in-law. The Torah says that the child who will be born *yakum al sheim achiv*. This seems to mean that he should bear the name of the dead brother.[13]

There is a principle that *ein mikra yotzei midei peshuto* — no matter how a pasuk is explained, the simple meaning is also always true, but this is one exception. Where *mesechta Yevamos* describes the *din* of *yibum*, there is no *remez* about naming the son after the dead man, and there is no such halachah. This is one instance where *halachah okefes es hamikra*, the halachah sidesteps the pasuk. The Gemara explains *yakum* to mean that the remaining brother becomes *like* the brother and he takes two *chalakim* of the *yerushah*, one for himself and one for his brother. The *peshuto shel mikra*, the simple meaning of the pasuk, however, is ignored entirely. The Torah doesn't actually require that you name the child for the dead man.

This man's death caused this child to come into the world, and it is a great *zechus*, merit, for him. Under other circumstances, his widow would be forbidden to his brothers; although it is an *issur kareis* to marry *eishes achiv*, in this one case the Torah permitted it. When a man dies, and because of that his brother had a child from his widow, then he is, very indirectly, a *gorem* for a child to come into this world. This man has gained the merit of something that is going to live on and on. Of course he didn't want to die, but nevertheless, by his death he caused a child to be born.

This is the meaning of what Naomi said about Boaz, *asher lo azav chusdo im hachaim ve'im hameisim*.[14] In fact, the halachah of *yibum* did not apply to Boaz, because Rus had never actually been married before. She became a *giyores* only after her "husband" died. The brothers took their wives in Moav *shelo kedin*. Still, when Boaz had

---

12. *Devarim* 25:5
13. See *Fortunate Nation* p. 281 (25:6)
14. *Ruth* 2:20

a son from Rus, that was because of the *meisim* — Naomi's husband Elimelech and his two sons; and they gained a *zechus*.

The Gemara says that *bera mezakeh abba*,[15] the father's mitzvos and *ma'asim tovim* are not on the son's record, but the son can do mitzvos for his father. Anything that the son does is a *zechus* for his father and his mother; if the son is a frum Jew, that is enough. If he is more than a simple frum Jew, if he is an *ish chassid oveid Hashem*, it is a very great *zechus*.

The better you are the more zechus you give your parents

YAHRTZEIT IS VERY IMPORTANT; *YIZKOR* AND KADDISH ARE IMPORTANT; but it is more important to know that the better you are, the more *zechus* you give your parents. If you learn *Mesillas Yesharim* or *Yevamos*, you are making yourself better. This is a tremendous benefit you can give your parents all your life, not only on their *yahrtzeit*, not only during the first eleven months after they die, but all your life, even if you are doing it just for yourself and not specifically for your parents' *zechus*. But as you acquire more and more *sheleimus*, as you behave with more *derech eretz* and *middos tovos*, as you gain more knowledge of *Toras Hashem*, you are bringing your parents great simchah.

Avrohom sings along with us at our Shabbos table

WE SAY ABOUT SHABBOS, "*AVRAHAM YAGEL, YITZCHAK YERANEN, Yaakov u'vanav yanuchu bo* — Avraham would rejoice, Yitzchak would exalt, Yaakov and his children would rest on it." What is it that our Forefathers are rejoicing about? They see that their descendants are sitting at a Shabbos table, singing *zemiros* and keeping Shabbos, and Avrohom sings along — literally. The *avos* sing together when we are happy. "That is what we wanted," they say. "This is nachas: our children are talking about *Bereishis bara Elokim eis hashamayim ve'eis ha'aretz ... ki vo shavas*, Hashem stopped the *beriah* and rested on Shabbos. Our children are doing such a great thing for us." The child is not thinking about his parents; he is thinking about himself, and still it benefits his *avos* — not only his father and his mother, but his grandparents and great-grandparents all the way back

---

15. *Sanhedrin* 104a

to Avraham Avinu. Everyone in the Next World is happy to see someone who is going *bederech haTorah* and making something of himself.

Large families — one of the biggest favors you can do for your parents

IF YOU RAISE A FAMILY OF *OVDEI HASHEM*, KNOW WHAT A GREAT *ZECHUS* that is for your parents — they become millionaires in *Shamayim*! When you have a big family with children and grandchildren, and everyone is putting on tefillin; everyone is keeping Shabbos and making *berachos*; everyone is being *mekayem kol haTorah kula*, fulfilling the entire Torah, then thousands upon thousands of mitzvos are being mailed to your ancestors in *Olam Haba*. When you bring a family into this world, you are doing one of the biggest favors you can do for your fathers and forefathers.

A child's name means a great deal, but it is important to know how to utilize a name, not just to give a name. When Leah Imeinu named her son Reuven, meaning "Look at the son who was born to me," she was actually saying, "Hakadosh Baruch Hu, look at my son; think about him and protect him always."[16] When she named Shimon, she was saying, "*Shema Hashem*, listen Hashem to the voice of my son Shimon." When she named Levi she said, "*Veyilavu alecha visharesucha*, I want my son Levi to be always connected to avodas Hashem and to talmidei chachamim, the Kohanim." And when she called to her son for any reason, she was thinking about what his name means. When the *kadmonim* gave a name, not only was it an honor for the person after whom the child was named, they were also translating the name, thinking about the *peirush hamilim*. When they said "Yeshaya," they were saying "Hashem should help you," and in the same way with every name they used they were giving thought to its meaning.

Utilizing the name of a child

THEREFORE, WHEN YOU NAME A CHILD AFTER YOUR FATHER OR mother, it would be worthwhile to get into the habit of thinking about the meaning of that name whenever you want to use it. If your father's name was Chaim, when you call your son Chaim, you should think of your father and also think that your child should have chaim. When you use that name, one of the functions you perform is honor-

---

16. See *The Beginning* p. 462 (29:32)

ing your parents. When a parent hears his name being used in this world, it is a simchah for him.

What if your wife wants to give the child a different name, taking the simchah away from your parents? The answer is that there is a greater simchah if you yield to your wife, for if you make that child go *bederech haTorah*, you are giving your parents the greatest benefit, one that is worth much more than the name. By training a child to be an *oveid Hashem*, to make *berachos*, to act with *derech eretz*, to wait six hours between *fleishig* and *milchig*, to do any mitzvos, you are giving your parents a great *zechus*, even though the name wasn't given to the child.

All our lives it is possible to remember our parents by saying their names. What happens after we ourselves pass on to the Next World? Then, even though the people who use those names forgot for whom the name was given — if, for example, a child is named after a great-grandfather you don't remember anymore — in *Shamayim* they know, and it is all recorded. So when they say in the synagogue "*Ya'amod* so-and-so," it rings in *Shamayim* and all the *neshamos* who had that name are very happy to hear it. *Yikaru al sheim avosai*, to be called by the name of my forefathers is a very great *chessed*; but it is an even greater *chessed* when those who carry that name — and even those who don't carry the name — behave in such a way as to add *zechus* to their forefathers.

Our happiness is gaining favor in Hashem's eyes

FOR MOST OF THE WORLD, THE PURPOSE OF LIFE IS THE ONE THAT IS stated in the American constitution — the pursuit of happiness. Everyone has the right to pursue happiness. That is the *derech* of the entire world, but it is not the Torah *derech*. We are looking not for happiness but for *retzon Hashem*. We say "*chayim birtzono*" — our lives and happiness all depend on gaining *retzon Hashem*, the favor of Hashem; that is what we want. Our aim is to do things that will cause Hakadosh Baruch Hu to smile at us. And once we know that this is the way Hashem approves, it becomes our happiness.

When people spend their lives pursuing pleasure they are running in the opposite direction and they never find the pleasure

THIS PREMISE THAT LIFE IS FOR THE PURSUIT OF HAPPINESS IS A BASIC error, because it is based on a materialistic approach. It ignores the most important part of our existence, the real goal of life, which is *Olam Haba*. When people spend their lives pursuing pleasure, they are running in the opposite direction, and they never find the pleasure they seek. They are always continuing to pursue happiness because they've never found it. It is a dream. Happiness is something you don't pursue; happiness has to pursue you. *Ach tov vachessed yirdefuni*[17] — happiness pursues me. You have to live in such a way that Hakadosh Baruch Hu causes you to become happy.

We find, however, that the Torah approves of happiness, as it says, *u'semachtem lifnei Hashem Elokeichem,*[18] you should rejoice, *besimchah u'v'tuv leivav,* serving Hashem with joy. The Torah speaks constantly about happiness. What are we saying when we speak about happiness? Happiness according to *da'as Torah* is when you know that you are accomplishing something in life.

Happiness is accomplishing something in life

SHLOMO HAMELECH SAID, "*AL SEDEI ISH ATZEIL AVARTI,*[19] I PASSED BY the field of a lazy man, *ve'al kerem adam chasar leiv,* and by the vineyard of a man who is lacking a mind." *Atzeil* and *chasar leiv* are one and the same. A lazy man has no mind. He doesn't understand — he is wasting his life; he has no *seichel*. But a man with *seichel* is not lazy, because he knows that life is for a purpose, it is for accomplishing things. A man who knows what life is for is always busy.

You must be busy in order to be happy

ONCE PSYCHOLOGISTS WERE DISCUSSING HOW TO DEAL WITH CERTAIN situations, and they came up with a very great chiddush: The most effective cure is for people to go to work. Take all the loafers who are hanging around on some park bench with nothing to do, who are sick in their minds, and give them jobs — that is the way to cure them. *Atzlus* and *atzvus,* laziness and depression, go together. The cure for depression is to abolish the *atzlus*. *Zerizus* means being energetic. If you are doing something, even something useless, but you think you are busy, it will save your mind; but if you are busy with something that is valuable, it will surely save your mind. You cannot be happy unless you

17. *Tehillim* 23:6
18. *Vayikra* 23:40
19. *Mishlei* 24:30

are a busy person. You may be busy all your life working to support your family — to pay *sechar limud* for them, to pay rent for them, to buy shoes for them, and whenever you have time, you go to the *beis hakenesses* or shiurim; if you are a woman, you may dedicate your life to bringing up your family. In either case, you are busy, and busy people are the happiest.

Traveling is bluff

THE TRAVEL BUREAUS ALL BLUFF THE WORLD WHEN THEY POST pictures of some island you can visit; they want to persuade you to buy tickets and travel there. And when you go there, you see that all the natives there want to come to America — the whole world wants to come to America, and America wants to travel all over the world! It is all *hevel varik* — happiness means you have to be busy. When people are busy with something that is worthwhile, such as raising a Torah family, it is real happiness and nothing in the world can compare to it. Accomplishing something that will be permanent is the greatest happiness and the greatest nachas. Of course it is a pleasure to spend time with your children and grandchildren, but there is a greater pleasure, and that is knowing that they are sitting in yeshivah or doing good things even if you don't see them.

The happiness of life is in knowing that you didn't waste your life. Learning Torah brings you success; when you learn Torah, *beda'as yemalu chadarim kol hon yakar vena'im*[20] — you are filling the chambers of your mind with beautiful furniture, and it is true happiness. Everything you learn in Gemara or Chumash or Mishnah is happiness, and that is what Hakadosh Baruch Hu considers success in this world. Running off to faraway places for a vacation is *rodef achar hahevel*.

There was a time
when the yeshivos never gave vacation

THE *GOYIM* MAKE SUMMER VACATIONS FOR THE SCHOOLS, SO THE yeshivos close down for the summer too. There was a time when the yeshivos never closed down; there was no vacation. *Einei kesil biktzei aretz*,[21] the eyes of the fool are at the ends of the world, looking for things beyond: maybe there the grass is greener; maybe there is

---

20. *Mishlei* 24:4
21. *Mishlei* 17:24

something that is happier there. And when he gets there he sees that it is nothing; he is always deceived. People pay money to go to a theater, and it is all *sheker* — when they walk out onto the dark street, the actors are no longer there. They gave money away and wasted three hours for nothing. Life is being wasted.

But when you come out of the beis medrash at night, you come home loaded down with valuable *sefarim!* Even though you won't remember it all, it is in your subconscious mind. What you've accomplished there is wealth that will last forever.

If you are raising children, that wealth will outlast all other things

IF YOU ARE RAISING CHILDREN, THAT IS A WEALTH THAT WILL OUTLAST all other things. You must understand how great is the task of bringing up a whole generation of *shomrei Torah* and mitzvos. We have to set ourselves a goal in what we do to make the best out of our children. Of course don't forget that the most important child is you. *Eileh toldos Noach, Noach* — the best child of Noach is Noach himself. But never neglect your children.

As soon as you start out, make sure you live in a frum neighborhood. The *sevivah* is very important.

Supervise your child's learning personally

THE SECOND PRINCIPLE IS THAT CHILDREN SHOULD RECEIVE HELP FROM you from the first day. When they start learning even siddur, you must help them out, because if a child is discouraged at the beginning, he will develop a distaste for his learning. Many times this will lead to his breaking away from Torah, because he feels like a failure in learning. Help out from the beginning, constantly. Supervise your child's learning personally. Don't rely on a melamed that you've hired to come to your house. You have to test your child constantly and see that your child succeeds in learning.

Speak to your children about tzaddikim and talmidei chachomim

THE THIRD PRINCIPLE IS ALWAYS TO SPEAK IN YOUR HOUSE OF THE Torah's ideals. Teach a child to think how great the tzaddikim are, especially the tzaddikim of today. Teach your child to believe in tzaddikim, and not only in "official" tzaddikim; there are plenty of "unoffi-cial" tzaddikim. Teach the child to appreciate the talmidei chachamim, the yeshivah people, and to respect them. In your house speak of talmidei chachamim only with admiration. Speak constantly of the greatness of their Torah learning, of the greatness of their *tefillah bekavanah*. Speak about Hakadosh Baruch Hu in your house. In some houses parents never mention Hashem at all. Speak about *chasdei Hashem* constantly. Tell your children, "Isn't this good, what you are eating now? Hashem gave it to us, *Mechalkel chaim bechessed*, He is giving it to us with kindness, *ba'avur Shemo haGadol*, in order for us to appreciate His great Name." Teach your children to be happy and grateful to Hashem.[22]

In the homes of tzaddikim there is true happiness

IF YOU PUT EFFORT INTO TEACHING THEM, THERE IS NO QUESTION THAT after 120 years, when you pass on to the Next World, your children will continue with what you put into their minds. It is a tremendous *zechus* for you. You will have raised up a *dor* of *bnei Torah* and *ovdei Hashem*, who will have families of their own. This is different from the *sheleimus* that a person can get on his own. Everyone who brings up a Torah family should know that it is true happiness — even though there is great effort involved and some people complain and they think they will find more happiness someplace else, don't be deceived. There are millionaires who have every kind of trouble in their homes; they have nothing to be happy about, only imaginary happiness. But in the homes of tzaddikim, *kol rinah vishu'ah be'a-holei tzaddikim*,[23] in the homes of those who live with the principles of the Torah there is true happiness, happiness that will last forever, in *Olam Haba* as well.

And so this is the beautiful pattern of our lives: We are in this world in order to utilize our *bechirah*, our free will, and the most important aspect of free will is what it is going to do for us after we leave this world. But even in the Next World, after we lose the opportunity to continue doing mitzvos, there is still a *kaparah* for *meisim*; our chil-dren are still doing mitzvos in this world, and that is as if we are doing

---

22. See *Career of Happiness* p. 84, See *Awake My Glory* p. 355 (1126; 1127)
23. *Tehillim* 118:15

them. *Bera mezakeh abba*, the child brings merit to the father, and that is success that goes on forever; children should know that this is their chance to do something for their parents. You can pay back your parents for what they did for you by becoming better Jews, becoming greater *ovdei Hashem*, greater talmidei chachamim, greater tzaddikim; and raise bigger families and make your families be the best you can make them.

Knowing that you are doing something solid is true happiness. When you live for a purpose, live for something that is a real pursuit of happiness, then Hakadosh Baruch Hu will reward you. The truth is, the degree of simchah in a Jewish home today is far greater that the simchah found in other homes, because nothing can compare to the satisfaction of a frum Jewish life. You can know *every* second that you are doing something good, even through the simplest mitzvos; *every* second, everything in the house is being done with *retzon Hashem*, and *every* second you are preparing merchandise to take with you to the Next World. Learning Torah, doing mitzvos, paying *sechar limud*, whatever you do is a solid achievement.

You can be the happiest person in the world but you have to work on it

YOU CAN BE THE HAPPIEST PERSON IN THE WORLD, BUT YOU HAVE TO think about it. *Ashrei ha'am shekachah lo, ashrei ha'am sheHashem Elokav*[24] — Hashem is waiting for you in the Next World and He is going to reward you for a lifetime of accomplishment. We don't pursue happiness; *Ach tov vachessed yirdefuni*[25] — it pursues us. What a person accomplished for himself in this world will last forever, and if he can accomplish for his parents, he should certainly continue. Drop a penny in the tzedakah box even for people who were kind to you — it is a great merit. And if you drop in a penny for yourself in this world, by training your children to continue to do *ma'asim tovim* long after you are gone, that is the greatest success you can have in this world.

---

24. *Tehillim* 144:14
25. *Tehillim* 23:6

LOVE THIS WORLD 7

When a person matures he should relearn all the things he learned as a youngster

HE *CHOVOS HALEVAVOS*[1] DECLARES THAT WHEN A PERSON matures, he should relearn all the things he learned as a youngster; otherwise, even if he is a *gadol beTorah*, all his life he will continue to think of these important things, such as the *beri'as ha'olam* and all the important lessons of *Bereishis*, in the way he thought when he studied them the first time as a child. Unless you relearn, you will never understand the concepts that the Torah intended to teach you.

Creation is a gift of such magnitude that it obligates us to pour out our thanks to Hashem continuously

BEREISHIS COMES TO TELL US THAT WE MUST APPRECIATE AND GIVE thanks to Hakadosh Baruch Hu because He created the world. In *Mizmor shir leyom haShabbos* it states, *"Tov lehodos laHashem*[2] — it

1. Section Eight Chapter 3:24
2. *Tehillim* 92:1-2

is good to give thanks to Hashem. *Ki simachtani Hashem befa'olecha, bema'asei yadecha aranen*[3] — for You made me happy with Your deeds, I sing at the works of Your hands." This refers to *ma'aseh bereishis*, and we learn here that it is a *chiyuv*, an obligation, to thank Hakadosh Baruch Hu for giving us this gift of *olam hazeh*. Creation is a gift of such magnitude of *chessed Hashem* that it obligates us to pour out our thanks to Hashem continuously for making the world. In fact that is what we do, but we do it like sleepwalkers. Every day we say *berachos* to Hashem — *roka ha'aretz al hamayim; Baruch Atah Hashem yotzer hame'oros* — but it is a pity that we do not say them with all our hearts.

The Mishnah states, *"Be'asarah ma'amaros nivra ha'olam"*[4] — the world was made with ten statements by Hashem." But, the Gemara asks, if you count you will find only nine, not ten![5] The Gemara answers, *"Bereishis nami ma'amar hu"* — Bereishis, the beginning of the world, is also a result of Hashem's statement— only it is missing the *tzivui*. The Torah didn't say, *"Vayomer Hashem yehi olam."* Why isn't that written? That first act, creation *ex nihilo*, is the most remarkable miracle of all. Nothing is as great as this *neis* of *yeish mei'ayin*. So why isn't Hashem's *tzivui* written — that Hashem said, "Let there be *shamayim* and *aretz*"?

The entire world is worthless unless you appreciate it

THE ANSWER IS THAT HASHEM WANTED THE COMMAND OF *"VAYOMER Elokim yehi ohr"* to be the first *ma'amar*, statement. Hakadosh Baruch Hu concealed the first *ma'amar* in order that *yehi ohr* should be the first. The reason is that *the entire world is worthless unless you look at it and see it*. The world was given to us to see and appreciate by means of the light. Light conveys objects to our eyes; it enables us to see, and seeing is so very important in this world, because we must appreciate that great gift. Therefore, *yehi ohr* is the first statement.[6]

Our function in this world is to look. We have to look at the sky, at the earth, at the trees, at ourselves — and be surprised at this miracle. It is only by seeing that a person can fulfill his obligation, which is to thank Hakadosh Baruch Hu for this world. Don't think that this obligation is a

---

3. *Tehillim* 92:5
4. *Avos* 85:1
5. *Rosh Hashanah* 32b
6. See *The Beginning* p. 20 (1:4), *Praise My Soul* p. 258 (750)

middas chassidus; don't think it is for *tzaddikim gedolim*. Every human being in the world is obliged to look at the world and thank the *Borei*.

The whole world is full of evil and falsehood

TODAY, THERE IS A GREAT CLOUD OF DARKNESS OVER THE WORLD — "*Hachoshech yechaseh aretz va'arafel le'umim.*"[7] The whole world is full of evil and falsehood, and many people and groups are trying their best to conceal from the eyes of man the truth of the *beri'ah*. They use every trick to make people blind to this great truth of the Torah, which is the truth of Hashem's word. Hashem tells us that the world was made in six days — *ki sheishes yamim asah Hashem es hashamayim ve'es ha'aretz*[8] — and it began with Hashem's command: *Bereishis bara Elokim eis hashamayim ve'eis ha'aretz,*[9] in the beginning Hashem made the world — out of nothing.

We have to look and recognize, "*Yoducha Hashem kol ma'asecha*[10] — all Your works praise You, they speak of the glory of Hashem's power." Everything Hashem made in the world — the sky, the sun, the earth — is all *lehodi'a livnei ha'adam gevuraso*[11] — to make known to people Hashem's power. *Lehodi'a* means to give *de'ah*. The purpose of the world is for us to gain *de'ah*: *Hashamayim mesaperim kevod Kel uma'asei yadav maggid haraki'a.*[12] If we open the Torah and read *Bereishis bara Elokim*, these thundering words resound in our ears and illuminate our minds to understand that the whole world is nothing but *bidvar Hashem shamayim na'asu*;[13] it was all made by the word of Hashem. *Vayomer Hashem, vayehi.*

It is a pleasure that your heart is pumping the blood through your system

WE HAVE TO UNDERSTAND THAT WE SHOULD SPEND OUR LIVES appreciating the great gift of this world. We have to appreciate the skies, the sun, the moon, the soil ... we have to study everything in the world in order to appreciate it. This world is a world of happiness. It is a pleasure to be alive; it is a pleasure to breathe air. It is a pleasure that

---

7. *Yeshaya* 60:2
8. *Shemos* 20:11
9. *Bereishis* 1:1
10. *Tehillim* 145:10
11. *Tehillim* 145:12
12. *Tehillim* 19:1
13. *Tehillim* 33:6

your heart is pumping the blood through your system; it is a pleasure that your kidneys are doing miracles, purifying all the materials that pass through the blood; it is a pleasure to be able to see. Every day you say *Baruch Atah Hashem pokei'ach ivrim.* You have to learn how to appreciate these things and spend your life expressing your thanks for them.

When Hakadosh Baruch Hu made them, He put a label on them: *Vaya'ar Elokim es ha'or ki tov*[14] — He labeled it *tov*, good, for two reasons. First, we should know that it is *tov*; otherwise you could pass through the world all your life without thinking about it. The second reason is that we should do what Hashem did. Hashem said *ohr* is *tov*, so we too have to say that *ohr* is *tov*. Did you ever say that in your life? You'd better say it at least once, because when you daven you are like a sleepwalker; you don't know what you are saying. Say it in English, in Yiddish, in any language — say that life is good. If you've never said it even once in your life, then you are neglecting an obligation. You should do it every day, and you should think what you are saying: *Baruch Atah Hashem yotzer ohr* — it is exciting. Why are *malachim* introduced in the berachah of *yotzer ohr*? To show you an example of how you have to be excited. The *malachim* are excited. They say *bekol ra'ash gadol* — they are excited when they look at the *ohr*. We look at them and we say, "*nekadesh es Shimcha ba'olam kesheim shemakdishim...,* we praise Your Name like the *malachim* do." We make a promise to emulate the *malachim*.[15]

We have to thank Hashem for the sun every day

A N AMERICAN BACHUR ONCE CAME INTO A YESHIVAH IN POLAND, AND the mashgiach asked him, "*Vos tut der Aibeshter aleh mal,* what does Hashem do all day?" The bachur did not know what to say. "Look in davening," the mashgiach told him. "What do the *malachim* do all day?" He didn't know what the *malachim* do. "The *malachim* are *me'orei ohr she'asisa, yefa'arucha selah,*" the mashgiach said. "They are always thanking Hashem for the light. That is what the *malachim* are doing." It is put there in davening for us to emulate; we have to thank Hashem for the light every day, all our lives. The light is pleasure.

Ohr vesimchah, light and joy, always go together. Darkness is sadness, light is happiness. The light of the sun gives us our food. We wouldn't have any apples or bananas to eat if not for the light of the

---

14. *Bereishis* 1:4
15. See *Praise My Soul* p. 271 (783)

sun. Hakadosh Baruch Hu made the sun a *shaliach* to help produce the food. Do you *every* think about that?

The sun provides heat — heat that costs no money. The sun provides vitamins — when the sun heats your skin it creates vitamins in you. The sun kills germs. This is just the beginning of the list of the *ma'alos* of the sun. The Torah doesn't mention the sun much; it only speaks about *ohr*, light — it doesn't want people to become too enamored with the sun because *ovdei avadah zarah* worship the sun. We are no longer in danger of the old foolishness of worshiping the sun, so we can talk about the sun, and it is a principle of life that we should understand how good it is. "*Umasok ha'ohr*, how sweet is the light," Koheles said. "*Vetov la'einayim liros es hashemesh,*[16] it is a pleasure to see the sunshine." Sometimes I say that pasuk in the street and start enjoying the sunlight. Practice it — it is there for that purpose.

There are many good things in this world. Eating is very good, and it is a pleasure. There is so much happiness in *olam hazeh* that *Mesillas Yesharim* has to prove that the world is not made only for *olam hazeh*. He proves that it is impossible to say that this world is an end in itself. It seems that without proof we would have been deceived, because it is such a good world. Of course the Torah reveals through the mouth of Bilaam that this world is not the final goal. Bilaam said, "*Tamos nafshi mos yesharim*[17] — I wish I could die like those righteous people over there, the Jewish people; *ure'isa es acharai* — my 'afterwards' should be like their 'afterwards.' " So Bilaam knew that there is an afterworld.[18] But *olam hazeh* is a good thing, and we have to spend time on that thought.

David Hamelech said (*Tehillim* 136), *Hodu laHashem ki tov ki le'olam chasdo, le'oseh shamayim bisevunah*; he gives thanks to the One Who made the sky with wisdom, and that is what we have to do. It is a *tzivui*, a command clearer than anything in *Shulchan Aruch*; there is no *machlokes* about it.

When you walk on the ground be happy

ROKA HA'ARETZ AL HAMAYIM KI LE'OLAM CHASDO — WE SAY THIS with a berachah every day. When you walk on the ground, be

---

16. *Koheles* 11:7
17. *Bamidbar* 23:10
18. See *Journey Into Greatness* p. 315 (2310)

happy. In many places in the world the ground caved in, and thousands of people lost their lives. As you walk on the ground and it doesn't cave in, think *roka ha'aretz al hamayim ki le'olam chasdo*.

When you eat you have to go wild with simchah

THEN DAVID HAMELECH SPEAKS OF THE LUMINARIES, *LE'OSEH ORIM gedolim, ki le'olam chasdo*, and he enumerates: *Es Hashemesh lememsheles hayom ki le'olam chasdo* — the sun — then *yarei'ach vechochavim* — the moon and the stars. And he goes on to enumerate a long list of things: *makkos* in Mitzrayim, *yetzi'as Mitzrayim, keri'as Yam Suf*...and at the end, he says, *Nosen lechem lechol basar, ki le'olam chasdo* — it is approaching a climax. The Gemara says, "*Kasheh mezonosav shel adam kekrias yam suf*[19] — a man's food is more difficult than *keri'as yam suf*." This means that *keri'as yam suf* was a tremendous *neis*, a miracle that Hashem made, but when you have food on your table that is a much bigger *neis*! So when you eat, you have to go wild with simchah.

This great man of our history is telling us that we have to look at the world and say, "Thank You, Hashem, for this world," and to realize that the purpose of the *chasdei Hashem* is *lehodi'a livnei ha'adam*,[20] to teach us *da'as*. *Da'as* is a feeling of conviction — we should be convinced that *ki le'olam chasdo*, and we must be happy. If we are not happy it shows that we didn't study and appreciate *olam hazeh*. When the *malachim* say *kadosh kadosh*, they are expressing their admiration for this world, not for *Olam Haba*. And then the *ofanim* and *chayos hakodesh* hear what the *serafim* are saying. They become so excited when they hear the *kedushah* of the *malachim* who are on top of the chariot, and they pick themselves up and face the *seraphim*.[21]

As much as you study the great happiness of this world it is only a hint of the great happiness of the Next World

IMAGINE A PALACE WITH ALL THE DOORS LOCKED AND ALL THE WINDOWS closed, and from the little keyhole a ray of light goes forth that illumi-

---

19. *Pesachim* 118a
20. *Tehillim* 145:12
21. See *Praise My Soul* p. 280 (809)

nates the whole neighborhood. One ant says to another, "Look at the great light!" The other ant says, "That is nothing — in the palace is a greater light." As much as you study *olam hazeh*, it is only a hint of the greatness of the happiness of *Olam Haba*.

Sefer Bereishis is the only one that starts without the letter *vav*. Almost every pasuk in the Torah starts with a *vav* — *Vayar, Vayomer*, etc. *Sefer Shemos, Vayikra,* and *Bamidbar* all start with the letter *vav*. What are all these *vavs*? Every "and" is for a purpose; they come to say that all the events and all the ideas expressed in the Torah are connected to one another. Each one is a result of the previous one and a preface to the next. The entire Torah is one series, a chain, and every *vav* in every pasuk is a link in that chain. When the world began, Hakadosh Baruch Hu described it in the Torah without a *vav*, so there is no link to the past. The letter *beis* (of *Bereishis*) has three sides and is open only on one side. This is telling us: go ahead. Don't look back. What is going on above, below, and behind is a waste of time. Just look ahead, and study our history that the Torah tells you. Don't bother your head over what was before this world. It is a waste of time.

Everything that came after *Bereishis* is a result of the thing before it. All the pesukim from *Bereishis* until *vayomer Hashem el Avraham lech lecha* are a preface to Avrohom Avinu. Everything that happened was necessary for the appearance of Avraham in this world. When Avraham came the world was still young. He was able to talk to people, and he did, and thousands listened to him.

Adam Harishon was created in the happiest environment, not in Gan Eden, which is the place where *neshamos* of tzaddikim are now, but in a *gan be'Eden*, a garden within Eden, and it was a glorious place of joy and happiness. Adam and Chavah were put in this world and they were able to live almost a thousand years and it was a gan eden, a garden of pleasure. The reason for this is that Hakadosh Baruch Hu wanted Adam to learn about the *Borei* and gain *da'as*, knowledge, of Hashem by means of pleasure. That was the original plan, because through simchah a person can become very great in awareness of Hashem. When Esav wanted a berachah from his father, Yitzchak said to him, *asei li matamim*,[22] prepare for me tasty food, the venison that you always make for me. I will eat it and I will enjoy

---

22. *Bereishis* 27:7

it and I will give you a better berachah. Did Yitzchak have to eat Esav's meal in order to give him a good berachah? He already loved and favored Esav. But Yitzchak wanted to give the best berachah that he could, and when he ate his son's venison he was in such a good mood that he gave him the very best berachah — only he gave it to the wrong son.[23]

When you are happy and enjoying yourself, that is the best opportunity to recognize the kindness of Hashem

WHEN YOU ARE HAPPY, WHEN YOU ARE ENJOYING YOURSELF, THAT IS the best opportunity to recognize the kindness of Hashem. From happiness a person can become great. If you are young and healthy, you are making a living, you are together with your wife, you have children, you live in freedom, Baruch Hashem, you have heat in the wintertime, maybe even air conditioning in the summertime, you have clothing, you have a bathroom in the house (*eizehu ashir, mi sheyeish lo beis hakisei samuch leshulchano*) — you have everything; you should be very happy and you should appreciate it. Hashem gave Adam Harishon all the good things of this world in order that he should learn to appreciate Hashem on the highest possible level. Happiness is the best way to come to avodas Hashem.

"*Ve'achalta lifnei Hashem ... vesamachta.*"[24] The Torah tells us constantly to eat the *korbanos* before Hashem and rejoice. Happiness is the best way to come close to Hashem. If a person doesn't utilize it, then Hakadosh Baruch Hu says: I will use another method — troubles — then he will cry out to Hashem. At least then he will remember that there is a Hashem. But the best way to remember Him is in happiness. That is why Adam was in Gan Eden. However, when Hakadosh Baruch Hu saw that Gan Eden caused Adam to err, that it caused a *cheit*, then He took him out of Gan Eden and put him in a different gan eden. After the *cheit* Adam lived a very happy life, but it was a different kind of life entirely. Hakadosh Baruch Hu gave happiness so that *ve'achalta vesavata*, it will make you more and more aware of Him and loyal to Him, but *hishameru lachem*, if you don't utilize it, *vecharah af Hashem*

---

23. See *The Beginning* p. 423 (27:4), *Fortunate Nation* p. 191 (12:7)
24. *Devarim* 14:27

ve'atzar es hashamayim velo yihyeh matar,[25] He will take away some of the happiness.

Did you ever thank Hashem for sanity?

For happiness to continue, we must thank Hashem for the good He is giving us

FOR THE HAPPINESS TO CONTINUE, WE MUST CONTINUALLY THANK Hashem for the good things that He is giving us. *Baruch Atah Hashem chonen hada'as*, You bestow *da'as* on me — I am sane. Did you ever thank Hashem for being sane? The purpose of the berachah is to thank Hashem for sanity. There is a very tiny difference between sanity and insanity. Baruch Hashem that He made that difference, and your job in life is to learn that; this is the purpose of *Bereishis bara Elokim*.

Seeing Hashem's Greatness

WHEN AVRAHAM CAME ON THE SCENE, THE *RAMBAM* SAY IN *HILCHOS Avodah Zarah*, Avraham looked at the sun and saw how wonderfully it works. The sun is just big enough to warm us. If it were bigger, we would be burned to a crisp; if it were smaller, we would be frozen. If the sun were a little closer, we would be burned; if it were more distant, we would be frozen. How did it happen that the sun was the exact distance and the exact size? Avraham was studying the happiness of this world, how good the sun is for us. With that he came to recognize that there is Someone in charge. That is Avraham's system. He looked at everything in the world and saw that nothing was accidental; everything is full of purpose, and from that he came to recognize the *Borei*. So now you know why the world was made in such a way — in order that an Avraham Avinu would recognize it. Now that an Avraham was destined to appear, in his *zechus* the world was able to eat and to have water, to sleep, to breathe air all those years.

This is a very great principle: all the *chasdei Hashem* were because of that tzaddik. The world was made because of him. Elsewhere it says, *kol ha'olam nizon bishvil Chanina beni*,[26] the whole world is supported because of the merit of the tzaddik Chanina ben Dosa. This is not a mashal. The whole world, the Eskimos in the north, the blacks in Africa, the Romans, the Greeks are all being fed because of My son Chanina.

---

25. *Devarim* 11:17
26. *Taanis* 10a

Do you want to do the world a favor?
Sit down and learn all day long

THIS PRINCIPLE IS STATED OPENLY IN THE TORAH: *VENIVRECHU BECHA kol mishpechos ha'adamah u'vezarecha*,[27] the whole world will be blessed because of Avraham. All the people in the north, in the south, in the east, and in the west all are being given happiness of *olam hazeh* only because of Avraham and his righteous descendants.[28] The Jewish nation that keeps the Torah is feeding the world. When you are acting like an *oveid Hashem* you are doing a very great favor for *olam hazeh*. All the gentiles should be grateful and love you for that. Avraham looked at everything and saw and learned from everything, and therefore everything is blessed because of him. Do you want to do the world a favor? Sit down and learn all day long! Learn *Mesillas Yesharim*; become a tzaddik; *netzor leshonecha mei'ra*, guard your tongue against *lashon hara*, or against talking in general; daven with *kavanah*; love your fellow Jews. Anyone who is a tzaddik is causing the world to be happy. Everyone in the world is eating and drinking and wearing clothing only because there is an Am Yisrael that obeys the Torah.

The Torah tells us, "*veru'ach Elokim merachefes al penei hamayim*[29] — the Spirit of Hashem is hovering over the waters," like a seaplane. Why over the waters? Why couldn't it rest on the land? Because there was no place to rest. Hashem was looking for a place to rest, looking for a nation with whom His Shechinah could rest. Maybe with Adam? No, Adam was a disappointment. Kayin and Hevel were also disappointments — they were both fighting, and in the end Kayin killed Hevel — to save his own life. (It says "*vayakam Kayim al Hevel*" — Kayin got up. Why did he "get up"? Because Hevel had knocked him down.) And so Hashem rejected them and chose their brother Sheis, who was born later. Sheis was the foundation, but Hashem kept on looking until finally, *ba Avraham Avinu venatal sechar kulam*;[30] when Avraham came Hashem said, "This is the man I was waiting for; I made the world for him." And later it says *veshachanti besoch Bnei Yisrael*[31] — that is when the *ruach Elokim* finally came to rest on Am Yisrael.[32]

---

27. *Bereishis* 12:3
28. See *The Beginning* p. 207 (12:3)
29. *Bereishis* 1:2
30. *Avos* 3:5
31. *Shemos* 29:45
32. See *The Beginning* p. 13 (1:2)

A wicked Jew is a misfortune to the whole world

However, there is another side to this picture. When people were expected to fulfill this great function of giving the Shechinah a place to rest, they proved a disappointment to Hakadosh Baruch Hu. A wicked Jew is a misfortune to the whole world. *Puraniyos* come because of *resha'im*. Sooner or later Hakadosh Baruch Hu eradicates the *resha'im*. And Hashem said, *keivan shenitan reshus lamashchis shuv eino mavchin bein tzaddik lerasha,*[33] once I give permission for the *mashchis*, the destroyer, to come and destroy, he makes no distinction. He wipes out whole communities. Hashem is an *ish milchamah* — if Hashem declares war, you have to look out.

One of the greatest methods of building up Am Yisrael is through frum schools

One of the great concerns we have today is that there are a great number of *poshei Yisrael*. One of the greatest methods of building up Am Yisrael as servants of Hashem is through the yeshivos and the frum girls schools, and they are doing a tremendous job. There are hundreds of day schools in America, which are producing Jews who are entirely different from the old generation that grew up in public school. And Baruch Hashem they are having families; they are filling up the world with tzaddikim, and Hakadosh Baruch Hu is waiting. But we are in great danger, because the other ones are causing the world to become *tamei*, infected, although the *resha'im* are dwindling and the tzaddikim are, Baruch Hashem, increasing.

Avraham Avinu is called Avraham Ha'ivri. *Kol ha'olam mei'eiver mizeh,*[34] *Avraham mei'eiver mizeh* — the whole world was against Avraham. *Echad hayah Avraham*, he was one man, and still Avraham with his great *zechus* was able to maintain the happiness of the world. Avraham went, *vayis'halechu migoy el goy u'mimamlachah el am acher,*[35] and he saw everywhere there were idol worshipers and all kinds of wicked practices. Avraham saw a world that was steeped in *avodah zarah*, but Hakadosh Baruch Hu said, "Avraham Avinu is so precious to me that even though he is only one,

---

33. *Bava Kamma* 60a
34. *Bereishis* 10a
35. *I Divrei Hayamim* 16:22

his merit is so great that he is *machria es kulam*, he outweighs all of them." Now we learn from this that the more the tzaddikim build themselves in mitzvos *bein adam lachaveiro* and in mitzvos *bein adam laMakom*, the more opportunity there is to save the world.

Today's booming frum Orthodox population is a big *zechus*, but is it sufficient to save the world? Who knows what is going to happen, *chas veshalom*? Germans were very polite and it was a law-abiding country, not a crime-infested country. It was much better than in America. Who dreamed that Germany would turn out to be a place of mass murderers and devils? Everyone admired the Germans and some emulated the Germans as their ideal. Germany was the apex of culture in Europe. Many Jews converted because they admired the gentiles, so Hashem said, I will show you who the gentiles are, what Germany is!

For America to continue to be a good place, it all depends on our virtue

WE SEE THAT AMERICA IS A GOOD PLACE TO LIVE IN, THERE IS tolerance, we can keep the Torah, there are many laws protecting us, Baruch Hashem, and most Jews are making a living. The question is, do you want to maintain that situation? Do you want to justify having such hatzlachah? It is important for us to know that it all depends on our virtue. The more elevated we become in the service of Hashem, the more we become tzaddikim and loyal *ovdei Hashem*, the better is our chance to save the whole world from the misfortune that happened in Europe.

Everyone knows that not all the Jews went out of Mitzrayim. *Vachamushim alu Bnei Yisrael me'eretz Mitzrayim*[36] — the Sages tell us *echad mei'chamishah*, one out of five left Mitzrayim. What happened? Six hundred thousand men between the ages of 20 and 60 left Mitzrayim, besides the women, the old and the young; millions of Jews. But there were many more. *Vayishretzu*, when the Jews were having children they used to have sextuplets. A woman who gave birth ten times had sixty children. There were so many Jews that *Vayakutzu*, the Egyptians couldn't take it any longer, they were so frightened. The land was cluttered with Jews. But not all were good. Nobody was bad, but they weren't good enough. Hakadosh Baruch

---

36. *Shemos* 13:18

Hu wanted more. So when the three days of darkness came, many Jews also died out, so only one out of five left Mitzrayim.

It is a great tragedy when Jews get lost

THE NAVI SAID (AMOS :9) *HINEI ANOCHI METZAVEH*, I AM GOING TO GIVE an order — *vahani'osi bechol hagoyim es Beis Yisrael* — I am going to move Beis Yisrael around throughout all the nations. I am going to shake them, *ka'asher yino'a bakevarah* — like you shake a sieve. And through the holes of the sieve will fall out all the dirt, all the ones that are no good. As they pass through the gentile nations, very many will get lost among those nations. *Bacherev yamusu kol chata'ei ami* — all the sinners of My people will die by the sword — and not only by the sword; they will die by assimilation — assimilation is worse than death. Hashem is making us go through all the nations and He is sifting us like in a sieve and He wants all the *pesoless*, the undesirable elements, to fall out. It is a great tragedy when Jews get lost. There were many Jews who became *mushumadim*, many more have become secular, and they follow the goyim; many Jews are lost in the culture of America today; many Jews move away to where there are no Jewish neighbors, and they get lost. But in the merit of the frum families, the *ovdei Hashem*, the world continues to exist.

If we are in the sieve, what effect does it have on us? You have to hold on and not fall through the holes. Become a frum Jew. Do something to save yourself! Marry your daughter to a talmid chacham; marry your son to a daughter of a talmid chacham. Do all you can to save yourself so you don't fall through the holes in the sieve. Hashem is sifting us, and the weaklings are falling through the holes.

The whole world depends on Bnei Yisrael

AND SO THIS IS THE WAY HISTORY GOES — ALL WITH A *VAV*, FROM THE beginning to the end; all tied up together. The world was created only because *bereishis* — *bishvil Yisrael, shenikra reishis*.[37] The first word in the Torah is *bereishis*, and the last word is *Yisrael*, which is the purpose of the Torah and the purpose of the world. The world is made *bishvil Yisrael, shenikra reishis*, and the whole world depends on us. Our function is *venivrechu*, we have to bring a blessing — a blessing to

---

37. *Rashi, Bereishis* 1:1

ourselves, and a blessing to all Am Yisrael, and we will bring a blessing to all the world, too — *kol mishpachos ha'adamah.*

All the birds will come and say that because of the Jews who kept the Torah the world is existing

SOMEDAY THE GENTILES WILL COME FROM AFRICA AND FROM ALASKA and from all over the world, and they will thank you for saving them with your righteousness. All the birds, the deer, and the trees will come and say that because of you Jews who kept the Torah the world has a *kiyum*. The more we do in the service of Hashem, the greater is the favor we are doing ourselves, right here in *olam hazeh*, and the greater is the favor we are doing everyone else. *Ilui gadol hu lebrios kulam*, it is a great elevation for all creatures, *sheyihyu meshameshim elyon*, that they serve the superior one — the Jew. The sun and the moon and the stars are all serving you, and you are improving the sun and the stars and all the universe!

DEEP TRUTHS IN A SHALLOW WORLD — UTILIZING THE WORLD FOR THE NEXT WORLD

OHELES EMPHASIZED THE EMPTINESS OF MANY THINGS in this world: *Havel havalim amar Koheles.*[1] Yet, the Midrash says, "*Bor'am meshabecham* — their Creator praises them; and Hashem said about *kol asher asah*, everything in the Creation — *hinei tov me'od,*[2] is very good, *ve'atah meganeh*, and you despise them." How can we say that it is all *hevel* when Hashem says it is all good?

Looking at wealth as something that is important in itself is false

IN FACT, BOTH ARE TRUE. EVERYTHING IN THIS WORLD IS FALSE, AND at the same time it is true. The falsehood of *olam hazeh* is when you look at things for their own value. People look at wealth as something that is important in and of itself; or even at life as important in and of itself. Consider the feeling of *kavod*; people desire glory just for the sensation, the feeling of elation at the honor that people give them.

---

1. *Koheles* 1:2
2. *Bereishis* 1:31

Consider victory — when the conquering general returns with his soldiers and receives a great ovation and a parade, and he sees that in itself as the purpose. In these cases, *hakol havel!* Feelings of love — a man's love for a woman, someone's love of nature, of beautiful scenery — when it becomes an end in itself, is *hakol havel.* This is what Koheles means when he says "*havel havalim hakol havel*" — it is all nothing.

But what about the *truth* of this world? In many ways, this world testifies to great eternal truths, if only you learn how to see them. This world can give us the ability to discern and to recognize truths that most people don't begin to think about.

There is not a space on this earth that is not for the purpose of chessed Hashem

FOR EXAMPLE, WHEN PEOPLE EXPERIENCE HAPPINESS, THEY SHOULD see it as evidence of the *chessed Hashem* that fills the entire world. There is not a space on this earth or in the oceans that is not for the purpose of *chessed Hashem.* When a person trains himself, he can see — in a nice day, in beautiful trees, in lawns and gardens and flowers, in the sun shining — that the world is full of *chessed Hashem*; it is all a demonstration of Hashem's kindliness. We don't see it unless we learn how to recognize it. For instance, things we enjoy in nature may stir in us a certain feeling beyond the ordinary attitude of interest in the scenery. We feel there is a mystery here, and in fact there is. All the beauty of nature testifies to the great principle that the world is full of Hashem's *chessed.*[3]

All forms of happiness have a higher function to help us realize that there is much more waiting for us in the Next World

ALL THIS, HOWEVER, IS ONLY A MASHAL; IT IS A FORETASTE OF something very great — it is a hint of the glory of the World to Come. Hakadosh Baruch Hu doesn't want us to live like sheep — who look at the luscious grass and chew it and enjoy their meal, and that is all they are thinking about. To mankind He has given a certain concealed emotion that tells us there is something very, very beautiful and great that is waiting for us beyond the horizon. We feel instinctively there is some vast happiness that is hinted at by what we see with our

---

3. See *The Beginning* p. 47 (1:31)

eyes. All the good things in this world, all the many forms of enjoyment and forms of happiness and well-being, all have a higher function; they are there to help us instinctively realize that there is much more waiting in the future.

What about wealth? People are greedy and want more and more; "*Oheiv kesef lo yisba kesef*,"[4] people who love money — which means us — never have enough; they always want more. But this particular statement was said about Moshe Rabbeinu; was Moshe Rabbeinu desirous of more money? Moshe Rabbeinu knew that *kesef* means desire — "*nichsof nichsafti*" — there is something to desire, and Moshe Rabbeinu did desire — he desired the most valuable money there is in the world: the money of perfection, of greatness of character. And he attained a tremendous amount in his lifetime; he became so perfect that no one even remotely approached his greatness. And yet when Hashem told him *hein karevu yamechah lamus*,[5] you are going to die soon — you lived 120 years and they were the most full and successful years that anyone ever lived — he put up the greatest protest; he wanted to live more. *Va'eschanan el Hashem*[6]— I begged Hashem: Please, Hashem, let me live longer! Here is a man who loved *kesef*; he wanted to become great, he had to achieve, to utilize his life — but he wanted more and more.

We have to dig into ourselves and keep on bringing forth the greatness which is within us

HASHEM TOLD THE JEWISH PEOPLE TO TAKE OUT THE WEALTH OF Mitzrayim, and Moshe saw some people who were very busy collecting the money there with great energy, and Moshe thought, these men are out for money, but it is not a waste. There is a purpose in it; it is a mitzvah, since Hashem said *venitzaltem es Mitzrayim*,[7] you should empty out Mitzrayim. Moshe Rabbeinu realized that a desire for money is a mashal for the great desire everyone has potentially within himself. You have a desire to become great, even to become perfect, and there is so much to develop. A human being is a gold mine. There are miners who come looking for gold, and they work day and night, digging in the ground. In the same way we have to dig into ourselves

---

4. *Koheles* 5:9
5. *Devarim* 25:11
6. *Devarim* 3:24
7. *Shemos* 12:36

and keep on bringing forth the greatness. There is no limit to how much we can bring forth. Even though Moshe Rabbeinu produced out of himself unequaled wealth — no one even came close to what he produced — still, *oheiv kesef lo yisba kesef*,[8] he wasn't satisfied; he wanted more.

The more you recognize the greatness of Hashem's kindness, the greater you are

THIS GIVES US AN IDEA OF OUR PURPOSE IN THIS WORLD. WE ARE HERE to take whatever we can and as much as we can, and there is so much to take from all sides. For example, you can take a whole shas with you; you could take the whole *Mesillas Yesharim*, *Chovos Halevavos*, Rambam, and *Sha'arei Teshuvah* with you. You could take realization with you: You can stand near a fruit stand and admire the miracle of red fruits, blue fruits, purple fruits, yellow fruits, and golden fruits, and each one has a separate taste; there may be a hundred different tastes, and the fruits are all so beautiful, wrapped in beautiful peels. You may not even eat them, but just looking at them can make you see *chessed Hashem* in the world, and that is wealth. The more you recognize the greatness of Hashem's kindness, the greater you are, and that recognition is a possession.

When Moshe Rabbeinu and the *asirei Bnei Yisrael*, the noblemen of Bnei Yisrael, came to *Har Sinai*, they had a remarkable vision. *Vayechezu es haElokim*,[9] they saw Hashem. And what did they do? *Vayochelu vayishtu*, they ate and drank. It seems strange: they were so full of joy when they viewed the Shechinah — not everyone was eligible to see that, and at that point they sat down to eat and drink. The reason is that it is not enough for our minds to be overjoyed at what we see; we want our bodies to participate as well, and this is what they accomplished by eating and drinking. Their *guf* and their *nefesh*, their body and soul together, were enjoying the scene. They gained an awareness of the great truths, and that *da'as* is wealth. Becoming aware of Hashem's Presence, of His kindness, of His *middos tovos*, and to feel it with the *neshamah*, is called wealth, and Moshe Rabbeinu wanted to live longer to get more wealth.[10]

---

8. *Koheles* 5:9
9. *Shemos* 24:11
10. See *A Nation Is Born* p. 355,356 (24:11)

Multimillionaires are put
in the world for a mashal

A ND SO, WHEN YOU HEAR OF MULTIMILLIONAIRES, YOU SHOULD
recognize that they are put in the world for a mashal — whether
they are learning anything from it or not. They may be investing all their
thoughts in *havel havalim*, but you are taking the *hevel*, the *sheker* of
olam hazeh, and utilizing it as a mashal, as a model for understanding.
Yes, it pays to amass as much wealth as we can in this world, to learn all
that we can of *yiras Hashem*, *Toras Hashem*, all good *middos*, praises
of Hashem, *berachos vehoda'os mei'atah ve'ad olam*. We can speak
about Hashem without even thinking: *Chanun verachum Hashem
erech apayim ugdol chassed; tov Hashem lakol verachamav al kol
ma'asav.*[11] A few words contain so much that will transform our minds
— it is wealth to gain these attitudes. There are millions in this world for
us to take, but the millionaire doesn't know which ones are valuable.

The Rambam[12] says that there are various names given to *Olam
Haba* in the *kisvei hakodesh*. For instance, in *Tehillim* it is called
derech hakodesh. It is talking about a road that leads to *kodesh*.
Many times you feel there is something interesting farther along a
road, and you feel like walking down that road to see what is there,
but when you get there, you see there is nothing; it is a deception.

The desire to travel
is a mashal to travel to Olam Haba

T HE ROAD IS A MASHAL. THE DESIRE TO TRAVEL ON THAT ROAD IS A
desire to see the road that leads to *Olam Haba*. The yearning to
travel is the secret of the road. This desire points to the fact that
mankind is looking for something. Others may be wasting their lives,
but we know we have to travel. A person can't stand still in life. All the
world is a road, and you keep on going and going to come closer and
closer to Hakadosh Baruch Hu.

So any time you come to a nice clean street, and farther down
you see houses and trees and you think, "Maybe I should go down
there and see what is there," know that it is a waste of time. Instead,
go down and see what there is in the *sefarim*, what is in *Mesillas
Yesharim*, for instance. There is wisdom in this world, *chochmah*

---

11. *Tehillim* 145:8-9
12. *Rambam, Hilchos Teshuvah* 8:4

and *chessed*. You can find all these things right now, where you are, but you have to travel, to keep on going. There is so far to travel in this world — so much to accomplish.

Another name for *Olam Haba*, says the Rambam, is *har*, a mountain: *Mi ya'aleh behar* Hashem.[13] Although that is a pasuk about the *Beis Hamikdash*, the Rambam says the mountain of Hashem is *Olam Haba*. *Har Habayis*, after all, is nothing but a little pimple on the surface of the earth. But there is another mountain you have to climb, a mountain that brings you closer and closer to Hashem, a mountain of *sheleimus*, greatness of character, nobility of soul, knowledge of Hashem. Therefore when we say *Mi ya'aleh behar Hashem u'mi yakum bimkom kodsho*, although the *pashtus* deals with the location of the *Beis Hamikdash*, the *neshamah* of that pasuk means, "Who will rise up to go on a *real* mountain of Hashem, where the Shechinah is, and come closer to Hakadosh Baruch Hu?"

Any banquet serves as a mashal

AND, THE RAMBAM SAYS, *OLAM HABA* IS COMPARED TO A *SEUDAH*, A banquet. Participating in a *seudah* can be a great mitzvah, but it is not enough. Any banquet has to serve as a mashal. There is a great *seudah* awaiting us — *hakol muchan laseudah*. "*Olam hazeh domeh liprozdor lifnei Olam Haba*,[14] this world is like a lobby before we enter the great banquet hall. *Hasken atzmecha biprozdor kedei shetikaneis latraklin*,[15] prepare yourself in the lobby in order to enter the banquet hall afterwards." We know that there is a big banquet hall waiting, and we are going to enjoy the meal there forever and ever. We will never tire of the happiness we will find in the World to Come, but we have to prepare for it.

When a woman is cooking or washing laundry it is all for the purpose of producing greatness and perfection in the world to come

THIS WORLD IS NOT THE PLACE TO STUFF YOURSELF WITH FOOD; IT IS a place to prepare yourself with as much perfection as you can. *Hasken atzmecha*, improve yourself, and there are thousands of ways to do it. You can guard yourself from *lashon hara*; you can do

---

13. *Tehillim* 24:3
14. *Avos* 4:21
15. *Avos* 4:21

chessed with people; emulate Hakadosh Baruch Hu by being kind to people; gain plenty of yedi'os HaTorah — *Bava Kamma, Bava Metzia, Bava Basra* — pack as much as possible into yourself. What a great success it is to bring up a frum family, children who are *shomrei mitzvos*. The mother who does that is like a mashal to Hakadosh Baruch Hu, Who created Adam and Chavah. Even when she is standing in the kitchen and cooking for her family, or when she is washing the laundry, it is all for the purpose of producing greatness and perfection in the world to come.

The *Tiferes Yisrael, Peirush Hamishnayos (Mesechta Sanhedrin)*, devotes a lot of space to the butterfly. The butterfly was a wormlike creature — a caterpillar — creeping very slowly on a branch, a clumsy and a rather ugly creature, too. Then it starts spinning out thread, and it weaves a funeral shroud — *tachrichim* — for itself, until it is entirely surrounded by *tachrichim* of its own creation. Then the caterpillar "dies" and parts of it decay, and then there bursts forth from the cocoon a beautiful butterfly with wings, which flies gracefully up in the air. What was once a poor, contemptible little caterpillar has become a beautiful, winged creature!

The *Tiferes Yisrael* cites this as a mashal for the great lesson of *techiyas hameisim*. Our little bodies are sometimes not so well; we get old and worn out and ready to leave this world, and we wonder, "What's going to be with us?" But someday we will come forth in a new, beautiful, shining edition, as the *sefarim* say. The body will be transparent like glass and the *neshamah* will shine through the body. *Techiyas hameisim* will be a great happiness, our existence will be infinitely superior to existence in this world. Those who were like unimportant little caterpillars — if they lived properly — will someday come forth in a way that will astonish everyone.

We must believe in techiyas hameisim in order to get it

WE SAY IN THIS WORLD, *VENE'EMAN ATAH LEHACHAYOS MEISIM* — we trust You, Hashem, that You are going to revive the dead. We had to learn to say these words every day and train ourselves with *emunah* — *Baruch Atah Hashem mechayeh hameisim*, we thank Hashem for the great gift of *techiyas hameisim*. You must believe in *techiyas hameisim* in order to get it, and the more you believe in it, the more you will be *zocheh* to it. Visualize it for yourself — remember that the butterfly was once a caterpillar, and picture how it is now flying with such beautiful colors. We too will someday be in a new form of existence, one that will be far superior to our existence in this world.

Gehinnom is worse than concentration camps

LET US LOOK AT A MASHAL OF A DIFFERENT KIND: WHEN HITLER, *ym"sh*, began gathering Jews and deporting them to concentration camps and torturing them, the news reached Reb Yerucham, *zt"l*, the Mirrer mashgiach, before the Nazis overran Poland. He understood the magnitude of the tragedy, and he commented: Because the world stopped believing in Gehinnom, Hakadosh Baruch Hu took it out of the Next World and brought it to this world and showed us an example of Gehinnom. Tragedy had no equal ever before in history, and Reb Yerucham said it is teaching us that there is a Gehinnom, and that Gehinnom is worse than Hitler's concentration camps.

The people who perished in the Gehinnom of the concentration camps died with suffering, and they died before their time; that is indeed a tragedy — but since they had been living in this world, they would have had to die in any case. But these very people can be eligible for the happiness of the World to Come. Those people who lose their right to *Olam Haba*, on the other hand, all the Nazis, for instance, are going to end up in Gehinnom, and you can be sure that their lot in Gehinnom is a thousand times worse than what they did to their Jewish victims, and you have to believe that *be'emunah sheleimah*.

Hitler is being subjected to the worse torture every day

RIGHT NOW HITLER IS SCREAMING — EVERY DAY HE IS BEING GIVEN back his coat of meat and bones and nerves and is being subjected to worse tortures, and he is screaming terribly; our blood would run cold if we could hear it. All the *resha'im* who persecuted our people are getting what they deserve in Gehinnom, and it is of such fearsome proportions that we couldn't even tolerate looking at it. Although we don't see it with our eyes, we must learn from the mashal of the concentration camps that there is a place of infinite punishment going on day and night, and there are plenty of customers there, of all nations, being tortured constantly.

Do you think Hitler could kill six million Jews and then just leave this world and it was all over? No — the "fun" began just when he died. You have to believe *be'emunah sheleimah* that every *rasha* who persecuted the Jewish people is now in Gehinnom and suffering terribly, and every minute spent there is worse than all the pain of *olam hazeh*; in this world there is no pain like the pain they experience in Gehinnom every minute.

Purim serves as a mashal that the resha'im are in Gehinnom

WE HAVE TO UNDERSTAND THE OCCASIONS IN THIS WORLD — Purim, for example. Purim is a tremendous mashal, it is a time of *venahafoch hu*,[16] a day when we see the world upside down. On Purim we saw the ten sons of Haman hanging, just as they were preparing to massacre all the Jewish people. Just a short time before, Haman had the king's ring on his finger; now Mordechai is wearing the king's ring. Haman had a crown on his head and had all the honor, then Mordechai goes out with *ateres zahav gedolah*,[17] a great golden crown on his head. That is a picture of the Next World. In this world we saw such an apparition only once; Hashem made it happen so that we could see that it is a mashal. The *resha'im* will be hanging, only a thousand times worse than you can imagine. Purim has to serve as a model for understanding what the next world is like. The *resha'im* in Gehinnom are getting what they deserve right now, but they are getting much more than what we think they deserve.

Identify with the Jewish people as much as possible

WE HAVE TO TRAIN OURSELVES TO SEE THE *EMES* OF *OLAM hazeh*, not the *sheker*. The *sheker* is that the gentiles have power; they hate us and belittle us and persecute us — but that is only in this world, which is so full of *sheker*. Many unfortunate, ignorant Jews are influenced by that, and they start despising their own people. Many of them try to conceal themselves and make themselves look like gentiles, hoping to get lost among the *goyim*. They don't realize that all this is a mashal. There will be another place

---

16. *Esther* 9:1

where everything is upside down, and then, when they come to the place of reward and punishment, they will try to say, "We are Jews," but it will be too late. Change your names back now, while you are still here — change Jeffrey into Yaakov, Marvin into Moshe. Identify with the Jewish people as much as possible, and then you will join with the happiness of the Jewish people. And all the nations that hate us will join their previous generations, and all will be burning in Gehinnom forever.

Don't think it is all talk. Yeshaya Hanavi said, "*Hinei avadai yocheilu*[18] — my servants are going to eat; *ve'atem tir'avu* — and you will be hungry." Picture a big banquet hall filled with the most luscious foods the best caterers couldn't equal, and we are all sitting there, and all around us are all the *resha'im*, but they are not eating. They will be standing there drooling, dying of starvation. "*Avadai yaronu mituv leiv*,[19] my servants will sing out from happiness of their hearts, *ve'atem tiz'aku mike'eiv*, but you will cry out in pain." That is the picture Yeshaya Hanavi gives us, and we have to put it into our minds. So every Purim when you read what happened to Haman, know that it is a mashal of what is actually taking place.

Kavod is for the Next World

WHEN SOMEONE WISHED TO GIVE *KAVOD* TO THE CHAFETZ CHAIM, *zt"l*, he said, "*Kavod* is kugel, and you don't eat kugel on erev Shabbos!" He was saying that *kavod* is for the Next World; *kavod* is not *sheker*, but you have to know where to use it. The next world is the place of *kavod*. "*Ashrei mi sheba lechan vesalmudo beyado*[20] — how fortunate is a man who comes into the Next World and brings along his learning with him. How fortunate you are if you can bring along even a *perek*; a *mesechta* or a couple of *masechtos* is so much better, and you will get *kavod* for that; *Olam haba* is a place where *kavod* is fulfilled. *Kavod* is both a reality and a *sheker* — a reality in the Next World and a *sheker* in this one. Honor is a great thing, and it brings people great happiness. When it is gained properly and then deposited to be drawn out of the bank in *Olam Haba*, then that *kavod* is a tremendous

---

17. *Esther* 8:15
18. *Yeshaya* 65:13
19. *Yeshaya* 65:14
20. *Pesachim* 50a

thing. If you lived decently, kept your mouth closed, were always kind-hearted to people, always thought about Hashem, about *Olam Haba*, about the Torah; if you always thought about helping people, about *emunah* in *techiyas hameisim*, about Gan Eden … you will receive a wealth of *kavod* in the Next World.

When kavod is visible in this world you should utilize it as a mashal for the Next World

THAT IS WHY, WHEN *KAVOD* IS VISIBLE IN THIS WORLD, YOU SHOULD utilize it as a mashal. If someone received the Nobel prize and collects the prize and the money that goes with it, he will come home very happy, but this *kavod* is nothing at all. Still, you can utilize that and realize that there is a *real* Nobel prize for real nobility — a prize that is worth something and lasts forever and is a million times greater than this prize that he got. Arafat got the Nobel prize too — the peace prize for a real peace lover! What is the value of that? The *kavod* in this world is worthless, but it is a valuable mashal. It is a *sheker*, but at the same time it is a great *emes*.

When the news comes out that Mashiach is here, everyone will go crazy with a happiness that will last forever

WHEN YOU ATTEND A WEDDING, THE CHASSAN PUTS A RING ON THE kallah's finger, and he breaks the glass and the band breaks out in a great blast of happy music. Everyone goes wild, jumping up and down and kissing each other with the greatest simchah. But you have to know that it is a mashal. Of course it is a mitzvah to make the chassan and kallah happy, but that mitzvah alone is not enough; it is a mashal for the future. You sing *Od yishama be'arei Yehudah u'vechutzos Yerushalayim*[21] — then, in the future, will be the real happiness. This tremendous happiness is nothing compared to what is to come. When the news comes out that Mashiach is here, everyone will go crazy with a happiness that will last forever; and the happiness of the Next World will be greater still — the happiness of *Olam Haba* is so great that it has no mashal. The Gemara says that Hakadosh Baruch Hu gives *koach* to the tzaddikim to be able to bear that happiness, which is so very great.

---

21. *Yirmiyahu* 7:17

Fire is a mashal of the fire of Gehinnom

WE ALSO HAVE TO UTILIZE EVERY UNPLEASANT EXPERIENCE IN THIS world as a mashal. If your finger accidentally touches a pot on the fire and it burns, don't let that get lost! It is a golden opportunity: *eish echad mishishim meiGehinnom*[22] — it is a little mashal of the fire of Gehinnom. Here you burned your finger for a moment; but in Gehinnom you will have to put your foot in the fire and keep it there; and you will have to put your tongue to the hot pot and keep it there, because you spoke wrong things. The experience of burning your finger on the pot is a tremendous *gilui*, a revelation; it is only a small mashal of the great fire of Gehinnom. If a woman was in the kitchen and had the experience, she should regret that she didn't utilize it. It shouldn't happen again, but if it *ever* does, make sure the experience doesn't go by unused — think, "This is the feeling of Gehinnom, a little mashal of the bigger Gehinnom." This lesson is extremely valuable.

Sleep is a mashal that a person will die one day

SLEEP IS VERY IMPORTANT; IT IS A BLESSING OF HASHEM. GETTING enough sleep is more important than getting enough to eat. Nevertheless, you should use sleep as a mashal. Every time you go to sleep, you have to know that there will come a day in 120 years when you will go to sleep for the last time. The Gemara says, "*Sheinah echad mishishim bemisah*"[23] — sleep is a small mashal of death. The Sages are telling us that because we should utilize it; not to make us unhappy, but to let us know that it will happen someday to everyone, without exception.

Every time as we go to bed and close our eyes, let us hope that tomorrow morning Hakadosh Baruch Hu will give us the experience of *techiyas hameisim*. In the morning when you open your eyes and you are alive, say, "*Modeh ani lefanecha*, I thank You, Hashem, *Melech chai vekayam*," and make a berachah, *Baruch Atah Hashem mechayeh hameisim*. This is a rehearsal of what is going to happen in the future. So every day in life, practice — as if you are dying at night. Let us hope you will live a full 120 years, but someday you will close your eyes for the last time, and eventually — no

---

22. *Berachos* 57b
23. *Berachos* 57b

one knows how long he will have to wait — we trust Hashem that we will open our eyes again — *Baruch Atah Hashem, mechayeh hameisim*. And at that time, Hashem will say, "Why didn't you thank Me when you still had free will? The mitzvah of thanking Me is not a mitzvah of free will anymore!"

Getting up in the morning is a mashal for techiyas hameisim

WE HAVE TO THANK HASHEM RIGHT NOW; WHEN WE OPEN OUR EYES in the morning, *Elokai neshamah shenasata bi*, He gave me my neshamah, *Baruch Atah Hashem mechayeh hameisim ... hamachazir neshamos lifgarim meisim*. We have to utilize this mashal every day, and feel the tremendous happiness of being alive again for the upcoming day.

All the world — every detail in it — is to be utilized as a mashal. If you see a bunch of ants running back and forth on the sidewalk, busy as could be — if you are a kindhearted person and step aside so as not to step on them, still, you have lost the opportunity. Shlomo Hamelech said, "*Leich el nemalah atzel*[24] — go to the ant, you lazy fellow." We are all lazy; we are not utilizing our lives properly. "*Re'ei deracheha vachacham*, look at her ways and become wise." An ant doesn't rest — *tachin bakayitz lachmah*,[25] she prepares her food in the summertime. She knows instinctively that in the wintertime there won't be any crumbs or kernels of grain to find, so the ant works day and night, sorting out as much as it can for the future.

We have to learn from ants

THE PASUK SAYS *RE'EI DERACHEHA*, LOOK AT HER WAYS; *VACHACHAM*, and become wise. The Alter of Slabodka said it is a pity that we have to learn from the ant; but the bigger pity is that we *don't* learn from the ant. In the summertime, if you go to a bungalow colony, look behind the bungalows and watch an anthill for a few minutes and say, "These ants are preparing for *Olam Haba*." We are the ants, and we have to run back and forth: when we learn all the time, when we do mitzvos, when mothers raise as many children as they can bring into this world,

24. *Mishlei* 6:6
25. *Mishlei* 6:8

we are preparing ourselves for *Olam Haba* in the very best way. Teach your children *yiras Shamayim, middos tovos,* Torah ... whatever you can do in this world to produce something. *Tachin bakayitz lachmah* — prepare your bread in the summertime; this world is the summertime and the next world is the wintertime. There are no more mitzvos to do in the Next World, no more opportunities. Whatever you bring with you from this world to the next is all that you will have there.

Summer and winter are meshalim

SUMMER AND WINTER ARE ALSO *MESHALIM*. IN THE SUMMERTIME THE trees are producing apples, pears, and peaches — we should thank Hashem for the hot weather; it is making all that luscious fruit ripe for us. Even though it is a little inconvenient sometimes, because your wife is baking a nice cake in the kitchen, don't complain that it is too hot; you are going to eat and enjoy that cake. Enjoy the heat! It is all part of your preparation. This is the only place where we can do mitzvos, and in the next world we take along whatever mitzvos we have prepared.

Mi shetarach be'erev Shabbos yochal beShabbos[26] — if you bake and cook and labor on erev Shabbos, you will eat on Shabbos. Shabbos is also a mashal for *Olam Haba*. If you sit at a Shabbos table and think, "I would like something else to eat now," it is too late. You should have ordered it before Shabbos; you can't cook on Shabbos. It is a mitzvah to enjoy Shabbos, and while you are enjoying it, you should think that it is a mashal for the Next World. There are plenty of people sitting in the Next World with nothing on their tables. Erev Shabbos of this world has already passed by — it is too late. You can't prepare anymore.

"*Me'ein Olam Haba yom Shabbos menuchah; kol hamisanegim bah yizku lerov simchah.*" This means that we should utilize the Shabbos for the purpose for which it was intended; think about *beri'as ha'olam yesh mei'ayin* — that Hashem made the world out of nothing. Enjoy all the good things that He made. You are eating the food that He created *yesh mei'ayin. Olam chessed yibaneh,* He made a world of *chessed,* and He made it for Bnei Yisrael — *beini u'vein Bnei Yisrael.* We are privileged; no one else has the mitzvah of Shabbos. If you think all these noble thoughts every Shabbos while

---

26. *Avodah Zarah* 3b

you are eating, that is utilizing Shabbos to prepare for the great Shabbos that will come after this *erev* Shabbos.

Pesach as a mashal for the next world

PESACH IS ANOTHER MASHAL. EVERYONE WORKS SO HARD GETTING rid of the chametz before sitting down at the Seder, but the seder itself is a mashal. *Olam hazeh* is Mitzrayim, and the Seder gives us a glimpse of what is going to happen when you leave this Mitzrayim of *olam hazeh*. We are slaving in this world in order to go out *birchush gadol*, with the great wealth we will come out of this world: *ve'acharei chein yeitzu birchush gadol*[27] — not the money that you got in Mitzrayim, but the wealth of understanding: that Hakadosh Baruch Hu has full power over this world; that He calls us His son — *Beni bechori Yisrael*.... There are many forms of *sheleimus* the Jews acquired in Mitzrayim. If we could have seen the *makkos*, we would have been completely transformed with *emunah* and gratitude to Hashem.

And so, when we are performing the Seder, or when we eat matzah anytime during Pesach, we should think about what matzah comes to tell us. The experience of *yetzi'as Mitzrayim* was a tremendous opportunity to prepare for the great event when they would see Hakadosh Baruch Hu and hear His Voice at Har Sinai. *Yetzi'as Mitzrayim* is a *hakdamah*, a grand introduction to the great experience of *Olam Haba*, when we say *veHu yashmi'einu berachamav sheinis* — another time He let us hear His Voice: Hashem will speak to us again someday, in *Olam Haba*. Therefore, Pesach is a mashal for something much greater than *yetzi'as Mitzrayim*.

Pesach also comes to teach us a great lesson: that this is a world where we are laboring and we are subject to the control of Pharaoh and the whole *olam hazeh*, and someday we will go free and be able to do nothing but enjoy the happiness of *Olam Haba*.

Rosh Hashanah is a very important occasion, and it is also a mashal. It is a day of judgment — that is extremely serious, but we have to know that there is a more important day of judgment. On Rosh Hashanah you don't actually feel or see that you are being judged, but you have *emunah* in what our Sages told us, and so you act in accordance with your *emunah*. But the day will come when there will be another judgment, called *ma'amad hadin*. The *sefarim*

---

27. *Bereishis* 15:13

say you should picture before you always a *ma'amad hadin*, a great day when you will have to be all by yourself before the Great Tribunal, and Hakadosh Baruch Hu will look down on you and say, "Why did you do this?" You won't be able to bluff or give alibis, and the embarrassment will be terrible.

Rosh Hashanah is a mashal for the great day of judgment in the world to come

ROSH HASHANAH IS A MASHAL FOR THE GREAT *YOM HADIN*, THE *yom hagadol vehanora*,[28] an experience that everyone will have to go through. The biggest tzaddikim will be able to answer more favorable answers, and Hashem will smile at them, and it is the greatest happiness. But if you have nothing to answer, then He will frown on you, and Hashem's frown is worse than Gehinnom.

The Gemara brings a tremendous mashal: When Yosef Hatzaddik was dressed like an Egyptian prince, and the king's ring was on his finger, the brothers thought that he was merely *mishneh lamelech*, and they fell down before him — they were afraid of him. When he finally opened his mouth and said in Hebrew, "*Ani Yosef*," they were absolutely overwhelmed that that was the Yosef they had wanted to sell into slavery. "*Velo yachlu echav la'anos*,"[29] they weren't able to answer him. Big brothers are never afraid before their younger brothers, but here all the big brothers lost their tongue and couldn't talk. This was Yosef, whom they had wanted to kill and then to sell. The Gemara[30] says, *amar Abba Kohen bar Dela, Oi lanu miyom hadin, oi lanu miyom hatocheichah* — the brothers said, "There will come a day that is even worse than this, when Hakadosh Baruch Hu will speak to us and say: This is what you are. All your life you thought you were something else — a prince, a good fellow, a tzaddik. Hashem will show you what you really are; He will point it out to you clearly with His finger, and you won't be able to answer. How terrible the embarrassment will be! You have to learn a mashal from the Chumash. Of course the story of Yosef Hatzaddik is a beautiful story, But Rabbi Abba Kohen bar Dela says it is more valuable as a mashal for the very great experience *oi lanu miyom hadin*.

---

28. *Yoel* 3:4
29. *Bereishis* 45:3
30. *Bereishis Rabbah* 94

This world is a world of *meshalim*. We are given many things in this world for the purpose of making us aware that there is something more important; there is a very great secret hiding behind everything in this world — the secret of Hashem and the secret of *Olam Haba*. And this world serves the purpose of making us aware of these secrets and getting ready for that great happiness awaiting us. Those who know how to utilize these secrets are taking this wisdom that they are learning and changing it into *da'as*, which is the highest form of perfection, and they take it with them into the World to Come.

THE MITZVAH OF OPTIMISM 9

ABBEINU YONAH IN *SHA'AREI TESHUVAH*[1] ENUMERATES SIX kinds of *lashon hara*, and the sixth is called "*nirganus*." A *nargan* is a complainer. The complainer does not speak about anyone in particular, and he does not belittle anyone; he merely tells you how unhappy he is. What connection does this have with *lashon hara*?

A complainer slanders Hashem

ACTUALLY, THERE ARE MANY CONNECTIONS. FIRST OF ALL, HE SLANDERS Hakadosh Baruch Hu's world. *Vayar Elokim es kol asher asah vehinei tov me'od*[2] — it is a very good world. If someone is unhappy, his personality and his words are proclaiming it.

This means that the sun does not make him happy; the air does not make him happy; the earth does not make him happy; his breakfast does not make him happy; his clothing does not make him happy; the

1. *Shaar 3 Os 631*
2. *Bereishis 1:31*

fact that he can walk does not make him happy; the fact that he can think does not make him happy; the fact that he can sleep at night does not make him happy. He is slandering all these things that Hashem made in order to make him happy.

Hashem made the world to enjoy

PAY ATTENTION TO THE VERY IMPORTANT WORDS OF THE *MESILLAS Yesharim:*[3] *Ha'adam lo nivra ela lehisaneg al Hashem* — Man was created only for the purpose of having joy from Hashem. This is a tremendous statement. Many years ago, I heard from a very great man how he understood that statement. *Ha'adam lo nivra ela lehisaneig* — Hashem made the world for joy. Do tzaddikim enjoy eating breakfast? Believe me they do. Do they enjoy breathing air? Certainly. Hashem created man for the purpose of enjoying this world. There is a great deal of joy and pleasure in being alive, more than you might think. But we are all *narganim*, complainers — all of us are guilty of *nirganus*; we are belittling what Hakadosh Baruch Hu is doing for us. Even if we are not complaining verbally, we certainly are lacking in our appreciation of all that Hashem does, and that is a passive form of *nirganus*.

There are two parts to this statement, and both are true. Hashem wants you to enjoy this world, but He wants you to take that joy further and enjoy *al Hashem* — He wants you to enjoy *Olam Haba* too. That is a much greater enjoyment.

Anyone who thinks about himself will discover that he has plenty of sins

WHAT DO *NARGANIM* SAY? THEY SAY *VATEIRAGENU BE'AHOLEICHEM.*[4] After the *meraglim* returned with their report, Bnei Yisrael said, "Because Hashem hates us He took us out to kill us in the midbar." Why does He hate us? It is not for nothing — it is because we are no good. They meant to say that they sinned.[5] Anyone who thinks about himself will discover that he has plenty of sins. It is only if you don't think about yourself that you can have a clear conscience, but when you start thinking, you discover that nothing is as clear as the fact that you have sins.

---

3. *Chapter 1*
4. *Devarim* 1:27
5. See *A Nation Is Born* p. 11 (1:27)

"So," they were saying, "because of our sins Hashem took us out into the midbar to kill us." That may sound good, but in fact the people who said that are faulted, because the truth is that Hakadosh Baruch Hu was taking them through the midbar in order to give them a land that is *zavas chalav u'devash*; it will be a land where you walk in the meadow and bend over and scoop up a handful of date honey and milk together. In Eretz Yisrael there are many fields where all you had to do was bend over and scoop up the honey from the dates that were so fat that they burst, and the honey dripped down onto the grass, and the goats were so full of milk in their udders that they dripped milk onto the grass.

Hashem says, "Do not blame Me because you are unhappy"

ERETZ YISRAEL WAS A LAND OF NOT ONLY *ZAVAS CHALAV U'DEVASH*,[6] of all good things, but also *arim gedolos vetovos asher lo banisa*,[7] they had large, beautiful homes, they had wells ... they had everything, and it was for this that Hashem took them through the midbar. When you are traveling toward a place of happiness, if you say that Hashem is punishing you for all your sins — that is called *nirganus*. And in our times, too, if someone is despondent and says, "I'm no good; that's why I have no mazal; that's why everything is a failure for me; that's why I'm unhappy; Hashem is punishing me for my sins" — this person is a *nirgan*. Hashem said: Do not blame Me for the fact that you are unhappy — it is only because you don't appreciate what I am giving you.

Despondency is a grave sin

WE CAN CALL *NIRGANUS* DESPONDENCY, AND IT IS A GRAVE SIN. I once met a tall, good looking young yeshivah man who gets plenty of spending money every week. He told me that nothing is going well with him. He is so despondent. What is wrong with this young man? He is healthy, he is tall and good looking, and he is in a yeshivah. Everything is normal for him — his eyesight, his hearing, his thinking is normal. You should know that this young man is speaking *lashon hara* about Hakadosh Baruch Hu's creation, although he doesn't know it.

---

6. *Yirmiyahu* 11:5
7. *Devarim* 6:10

Laziness means you are forgetting about Hashem

WE HAVE TO STUDY AND UNDERSTAND THIS SUBJECT. THE SAGES TELL us: *Ein omdin lehispallel lo mitoch atzvus velo mitoch atzlus*[8] — a person should not stand up to daven *Shemoneh Esrei* if he is in a mood of sadness or laziness. Hakadosh Baruch Hu says if you are lazy or sad, you are a victim of the *yetzer hara. Atzlus*, laziness, means you are forgetting about Hakadosh Baruch Hu. Every person should know that he is enlisted in military service in this world — in Hashem's service — and when a man has service to do, he has to keep in mind that he is a busy man and he cannot be lazy. If the sergeant says, "Charge," you have to start running carrying a heavy rifle. In the morning you have to get up from your bed; You can lie in bed for a minute or two until you gather your energy, but no more. You are in the army now, and every morning "*Modeh ani lefanecha*," I am happy, Hashem, that You took me back in Your army.

Hashem is your very best friend and is doing the very best for you

THE SIN OF *ATZLUS*, LAZINESS, MEANS FORGETTING THAT YOU ARE THE servant of Hakadosh Baruch Hu. *Atzvus*, sadness, means forgetting that Hakadosh Baruch Hu is your very best friend and that He is doing the very best for you. *Ki Atah Hashem tov u'meitiv* — *tov* means that He is good, and *meitiv* means that all the good that comes in the world comes from Him. A person has to have *emunah* that Hakadosh Baruch Hu is doing the very best for him.

Our service to Hashem is to be humble

YOU MAY NOT FEEL LIKE DAVENING, BUT IF YOU DAVEN ANYWAY, IT will accomplish two things: First, you will concentrate on your avodas Hashem, which means thanking Hashem. That is our service. The *Chovos Halevavos* asks, How can you be a servant to Hashem? There is nothing you can give Him as His servant. But your avodah is to be humble before Hashem, to say, *Ma ashiv laHashem kol tagmulohi alai*,[9] what can I pay Hashem back for all that He does for me? *Baruch*, bending our knee to Hashem, means *hachna'ah*, humility, and that is

---

8. *Berachos* 33a
9. *Tehillim* 116:12

our thanks to and our service to Hashem. Tefillah is called avodah because through it we show our gratitude by being humble before Hashem. We are awake; we are alive; we can think. How many people are in the cemetery? How many people are in the insane asylum? How many people cannot see? So we say *Baruch*, I can bend my knee, *Atah*, to You, Hashem. That is avodah.

The second accomplishment of davening is that you will be able to overcome *atzvus*, sadness, because if a person is sad he is not grateful, and the entire tefillah consists of *Tov lehodos laHashem*, thanking Hashem. Tefillah is not only asking Hashem for benefits — that is *agav urcha*, "by the way." The main purpose of the tefillah is to say, "You, Hashem, are a *gomel chassadim tovim*," You are the *magen Avraham*; You are the *mechayeh meisim*; you are the One Who is *chonen da'as*. If a person is sad, he will not be eligible for the avodah of tefillah, which requires gratitude.

So we see that these two traits of being happy and being energetic go together: *lo mitoch atzvus velo mitoch atzlus*.

A busy person is never sad

APERSON IS SAD WHEN HE IS NOT DOING ANYTHING; A BUSY PERSON is never sad. If you are walking in a bad neighborhood and a rough-looking character is working at repairing cars in the garage, even though you have a beard and peyos, the rough character won't say a word — *be'avidatei tarid* — he is busy with his work, and he has no time for the *yetzer hara*. When a man is busy he is a good man, but don't trust him when he is not at work, because *atzvus* and *atzlus* go together.[10]

Talk to your children

YAAKOV ISH TAM YOSHEIV OHALIM,[11] YAAKOV WAS BUSY LEARNING IN the tent. He had shiurim from both his father and his mother. *Shema beni mussar avicha ve'al titosh toras imecha*; his father and mother were busy investing in him. They put all they could into him. It is important to talk to your children, even little children — it is not a waste of time. Tell them things, even though right now they might not

---

10. See *Awake My Glory* p. 162 (553); *Rejoice O Youth* p. 195 (412), p. 267 (566); *Sing You Righteous* p. 206 (464)
11. *Bereishis* 25:27

appreciate it. It goes into their head and they will remember what you said to them when they were 2 years old, and they will listen even when they are grown.

Yaakov listened and listened, and he was a happy man. He didn't look for any recreation; he didn't need to — he was busy sitting and learning. But Esav didn't want to listen. He was unhappy. He was looking for something to do. He went out into the *sadeh* and he became a hunter. At least he did something, but hunting is a very poor substitute for being a yeshivah bachur. Even so, at least you won't go crazy if you are doing something. That is why a *ben sorer u'moreh* is not punished only for being disobedient. In addition, he has to be a *zolel vesovei*. He drinks wine and eats meat in excess. Why does he eat and drink so much? It is because he has nothing else to do; he is sad. Many depressed people eat and become overweight.[12]

As soon as a person feels depressed he should stop it at the very beginning

IT IS IMPORTANT TO KNOW THAT DESPONDENCY AND DISCOURAGEMENT can turn into chronic depression, which is a severe illness. The time to stop it is at the very beginning, without delay. As soon as a person feels depressed, he should know that he is doing something wrong and immediately snap out of it.

Say good words and your mind will begin thinking along those lines

SOMETIMES WHEN YOU START TO HICCUP, FOR EXAMPLE, IT MIGHT LAST days. So at the very first hiccup, you should deal with it. Take a deep breath and hold your breath for as long as you can. Then breathe out and take another deep breath and hold it. Do that three times, and the hiccups will stop. If you don't take care of the problem, it can lead to trouble; people have become sick from hiccuping too much. Despondency is no different. You have to stop it from the very beginning. As soon as you are discouraged, say, "I am speaking *lashon hara* about Hakadosh Baruch Hu's creation — it is a very good world." Just say the words, and *machshavah nimsheches achar hadibbur*, One's thoughts, the *Chovos Halevavos* says, follows one's words. Say good words, and your mind will begin thinking along those lines.

---

12. See *Fortunate Nation* p. 253 (21:20)

You must fight against despondency at the very beginning. The Gemara describes the case of a man who married a very wealthy woman. She was not looking for a job — she doesn't need any money. The husband should stipulate in advance: You have to get busy working in the house. What should you do? I'll give you wool, and you'll spin the wool and be busy all day long.

She said: I have servants to do that for me, but he said, "No, *batalah meivi'ah lidei shi'amum*,[13] being idle brings a person to depression, making him confused and despondent. I don't want to have a wife who is mentally ill. A husband has the right to demand that his wife spin wool.

Anyone can succeed in learning

WE HAVE TO KNOW THAT WHEN A PERSON SITS IN THE YESHIVAH AND is not learning anything, he is in danger of becoming discouraged. I have seen it happen again and again. When he is not doing anything, he becomes unhappy. The truth is that anyone can succeed in learning if it is done with a system. If you learn, say, even ten lines a day without Tosafos, at the end of the year you have learned 3,000 lines. Three thousand lines are forty *blatt* Gemara. Forty *blatt* Gemara is one *masechta*, even without Tosafos. If you know forty *blatt* Gemara by the end of the year, *ashrecha*! It is so easy that you will review it again and again. Learn it even if you don't understand everything. You are allowed to have unanswered questions. Many times Tosafos has questions too. Even the Gemara has questions. After a few years, you leave the yeshivah with a few *masechtos* you have learned under your belt. There are bachurim who have listened to shiurim for hours and hours and don't know anything. Once a bachur in yeshivah came over to me and said, "I've been here for five years but didn't learn one word" — and he was a *good* boy!

There is no reason for the yeshivah man to be discouraged.

Whenever you are unhappy you have to know that you are doing a sin

HA'ADAM LO NIVRA ELA LEHISANEIG — HASHEM WANTS YOU TO BE happy in this world; you have a *chiyuv* to be happy. Don't think that to be a tzaddik you have to be unhappy. As the Kuzari says, the

---

13. *Kesubos* 59b

tzaddik looks at the apple and thinks, "What a beautiful gift Hashem has given me. *Baruch Atah Hashem, borei peri ha'etz.* What a luscious gift! I am not running after *ta'avos*, but You gave this to me. I have to thank You for it. And if I don't enjoy it, then I am being ungrateful to You." You have to enjoy what Hashem is doing for you. You may not be chronically depressed, but whenever you are in an unhappy mood, you have to know that you are doing a *cheit*: you are not appreciating what Hashem is giving you right now.

Do you have a headache? A man in my kehillah had a headache every morning. If one day he would wake up without a headache, it would be a *simchah gedolah* to him. You have no headache — what are you so sad about? Many people have aches in their shoulders each time they move. They are missing lubrication in their joints, and the bones rub against one another and cause great pain. There are special hospitals for joint diseases, and operations on joints are very difficult. But Baruch Hashem, *chilutz atzamos* — try it! The bones are moving in their sockets — it is a happiness. I once was walking with a man from Bangor who was limping as he walked. He told me, "My hip is becoming fused with my pelvis." His body is depositing calcium in the joint, so the thigh and the pelvis are rubbing together. Eventually he won't be able to move his leg at all. Baruch Hashem, this is not your problem; so what are you sad about?

You have two kidneys, so why are you unhappy?

YOU MAY SAY THERE ARE OTHER THINGS YOU WANT — A MILLION dollars on Wall Street, perhaps. I know a very wealthy man who had no kidneys at all, and three times a week he had to have dialysis. He had a big machine for it in his house, and he could afford a private nurse, too. But each time he needed treatment, they had to put the needle for dialysis in a different place. His whole body was full of holes; there were no places left to put the needles. He spent his life searching for someone to give him a kidney. His mother gave him a kidney, but it didn't work. His brother gave him a kidney, but it didn't help. You have two kidneys, and one is a spare, so why are you dissatisfied and unhappy? Hakadosh Baruch Hu has a *ta'anah* on you for that. There is no question that it is a sin to be unhappy.

I was once talking to a man in the yeshivah who told me, "I don't see any future for myself. I have nothing."

I told him, "Don't worry, you'll have a car someday, you'll have a home someday, and you'll have a family." That was forty or fifty years ago. It was hard for him to believe, but now — I meet him every day; he comes to learn here, and he has everything — just as I told him he would.

Some people will ask: Why should you tell him only that he should not worry, that he will have everything? Why don't you say that it is a *chiyuv* to have *bitachon* in Hakadosh Baruch Hu, and that it is a sin not to have *bitachon*?

But this is not always the best way to encourage people. There are two paths in life: one we can call the "high way" and the other the "low way." The "high way" is *bitachon*, and it doesn't come so easily. You can talk about it, but the "low way" comes first.

The "low way" works like this: Most families in this country have cars. That is not a matter of *emunah*, but simply common sense. Hakadosh Baruch Hu doesn't want you to be unhappy, so the first thing for you to do is to take away the source of the unhappiness. First say, "Most people get cars eventually anyway, so why shouldn't I get one? Most people end up with a house to live in eventually." If a person is worried about his health, he should say that he will get well — *rov cholim lechaim*,[14] most sick people become well. So you ask, why didn't you tell him to have *bitachon baHashem*? That is the "high way," and it is a hard way. First use the simple, common-sense approach.

Once there was a king who wanted a gift that would be more valuable than anything else he had, so a wise man came and gave him a ring on which was engraved the letters *gimel, zayin,* and *yud*. When the king asked what it meant, the wise man explained that it stands for "*Gam zeh ya'avor* — This too shall pass."

Most of our troubles and worries eventually turn into nothing

MOST OF OUR TROUBLES AND WORRIES EVENTUALLY TURN INTO nothing. *Gam zeh ya'avor*, it will go away. *Bitachon* in Hashem is very good, but it won't work immediately. The first thing to do is to say *gam zeh ya'avor*. It is a very important principle: in order to make yourself free of worry and despondency, you have to use common

---

14. *Gittin* 28a

sense; Hakadosh Baruch Hu wants you to use your mind. Included in common sense is the idea that *sof kol sof* you will be settled, you will have money, your problems and those of your children will be solved.

You don't have to be unhappy because of one incident. Forget it! It is like the hiccups — stop it at the beginning. Look for happiness, not unhappiness.

There shouldn't be a day of unhappiness

IT IS EASIER FOR PEOPLE TO TRAVEL ON THE "LOW WAY" AND TO USE their *seichel hayashar*; and the truth is that there is no reason to be unhappy in this world. If, *chas veshalom*, a person is at the end of his life, and he has done many wrong things and has failed to do good things, then he should worry. Still, even then it is possible to encourage him to thank Hakadosh Baruch Hu that he has lived so long — no matter how long it was — and thank Hashem in retrospect. Thanking Hashem even for what is in the past is a very great avodas Hashem. We can look back on how many years we ate breakfast and supper, how many years we slept a good night's sleep. We have to thank Hashem for that — it will make Him happy. We say *bechol nafshecha*, love Hashem with all your life, and it means *afilu besha'ah shenoteil nafshecha* — even when you are about to die. If you love Hashem at that time, it is a big *zechus*. It is a tremendous thing to die in the right way, and to say *vidui*. But the best thing is for a person to change right away, when he is younger, before he has to say *vidui*. Don't waste any more time. Get busy understanding how fortunate you are in this world; there shouldn't be a day of unhappiness.

The more children one has, the wealthier he is

THE *RAMBAM* SAYS, *KOL HAMOSIF NEFESH ACHAS BIVNEI YISRAEL ke'ilu mosif olam malei*,[15] one more child is like a whole world full of people. What a *zechus* it is! That child you have now will have children, grandchildren, great-grandchildren, and eventually thousands and thousands of people will come out of him. How happy a mother is that she has a child. The more she has, the wealthier she is. It is a great happiness to have children. Everyone says she is so worried and so harassed. A childless woman tells me, "I wish I were harassed." If you are harassed

---

15. *Hilchos Ishis* 15:16

with many children, say "Baruch Hashem" for this great wealth. I knew a man with fifty apartment houses; each one had two hundred tenants. The tenants call up complaining. He has a manager for each apartment house, but he has to manage the managers. He is a very busy man — he is busy all the time. I asked him, "What about selling them?" He said, "No, why should I sell them?" It is better to be unhappy, but with a lot of property, and children are far greater wealth than property is.[16]

Being unhappy makes you physically sick

BEING UNHAPPY IS A BIG AVEIRAH. THE TORAH STATES: *VE'ASISA hayashar vehatov be'einei Hashem,*[17] you should do what is right and what is good in the *eyes* of Hashem, which includes all the things that are not written openly. Some of the most serious aveiros come under the heading of being contrary to what is *yashar* and *tov be'einei* Hashem, and being despondent is among them. When a person is despondent, his glands start producing the wrong kind of secretions. All the secretions the glands make are beneficial for the body. Hakadosh Baruch Hu made everything work out for good, when it all works normally. But when unhappiness enters the picture, the body starts working in the wrong way, and the secretions are harmful and lead to illness. As it says in *Malachi, Miyedchem hayesah zos*[18] — you brought it upon yourselves, and now Hashem is angry at you. You shouldn't have allowed yourself to fall into that.

One of the first things for a person to do when he is afraid of falling into deep depression is to get busy

ONE OF THE FIRST THINGS FOR A PERSON TO DO WHEN HE IS AFRAID of falling into depression is to get busy. Many times I have advised parents to give a man money to have his son do something. A man should hire his son and pay him a little salary, but the son shouldn't know it is his father's money he is paying with. Or the father can tell his son, "I want you to learn with this man; this man likes to teach young men." The father then gives the older man money to give to his son, but the son doesn't know it is from his father. When your son is getting money, he is already happy.

16. See *Awake My Glory* p. 359 (1135), p. 376 (1189)
17. *Devarim* 6:18
18. *Malachi* 1:9

So one cure is to get busy making money — don't think it is a small thing. Making money is very important in life — on the "low way" it is important to save money and to make money. You may disagree and say that one should just become a tzaddik, a talmid chacham. But that is the "high way." Right now, make money. We save peoples' lives that way.

By the way, all children should be taught to save money, even to put a nickel into a little bank every day.[19] Teach your children to be frugal. Money helps a person to have simchah. Do you think you don't need money, because Torah is simchah? That is a hard lesson to learn, it is an avodah. The simchah of money, however, everyone can understand. A child likes money, so you should get your child to do good things with money, including learning for money. It is not wrong when people do things because of money. Hakadosh Baruch Hu wants you to be busy and happy in this world. If money is the *refuah*, it is certainly not worse than a chemical or a prescription.

Of course, there is a "high way," too. If you can add to the "low way" the incentive of serving Hakadosh Baruch Hu, doing mitzvos and having *bitachon* in Hashem, by all means do it. But don't neglect any *eitzah* that comes your way in order to rescue yourself from the illness of depression.

The biggest reason to celebrate is because you are alive

IN LOMZA ONCE THE MASHGIACH CALLED OVER A BACHUR, TOOK HIM BY the lapel and said, "Mazel tov!" The bachur wanted to hear the good news. The mashgiach said, "Mazel tov — you are alive!" That was the big reason to celebrate.

Once a man was told that he had a dangerous illness and that he wouldn't live more than eighteen months, *chas veshalom*, and he was so worried. When he came home, he and his wife were weeping. For eighteen months they said good-bye to each other. Many years have passed, and they are still alive. But even now he is not happy. Had he known at that time that he would have lived so many years after the diagnosis, he would have been very happy.

Now we have to learn how to be happy retroactively. Baruch Hashem, you are still alive — be happy that you are alive, because

19. See *Awake My Glory* p. 350 (1117)

there is so much that you can accomplish. If you learn a little bit every day — say you learn one *sa'if* of *Choshen Mishpat* while you are eating lunch, in twelve years you will know the whole *Choshen Mishpat*. It doesn't mean you will be a *Shach*, but you will be somebody. When we recognize opportunities that are ours just because we are alive, it can serve us as a means of combating that great *yetzer hara*, the great aveirah of depression.

One form of depression is lack of emunah

ONE FORM OF DEPRESSION IS A LACK OF *EMUNAH*. PEOPLE WITHOUT *emunah* are full of *shtus*. Anyone with a little sense can see how ridiculous their ideas are.

I'll give you one example. The New York Times came out with headlines congratulating a *rasha* — the head of the Education Ministry in Eretz Yisrael — who was trying to close down the Torah schools. They congratulated him for his efforts to stop teaching children ancient myths and fairy tales. The word *ancient* is very important here. Josephus lived 2,000 years ago. He writes in his historical accounts all the details that are found in the Tanach, all the *nissim*, the *makkos* in Mitzrayim, *keri'as Yam Suf, mattan Torah*, etc. In his times, these things weren't so ancient. They happened 3,000 years ago, but 2,000 years ago Josephus recorded it all, and no one said it was "ancient" at that time. Three hundred years earlier than Josephus, they had already translated the Chumash into Greek — the Septuagint, the *targum hashivim* — and then the Chumash was in the hands of the goyim. So the goyim are testifying that even hundreds of years before Josephus the Jews had the Torah.

In fact, even earlier than that, from five hundred years after *matan Torah*, there is proof of the Torah's validity. The Gemara speaks about the *issur* to return to Mitzrayim. The Torah states, "*asher re'isem es Mitzrayim hayom, lo sosifu lirosam od ad olam,*" As you saw Mitzrayim today — drowning — you won't see them again. The *sefarim* of *Yehoshua, Shoftim, Shmuel I* and *Shmuel II* cover hundreds of years of history, and not once in all those books is Mitzrayim mentioned. There are all kinds of stories about wars with Ammon, Aram, Edom, Moav, Midian, and others, but none with Mitzrayim. Mitzrayim is Eretz Yisrael's next-door neighbor, and Mitzrayim was the most powerful kingdom, yet nothing is mentioned about the country or its people. This is clear testimony that Mitzrayim did not speak up to say anything to their neighbors in Eretz Yisrael, and the reason is that Mitzrayim had learned its lesson already.

There is so much evidence of the Torah's truth. For example, there are so many scientific proofs that the world is young. If plenty of scientists say that the world is only a few thousand years old, why do you even consider that evolution is possible? Carbon 14 dating is already out of style. It is so unreliable that the scientists themselves stopped using it and don't refer to it anymore. Some say that Carbon 14 dating can indicate that something is 800 years old, and others use the system to show that the same object is 2 million years old. There is no reason to believe in this system.

When we speak about our obligations as *ovdei Hashem*, of course we should say that Hakadosh Baruch Hu wants us to believe that He is in charge of the world and that everything will turn out well. And we have to exercise *emunah*, *bitachon*, and tefillah constantly, and of course we should add whatever we can so that we travel on the "high way," too. But at the same time, don't stop traveling on the "low way." You need both of these roads, because both of them are true.

Every day you can say, I love You, Hashem. It is worth living just for that alone

AND WHILE YOU ARE STILL ALIVE, THINK EVERY DAY HOW LUCKY YOU are that you can accomplish something. Every day you can say, "I love You, Hashem." It is worth living just for that alone. It is a *mitzvas assei min HaTorah* to love Hashem, and *machshavah nimsheches achar hadibbur*. Every day say, "I love You, Hashem." Every day say, "I love my people Yisrael; I love my nation Am Yisrael." Hashem loves them — *oheiv Amo Yisrael* — so why shouldn't you?

Utilize your life to accomplish things. If you are a ben Torah, learn every day and add to your knowledge of Torah. There are so many things you can do, and it is so easy to do them while you are still alive. Everyone who has the ability to function and to think and to live normally can do so many good things in his life, every day. His life should be full of joy because he has the opportunity to continue to accomplish and gain more perfection, even in the smallest ways.

LUBRICATION OF LIFE 10

Lubrication of Life — Preparing for Olam Haba

UR GREAT TEACHERS GAVE US THE VERY FUNDAMENTAL *eitzah*, "*Hasken atzmecha baprozdor kedei shetikaneis latraklin*"[1] — you have to utilize your life to prepare yourself to be worthy of entering the great banquet hall. This world is only a lobby; there are light refreshments in the lobby, but the big meal is in the banquet hall. Here, we work to gain those qualities that give us the right to be admitted to *Olam Haba*, and this should be always on our minds.

The Mishnah continues, *hakol lefi rov hama'aseh*, everything depends on doing many good deeds. The *mefarshim* explain that this means that instead of giving all your tzedakah money to one place (which is a very valuable thing to do), you should give it at various times. Each time is a separate *nisayon*, a difficult trial. Each time you give, you have to overcome your will to hold onto the money. Something that you do many times is a fundamental preparation for *Olam Haba*.

---

1. *Avos* 4:16

Mitzvos are made to change your personality

THE SAGES TAUGHT US, "*LO NITENAH* MITZVOS *ELA LETZAREF bahen es haberi'os*,"[2] the mitzvos were given to us only to refine us, to purify us. There are many reasons for every mitzvah, but this is a reason that applies to all the mitzvos. Doing mitzvos makes you a different personality, for the mitzvos are intended to change you. Of course, if you understand the *kavanah* of a mitzvah, or you add *kavanos*, you accomplish great things in this world.[3]

Let us say that when you put on tzitzis, you are you doing it only because Hakadosh Baruch Hu said to put on tzitzis. Then each time you put on your tzitzis, it makes you *kadosh*. *Va'asisem es kol mitzvosai vih'yisem kedoshim*,[4] each time you do the mitzvah of putting on tzitzis, you become holy. But if you add a *kavanah* to it, you have gained so much. If you think, for example, that one corner of the tzitzis is to remind you "*es Hashem Elokecha tira*" — to fear Hashem, to have *yiras Shamayaim*, how much more have you gained! We have to learn how to fear Hashem, to feel the Presence of Hashem.

Each tzitzis should remind you of a different mitzvah

IF ANOTHER CORNER OF THE TZITZIS REMINDS YOU "*VE'AHAVTA EIS Hashem*," to love Hashem, that is *tikkun*, it is preparing yourself for the Next World. He loves you more than anything else in the entire world. He calls us His children, and He is more our father than any real father. He loves us tremendously, so we should love Him. We have to work on loving Hashem.[5]

Another corner of *tzitzis* should remind you to thank Hashem. Thank Hashem that you are alive; that you have two good eyes; that you have a normal mind; that you have teeth; that you can walk, that you are able to function in life, and sometimes you can do better than function — you can accomplish things. Baruch Hashem, He gives us clothing to wear, food to eat, a place to sleep at night. He gives us warm houses and cold and hot running water in the house. People don't realize that most of the world's population don't have running water in the house. Most people have to go out and draw it from the

---

2. *Midrash Vayikra Rabbah* 13:3
3. See *Rejoice O Youth* p. 330 (746), p. 336 (762)
4. *Bamidbar* 15:40
5. See *Journey to Greatness* p. 198 (15:39)

well. There are so many things for which to thank Hashem in this world; you cannot neglect the opportunity.

The fourth corner of tzitzis can remind you to love Am Yisrael, because Hashem loves them. In the Torah there are only fifty-six pesukim about *beri'as ha'olam*, but the whole Torah is about Am Yisrael. The *Toras Hashem* is the "thought" of Hashem. Hashem thinks about everything in the world, but we can say that Am Yisrael is "on His mind" more than anything else. Hashem made everything, but "*rak ba'avoseichem chashak Hashem,*[6] only in your Forefathers Hashem delighted, to love them, *vayivchar bezaram achareihem bachem kayom hazeh.*" If you put on your tzitzis with that thought in mind, surely it is a *tikkun*. All mitzvos and *ma'asim* are *tikkun*, preparation for *Olam Haba*.

What is Olam Haba?

THE *RAMBAM*[7] SAYS ON THE *MA'AMAR CHAZAL*,[8] "WHAT IS *OLAM HABA*? *Tzaddikim yoshvim*, tzaddikim are established there." *Yoshvim* means that they are there forever. In *Baruch she'amar* we say, *Baruch meshalem sachar tov lirei'av*, Hashem gives reward; *Baruch chai la'ad vekayam lanetzach*, and the reward is forever and ever. The reward in *Olam Haba* is *nehenim miziv haShechinah*, to look at the Shechinah, which is *la'ad vekayam lanetzach*. You are thanking Hashem that *Olam Haba* is forever.

Olam Haba is the *sachar tov* that He promised to Avraham Avinu: *Al tira Avram, secharcha harbei me'od.*[9] The added word *me'od* refers to *Olam Haba*, which his children will have. To receive that very great *sachar*, you have to make certain preparations.[10]

A bachur once came to me asking for guidance in avodas Hashem. I asked, "For example, what?"

He said, "Tell me how I should stop eating too much and sleeping too much."

I told him that there is better guidance than that. One is to learn *Mesillas Yesharim*. First you will get a Torah mind, a *lev tov*, and that is more important. Hakadosh Baruch Hu is not so interest-

---

6. *Devarim* 1:15
7. *Rambam, Hilchos Teshuvah* 6:2.
8. *Berachos* 17a
9. *Bereishis* 15:1
10. See *Rejoice O Youth* p. 111 (200-203), *Awake My Glory* p. 271 (879)

ed in *inuyim*, self-afflictions. He is interested in your changing your mind. The Rambam says *tzaddikim yoshvim*, the tzaddikim sit forever in *Olam Haba*. They never get tired of it — every minute the simchah in *Olam Haba* gets bigger and bigger, *Va'atroseihem berasheihem*, and their crowns are on their heads. Those crowns are very important. What are their crowns? The Rambam says they are the *da'as Hashem*, the understanding that you gain in this world. You have to know that Hakadosh Baruch Hu is the *Borei*; He is the *Mehaveh*, the One Who brings into existence — that is why we call Him *Havayah*. *Bidvar Hashem Shamayim na'asu*[11]— the whole world was made *bidvar Hashem*, and not only did He make it, He maintains it all the time. Every moment Hashem says, "It should be." *Ki Hu amar vayehi*[12] — He said it not once but all the time. That is why we say *Baruch Gozer u'Mekayeim*, He decreed that the world should come into existence, and He maintains and upholds the world's existence.

The more knowledge of Hashem you gain in this world the more happiness you will enjoy in Olam Haba

ALL THESE THINGS ARE PART OF *ATROSEIHEM*, THE CROWNS OF *DA'AS* — the love of Hashem, going in the ways of Hashem, and other things that make your crown on your head. The Rambam explained that in *Olam Haba*, tzaddikim are *nehenim miziv haShechinah*, they have pleasure in proportion to the kind of crown they have. If they gained more *da'as* in this world, they will have a bigger crown and they will have more happiness in *Olam Haba*.[13] The *sachar* in *Olam Haba* is measured by *dei'ah*, how much knowledge of Hashem you gain. Mitzvos are very good, but if you want to get more *sachar*, do mitzvos with *dei'ah*, and *dei'ah* is something you have to work on. That is why *talmud Torah* is so important. You have to learn *hashkafah* and *emunah* and all the topics dealt with in the *Chovos Halevavos*, in order to recognize Hakadosh Baruch Hu's *chessed* and *chochmah* in the world. You have to learn all the *sefarim* that tell you how to respond with gratitude and love for Hashem for everything He did for you. Learn Gemara, *sifrei Rishonim*, *Rambam's Hilchos Dei'os* and *Hilchos Teshuvah*, *Sha'arei Teshuvah leRabbeinu*

---

11. *Tehillim* 33:6
12. *Tehillim* 33:9
13. See *Awake My Glory* p. 285 (920)

Yonah, *Mesillas Yesharim,* and *Orchos Tzaddikim*; and the Gra said to learn *Kuzari.* He said "*Hishamer lecha pen ta'azov es halevi,* don't forsake the Levi," meaning the *Kuzari.* These things give you *dei'ah.* When you have *dei'ah,* you will enjoy *Olam Haba* all the more.

Many years ago, I went to the U.N.; I didn't know any Russian or French, so I put on earphones. You can turn to any language you want by pushing buttons, and then you can understand what is going on. Without the earphones, you sit there like a dummy. *Olam Haba* is the same thing: you need earphones — you need *atroseihem berasheihem.* Without the crown on your head, you won't appreciate *Olam Haba* much.

If you are a *yeshivah* man, sitting in *yeshivah shel mata,* you have to prepare yourself for your career in *yeshivah shel ma'alah.* The way you behave here is a preparation for *yeshivah shel ma'alah,* so *hasken atzmecha beprozdor,* prepare yourself in this lobby. Be a loyal talmid; respect your rebbis; be interested in learning. In this world everyone is a yeshivah bachur, even women, because they are also learning in this world. You are a talmid in *yeshivah shel mata,* and when the time comes, you will be *zocheh* to be in *yeshivah shel ma'alah,* and there will be tremendous *sachar* there for everyone.

Be loyal to the gedolei Yisrael

ANOTHER IMPORTANT INGREDIENT OF *TIKKUN,* PREPARING FOR *OLAM Haba,* is to be loyal to the *gedolei Yisrael.* Every *dor* has great leaders. We have Roshei Yeshivos, great Rebbes and big tzaddikim. The best way to utilize them is to respect them, to look up to them. Even if you don't always go to see them, because you are busy, you should have in your mind to be loyal to the *gedolei haTorah.*

Moshe Rabbeinu was considered a model for all the gedolim in every generation. In the times of the Talmud, when someone said something good in the Gemara, people would call him Moshe. They would tell him, "*Moshe shapir ka'amart,*[14] Moshe, you are speaking well." In every generation we have to look up to our leaders — they are our Moshes. Many people make the terrible mistake of thinking, "What is so great about him? He wears pants like I wear pants; he is a human being." *Hibitu acharei Moshe,*[15] some looked after Moshe and said, *kamah avim shokav,* look how thick his thighs are. Moshe

---

14. *Shabbos* 101b
15. *Kiddushin* 33b

was a big strong man, and some people thought about how he was built. Of course they wouldn't say such a thing, but they thought about it subconsciously. We look at Moshe Rabbeinu and see only a *malach Hashem*. When you see the *gedolei haTorah* of every generation, don't see a human being, see a *malach Hashem*. Baruch Hashem, we have true tzaddikim in this generation. I know some personally. We have to learn to appreciate the gedolim we have.

I remember when the Chafetz Chaim was still alive, people respected him, but only when he was *niftar* did he become very great. Then people understood what they had lost. I went to the *hespedim* of the Chafetz Chaim in Kovno, and when the *gedolei haTorah* spoke there about the Chafetz Chaim, people realized what he had been. They had missed that understanding during his lifetime. Some people would buy *Mishnah Berurahs*, but after he was *niftar*, the *Mishnah Berurah* became very popular. We should recognize the gedolim while we have them. That is one of the ways of preparing for *Olam Haba*.

Anger causes so many kinds of sins

INCLUDED IN OUR PREPARATION FOR *OLAM HABA* IS PREPARING TO AVOID Gehinnom. One of the ways of keeping out of Gehinnom is by not getting angry. "*Kol hako'es,*[16] Anyone who becomes angry frequently, who is a *ka'asan, kol minei Gehinnom sholtin bo*, all the kinds of Gehinnom will have a power over him." Gehinnom is like a big hospital that delivers all kinds of treatments, and all the treatments hurt. The person who goes to Gehinnom is purified; then he goes to Gan Eden to enjoy his mitzvos. People have to be purified in Gehinnom in various ways. For a person who is a *ka'asan*, all the ways of Gehinnom have to be worked. He has to suffer all the treatments of Gehinnom. Because *ba'al cheimah rov pesha,*[17] a person who is angry does many, many sins. Anger causes so many kinds of sins, and each sin calls for a different kind of treatment. A *ka'asan* will have to undergo all the various treatments before he can go to *Olam Haba*.

Your Rabbi should have a good opinion of you

RAV YISRAEL SALANTER HAS ANOTHER *EITZAH* TO PREPARE FOR *OLAM Haba*: He said that the *beis din* of your town should have a good

---

16. *Nedarim* 22a
17. *Mishlei* 29:22

opinion of you. Did you *ever* go to the *dayanim* and ask, "Rabbanim, what do you think of me?" Hakadosh Baruch Hu considers their opinion seriously. The *dayanim* of the *beis din* of your community see your behavior and know you better, because they live in the same community. The opinions of the rabbanim of your neighborhood with whom you have contact can be the deciding factor in whether you are a *ben Olam Haba*. So it is very important to make sure that you are behaving in such a way that the *beis din* of your town approves of you.

I was a mashgiach for many years, and in all that time it happened only *once* that a bachur approached me and said he wanted me to tell him whenever I saw something wrong with him. I was looking at them all day. For years and years I watched the same boys, so I knew them well; they could have come to me and said, "If you have any criticism let us know, so we can improve ourselves," but it never entered their minds. Only one bachur thought about that.

The Mishnah states, "*Kol Yisrael yeish lahem cheilek le'Olam Haba*, which means that *Olam Haba* is not a reward promised to you individually. You are going to get it only because it is a promise to *kol Yisrael*. Therefore, to the degree that you are connected with *kol Yisrael*, in that measure you are going to be *zocheh* to share in the reward of *kol Yisrael*. Suppose you decide to move out of Boro Park, say to Nantucket, a small town in Massachusetts with no frum Jews. You say, "I am going to keep the whole Torah. I will live by myself and have no connection with Jews, but I will learn mussar and do mitzvos." *Kol haporesh min hatzibbur*,[18] those who separate themselves from the community, will not see *benechamas hatzibbur.* You have to be together with Klal Yisrael.

Be loyal to frum Jews

I ONCE SPOKE TO A MAN WHO LIVED IN A SUBURB FAR AWAY FROM HERE. I asked his wife, "Why don't you move back to Brooklyn? Why do you live among the Italians?" She answered, "I should move back to the ghetto?!" I wanted to tell her, *You despise the Jewish people.* I didn't tell her that she won't have a *chelek* in Olam Haba, because Olam Haba is promised to the Jewish people only if they are connected with the Jewish people. *Kol Yisrael* — you have to have a connection with them, and *kol Yisrael* means frum Jews. Be loyal to frum Jews; always

18. *Tanna D'Vei Eliyahu Zuta* 1:15

speak highly of them and always try to be together with them and live among them, and train yourself to look at them *be'ahavah*. The Torah mentions the word *ve'ahavta* twice — "*ve'ahavta eis Hashem Elokecha*,"[19] you have to love Hashem, and "*ve'ahavta lerei'acha kamocha*,"[20] you have to love your fellow Jew. As we've stated, Hakadosh Baruch Hu loves Am Yisrael with a tremendous love, and therefore we have to learn how to love our fellow Jews. To be *zocheh* to *Olam Haba* you have to have a connection with Klal Yisrael, to learn how to love your fellow Jew.

When you look at a Jew you have to keep in mind that he is holy

YOU HAVE TO RECOGNIZE WHAT IS MEANT BY *YISRAEL*. *YISRAEL AM kadosh atah laHashem Elokecha*,[21] you are a holy nation. This doesn't mean you make fast days and do things *lifnim mishuras hadin*; every Jew who keeps the Torah is *kadosh*. If you don't eat milchig and fleishig together, you are *kadosh*. You shouldn't eat what is not kosher, because *am kadosh atah*, Am Yisrael is a holy nation. You have to study that and think about it. When you look at a Jew, you have to keep in mind that he is *kadosh*, otherwise you are underestimating him, and you are not connected to Klal Yisrael as Hakadosh Baruch Hu intended.

Not only are the Jewish people *kadosh*, they are Hashem's children. "*Banim atem laHashem Elokeichem*,[22] You are My children," said Hashem. More than you are the children of your father and your mother, you are Hashem's children. A Jew is a child of Hakadosh Baruch Hu. *Ka'asher yisa ha'omein es hatinok*,[23] as someone carries a baby in his arms, Hashem carries you in His Arms. A Jew is more important than the *malachim*. "*U'kedoshim bechol yom yehalelucha selah*," every day *kedoshim* praise Hashem. There are two sets of *kedoshim*: One is the *malachim* who say *kedushah* every day, and the other is Am Yisrael who say *kedushah* every day. But the *kedushah* of Am Yisrael is more important, for the *malachim* cannot say *kedushah* until *Yisrael* have said *kedushah* first.

---

19. *Devarim* 6:5
20. *Vayikra* 19:18
21. *Devarim* 7:6
22. *Devarim* 14:1
23. *Bamidbar* 11:12

When Yaakov Avinu was going away from Lavan's house, the Torah says: *vayifge'u bo malachei Elokim*,[24] he encountered a company of *malachim*. He said *machaneh Elokim zeh*, it is a camp of *Elokim*, and he called the place *Machanayim*, "Two camps" — because the truth is, it was two camps: *machaneh Yisrael*, the camp of Yaakov's family, and *machaneh Elokim*, the camp of the *malachim* that came there. The *malachim* came there only because of Yaakov Avinu's family, so Yaakov's family are the first great "*malachei Elokim*." They are more important.[25]

When you look at a Jew say I love that man because he is a tzelem Elokim

WHEN YOU LOOK AT A *YISRAEL*, TRAIN YOURSELF TO SAY, "I LOVE that man because he is a *tzelem Elokim*, and besides that he is a *kadosh*, a holy man." Every Jew is a holy person and a child of Hakadosh Baruch Hu. No one else in this world is called *avdei Hashem* — Hashem's servants — except us, and therefore the connection between us and Am Yisrael is of the utmost importance in preparing us to share with Am Yisrael a *cheilek le'Olam Haba*.

All these preparations for *Olam Haba* that we have mentioned, and all those we haven't mentioned, are actually preparations for *olam hazeh*. If you make the preparations for *Olam Haba*, it is guaranteed that you are preparing yourself for a career of happiness in this world as well.

Once David Hamelech made an announcement: "*Lechu banim shimu li*,[26] come all my talmidim, and listen to me, *Yiras Hashem alamedchem*, I will teach you *yiras Hashem*." People heard that and started running to hear a shiur in *yiras Shamayim* by David Hamelech. And he asked them, *Mi ha'ish hechafetz chaim oheiv yamim liros tov?* They were thinking, "What is this? We came to learn *yiras* Hashem, and he is telling us how to enjoy this life." They thought this was only an introduction, that they should listen further. They thought *Netzor leshonecha mei'ra* was the beginning of the shiur, but in fact the shiur had already begun when he said *Mi ha'ish hechafetz chaim*. That is the first lesson in *yiras Hashem*. *Yiras Hashem* makes you successful in your life. If you have *yiras Hashem*,

---

24. *Bereishis* 32:2
25. See *The Beginning* p. 487
26. *Tehillim* 34:12

if you are *oheiv yamim*, you want to live long to help you enjoy life, *liros tov* — if you fear Hashem, you will enjoy life more.

Yiras Shamayim helps you enjoy Olam Hazeh

Dᴀᴠɪᴅ ʜᴀᴍᴇʟᴇᴄʜ ᴛᴇʟʟs ᴜs ᴛʜᴀᴛ *YIRAS SHAMAYIM* ɪs ᴀ ᴡᴀʏ ᴏꜰ preparing for *Olam Haba*, and it is another method of helping us enjoy *olam hazeh*. Believe me, you need *olam hazeh* more than you need *Olam Haba*. In *olam hazeh* you can do mitzvos. Moshe Rabbeinu is so sorry that he can't come back to this world again and do mitzvos. Learning how to enjoy *olam hazeh* is a big success, and one of the ways of preparing for *olam hazeh* is by preparing for *Olam Haba*.

Chaim means all kinds of life — life in this world and life in the Next World. A very important prescription for preparing for both worlds is *Netzor leshonecha mei'ra*, guard your tongue against bad. Everyone knows it means not to speak *lashon hara*, but *ra* means much more than that. It means don't say words that hurt people; don't say mean words that hurt your brother or your wife. *Lashon hara* is also forbidden, but *ona'as devarim* — words that hurt people — that is the real *lashon hara*. Guard your tongue against words that hurt. *Bakesh shalom*, look for shalom. If shalom comes to us and says *shalom aleichem*, we are willing to say *shalom aleichem*, but that is not enough. We have to run after the shalom.

Run after peace

Iꜰ ᴀ ʜᴜsʙᴀɴᴅ ǫᴜᴀʀʀᴇʟs ᴡɪᴛʜ ʜɪs ᴡɪꜰᴇ ᴀɴᴅ ᴀꜰᴛᴇʀᴡᴀʀᴅs ᴛʜᴇ ᴡᴏᴍᴀɴ brings her husband something to eat, a piece of cake or something else, it is already the beginning of making shalom. You have to be *rodef shalom*.[27] Even if the other party is wrong, still be a *rodef shalom*. If he comes to you and asks *mechilah*, it's very good, but even if he doesn't, still try to get close to him and make shalom. If you are *rodef shalom*, you are doing what Hakadosh Baruch Hu wants us to do all the time. He said that is the way to prepare for *Olam Haba*. You have to be together with My people, meaning with every one of My people. As we said earlier, *hakol lefi rov hama'aseh*. If the same thing is done many times, there is much more *sachar* for it. If a man comes in contact with many people — his wife and others, and some-

---

27. See *Career of Happiness* p. 159

times they insult him — he can be a *rodef shalom*. In some cases the husband and wife have a thousand incidents like that. If the other party is willing to overlook and forget the insults, that is *rodef shalom*, and that is a preparation, a tremendous *tikkun*, for *Olam Haba*. How great is shalom? Hakadosh Baruch Hu says, "That [Shalom] is My Name."

One who suffers from his wife is a lucky man

SOME PEOPLE DON'T UNDERSTAND WHAT A GREAT OPPORTUNITY THIS is. I received a letter from a man who wrote that he suffers from his wife. I was thinking, *He is a lucky man; each time he keeps quiet, he is preparing for Olam Haba.* Hakadosh Baruch Hu says, "He is a *rodef shalom*." That is the man Hakadosh Baruch Hu is looking for. Many times a wife like that gives you *rov hama'aseh*, many good deeds to do, and it is a great *takanah*. Each time you are refining yourself.

I know a man who had a mean *mechutan* who wouldn't speak to him. On Purim this man brought *shalach manos* to his *mechutan*. That is how you should be: you do your part. A *mechutan* like that is an opportunity. You gain so much *zechus* and so much perfection from dealing with people like that. We should consider all such incidents as opportunities from *Shamayim*, and utilize them properly to gain the *sheleimus* that will help prepare us for *Olam Haba*.

In the body, the bones rub against one another constantly, causing friction. Hakadosh Baruch Hu puts a substance between the bones so they never touch one another. The bones keep moving very close to one another, but this substance separates them. Sometimes a person gets sick, *chalilah*, and this substance disappears; then the bones start rubbing against one another and it hurts terribly. He has to go to a hospital for treatment and maybe surgery.

Baruch Hashem, all our bones are lubricated so that they don't rub each other. Lubrication is a very important principle in the body. It makes your life much happier. You couldn't live without lubrication.

In the life of every person there is lubrication. That lubrication is what it says in *mesechta Sanhedrin*:[28] If anyone insults you, keep quiet. The Gemara tells us: "Happy is the man who hears people insulting him, and he ignores it; a hundred evils will pass him by."

---

28. *Sanhedrin* 7a

Learn to ignore insults

LEARN TO IGNORE ANY INSULTS. IF YOU ARE WALKING IN THE STREET and a bum insults you, don't turn around and look at him. That is dangerous. I know a man who did that and was beat up. Keep on walking as if you didn't hear it. In another minute you are out of danger. Once when I was walking in the street, four goyim blocked the sidewalk, so I couldn't walk. I walked to the side and continued without looking back or saying anything. That is lubrication. Keep quiet! If anyone says something you don't like, pay no attention — unless your Rebbe is criticizing you — then listen to him. If your husband is mean to you, pay no attention. If your wife is mean to you, pay no attention, and a hundred evils will pass you by. You will live together happily for the rest of your lives.

Shlomo Hamelech's advice for all troubles

SHLOMO HAMELECH GAVE ADVICE FOR ALL KINDS OF TROUBLES. HE said: I'll give you a ring inscribed with three letters — *gimel, zayin, yud* — always look at that. It stands for *gam zeh ya'avor*, this too will pass. No matter what happens, look at the ring and remember that everything will pass. Don't become too depressed; *gam zeh ya'avor*. When a man lives with an attitude of *gam zeh ya'avor*, he is lubricating his life in such a way that eventually he will be successful, not only in *Olam Haba* but in *olam hazeh* as well.

There was a nice young man — I knew him well — who ran away from home. His father-in-law lived upstairs from him and used to mix in and tell him what to do. When he fought with his wife, the father-in-law always said that the wife was right. One day the man got fed up and ran away. Another man might have run away, but when he was on the train he would have changed his mind and come back again. The wife asks where he was and he doesn't say anything, and it is forgotten. But this man boarded an airplane and went to France. Afterwards he was sorry, but it was too late. He called his wife long distance and she said, "Where are you?" He should have said he was in Philadelphia, but he told her he was in Paris. She said, "Stay there."

They both made mistakes. He made a mistake by running away. What do you care what your father-in-law says? *Gam zeh ya'avor!* In another minute you could have forgotten about it. She made a mistake and said, *Stay away*. She should have said, *Come back as soon as possible*. He died young, and she married again and was divorced. Both had tragic lives. You have to lubricate your life. People make mistakes all the time. A little bit of patience is the lubrication that keeps friction away. *Gam zeh ya'avor*, it too will pass.

Don't prolong a fight
Always apologize as soon as possible

WHEN THE TORAH WAS GIVEN, IT WAS A TREMENDOUS, HISTORIC event. Some of Bnei Yisrael didn't want to leave; they wanted to stay there forever. But Hakadosh Baruch Hu told Moshe to tell them *Shuvu lachem*,[29] go back home. This is a principle of the Torah: *Go back home*. Don't break up your home, not even for good purposes, not even to stay at *Har Sinai* forever. Go back to your wives and to your homes. If someone wants to run away, even if he bought a ticket already, he should tear it up and go back home as soon as possible. If there is a fight, don't prolong the fight — put in some lubrication as soon as possible. If you feel embarrassed, write a little note and say I am sorry, and hand the paper to your wife. It is better than nothing. Even if she throws the note away, it is still a good beginning. Do something! *Bakesh shalom*, look for shalom. It is never too late! Always apologize if you can, as soon as possible.[30]

The whole Torah emphasizes that. *Deracheha darchei no'am vechol nesivoseha shalom*,[31] all the paths of the Torah lead to shalom. Shalom means *sheleimus*, and it keeps its simple meaning — peace. Hakadosh Baruch Hu gave us the Torah for the purpose of making shalom, and that *shalom* is for the happiness of *Olam Haba* and for successful living in *olam hazeh*. A man should understand that *hakol lefi rov hama'aseh*, all the things that happen are glorious opportunities and gifts from *Shamayim*, and you are utilizing that gift by keeping quiet and, even more, *bakesh shalom*. Try your best to make shalom, and eventually shalom will come.

Once a bachur went out in Madison Square Garden with a group of boys. Two 20-year-old goyim were ridiculing their yarmulkes. He looked at the goyim with anger, and they started getting angry at him.

---

29. *Devarim* 5:27
30. See *Fortunate Nation* p. 77 (5:27)
31. *Mishlei* 3:17

They took a hammer out of their car and pounded him on the head and killed him. When the case came to court, the judge postponed it to let the matter cool off. The judge didn't want to sentence any gentile boys. Half a year later they appeared in court, and the judge said the court system is no place for revenge. He let the murderers go on probation.

This poor fellow would have lived had he been at this lecture a little sooner and learned that *gam zeh ya'avor* — in one minute he would pass by them and it would have been all over and he would have been alive today. Who cares what they say?

How many women ruin their marriages over something that was worthless?

HOW MANY WOMEN RUIN THEIR MARRIAGES OVER SOMETHING THAT was worthless? If they would have waited a little while, the incident would have passed. Everyone makes mistakes sometimes. I am not justifying a husband who is mean, but *gam zeh ya'avor*, it will pass, and you will save your marriage. Although *hasken atzmecha*, improve yourself in this *prozdor*, is good advice, you also have to learn how to be happy in this *prozdor*. It is important to succeed in this world. You have to have a successful marriage. Many people fight and fight, yet in their old age they take their grandchildren to the chuppah together and they are buried together, despite the fact that they fought. How much better would it have been if they had each utilized the other's mean temper, or depression, or anxiety, and they would have thought *gam zeh ya'avor*, it will pass.

This *eitzah* of learning how to be able to lubricate life is one of the greatest *eitzos* to prepare for our career in *Olam Haba*.

A husband and wife should thank each other

AMONG THE LUBRICATIONS ARE TO SAY THANK YOU TO YOUR WIFE OR husband. If she asks him for money and he gives it, she should say thank you, even though she may think, "Why should I say thank you? He has to give me the money — I need it for the house." Still, she says thank you. When she serves supper, he says thank you. These things cause people to be more tolerant of each other and get along more easily. There are many different ways of creating lubrication. There is no need to cause unnecessary tragedies, abrasion, and friction that cause problems. If you make up your mind to lubricate life, you are doing yourself a great favor, and you are also preparing yourself for a long, happy career in this life.

How fortunate is a person who listens and doesn't pay attention. One hundred evils will pass him by, and Gehinnom will also pass him by. If he gets angry, there is a big Gehinnom waiting for him. Each time he gets angry, *kol minei Gehinnom sholtim bo*, he needs treatment for each time. Each incident of anger calls for a different treatment in Gehinnom. These women and men who keep quiet are not only earning redemption from Gehinnom, they are gaining *Olam Haba*.

THE MARRIAGE BOND — LOYALTY TO EACH OTHER

11

HEN NAOMI WAS LEAVING THE LAND OF MOAV, SHE WAS accompanied by Rus and Orpah, both of whom intended to accompany her all the way back to *Beis Lechem* in *Yehudah*. It was a noble intention, because it meant leaving their homeland and going as beggars into a foreign land, a foreign people and a foreign religion. Despite the fact that Naomi pleaded with them and urged them again and again to return, they persisted. Finally, though, Orpah broke down and yielded. She wept and Naomi wept and they kissed each other farewell: "*Vatishak Orpah lechamosah*,[1] Orpah kissed her mother-in-law, *veRus davekah bah*, but Rus clung to her." Rus refused to turn back.

The Sages[2] tell us that many years later, the descendants of Rus and Orpah met again; David Hamelech, the descendant of Rus, and Golias, the descendant of Orpah, met in battle, and the unarmed youth David conquered Golias. The Sages say, "*Yavo ben*

---

1. *Ruth* 1:14
2. *Sotah* 42b

haneshukah veyipol beyad ben hadevukah, let the son of the one who was kissed come and fall into the hands of the one who was *devukah* — who clung and persisted." Orpah and Naomi had a strong bond of affection — they didn't kiss for appearance sake; that kiss was an honest, heartfelt expression of emotion. Yet there is something more genuine than genuine emotions, and that is remaining. Saying farewell with sincere tears is not as good as remaining.[3]

Sincere emotions are certainly precious but it is the loyalty that really counts

IF A YOUNG MAN TELLS HIS REBBI THAT HE IS GOING TO LEAVE THE yeshivah and that his heart is broken, and he walks out with tears flowing from his eyes as he says good-bye to the *chatzros Hashem*, in the courtyard of Hashem, even though his rebbi sees that he is truly heartbroken, the rebbi is thinking, "How much better would it have been if he wouldn't have kissed me good-bye, if he had remained, like all the rest who are here." *Yavo ben haneshukah veyipol beyad ben hadevukah* — the one who remains is the one who is favored. Sincere emotions are certainly precious, but it is the loyalty that really counts.

In relating the story of Rus, the *navi* could have written simply that Rus didn't leave Naomi, but he used the word "*davekah*." This word is reminiscent of its great sources, "*ledovkah bo*[4] — to cling to Hashem," and "*uvo sidvak*[5] — and cling to Hashem." The plain meaning of this phrase is that your mind should dwell on Hakadosh Baruch Hu — you should think about Him, as the Torah tells us, "*Ve'ahavta eis* Hashem[6] — you should love Hashem," and "*Vehayu hadevarim ha'eileh*[7] — these words should be on your mind."

As you walk in the street snatch one second to think about Hashem

SOMEONE WHO THINKS ABOUT HAKADOSH BARUCH HU MORE frequently is a "*davek baHashem*" — he is clinging to Hashem. As you walk in the street, of all the things you think about, snatch just one second to think about Hakadosh Baruch Hu — that is a great achieve-

---

3. See *Career of Happiness* p. 108
4. *Devarim* 11:22
5. *Devarim* 10:20
6. *Devarim* 6:5
7. *Devarim* 6:6

ment! Thinking about Him for one second in the day already makes you exceptional; you are *dagul mei'revavah*, standing with your head higher than the rest of the multitudes. If you remind yourself of Hashem another time, another second later in the day, you are twice *dagul mei'revavah*. This is the fundamental *deveikus*; it is the way to cling to Hashem.[8]

Walking home with your rebbi is of great importance

BUT *DEVEIKUS* MEANS MORE THAN THAT. THE SAGES[9] TELL US that *ledovkah bo* means *lehidavek bechachamim u'vetalmidei-hem* — cling to the chachamim. This doesn't mean that we should only *think* about the chachamim (although thinking about talmidei chachamim is a good thing). The meaning of this statement is that we should be found close to them in the literal sense. In the berachah about tzaddikim, we ask Hakadosh Baruch Hu, "*vesim chelkeinu ima-hem*, put our lot together with them." How much are you found in the company of the chachamim? Walking home with your rebbi is *ledovkah bo*; as it says, *Holeich es chachamim*[10] — *walk* with chachamim, and you become a chacham. *Holeich* means to walk in their ways, but it also means to walk physically; because how can you learn their ways if you don't walk with them?

There was one boy named Yisrael, from the town of Salant, who tagged along with his rebbi and he became very great. A man there named Reb Yosef Zundel used to walk alone outside the town fre-quently. Yisrael was a sharp-witted boy, an *illui*, in fact, with an eagle eye, and he surmised that Reb Yosef Zundel was no ordinary man. The townspeople were simple, poor people, and they thought that Reb Yosef Zundel was just another poor baalebos. But whenever Reb Yosef Zundel went out on the countryside, Reb Yisrael would follow him at a respectful distance, and he tried to spy on him. He saw that Reb Yosef Zundel was doing something very unusual in his walks: he was thinking and meditating and talking, and sometimes Reb Yisrael was able to come close enough to get a snatch of the words of his monologue.

One day, Reb Yosef Zundel noticed that this young fellow was trailing him, and he understood that this young man was a "some-

---

8. See *Fortunate Nation* p. 160 (10:20)
9. *Sifrei Devarim*
10. *Mishlei* 13:20

body," just like the young man had understood that Reb Yosef Zundel was a somebody. Reb Yosef Zundel turned around and said, "Come here, Yisrael … you want to become a yerei Shamayim — learn mussar."

Reb Yisrael testified that these words entered his heart like an arrow. From that day on, his way in life was pointed out for him, and that remained his derech for the rest of his life. Because he had tagged along, because he was holeich es chachamim, he had walked with the wise, he too became wise. In fact, Reb Yisrael Salanter became the generation's rebbi in mussar, but his rebbi was Reb Yosef Zundel.[11]

This quality of vesim chelkeinu imahem, putting our lot together with them, means not merely to agree with their shittos, opinions, or to approve of their ways; it involves wanting to be with them. This, the Gemara says, is the way to fulfill ledovkah bo, to cling to Hakadosh Baruch Hu.

The Gemara[12] says, for instance, that you should eat with chachamim. If the Rosh Yeshivah eats in the dining room, try to get as close to him as possible without disturbing anyone. It also says walk with them and, if possible, do business with them.[13] If they have things to sell, patronize their shop frequently. Walk in all the time, find an excuse to talk to them. There were gedolim, such as the Chafetz Chaim, who had little shops. The Chafetz Chaim sometimes came to help his wife when it was busy, and if a man was smart, even if he didn't need anything he would go in to buy something, in order to exchange a word with the Chafetz Chaim. The best way to become close to a chacham and to fulfill uvo sidbak is yisa bas talmid chacham, if you can, marry his daughter.[14]

When we talk about the quality of deveikus, persistent clinging, it is worth reminding ourselves of what that great teacher Rabbi Yochanan ben Zakkai once said when he was in the company of his five great disciples: "eizohi derech tovah sheyidbak bah ha'adam[15] — what is the good way to which a man should cling?" He instructed them, "tze'u ure'u — go out and see what is the good way to which a man should cling." He didn't tell them to investigate and bring him back a report of what is the best way in

---

11. See Career of Happiness p. 110
12. Berachos 64a
13. Kesubos 112b
14. Pesachim 49b
15. Avos 2:13

life, because that would have been only half of a job accomplished. He told them to investigate what is the good way *sheyidbak bah ha'adam* — to which a man should *cling*. He wanted them to find the way in which one should *persist*. He did not want a theory or an intellectual accomplishment; but in fact the result turned out to be just that — theory.

The one who found the right answer was Rabbi Elazar ben Arach, who said it was a *leiv tov*, which means a *Torahdikeh* mind, a *Torahdikeh sechel*. When the rebbi heard his response, he said, "*Ro'eh ani es divrei Elazar ben Arach medivreichem*, these words I approve of above all your words." They all said good things, and whatever they said was true; all their words are like the titles of *sefarim* — each statement that was brought in at that time was like a *sefer* in a nutshell. But Rabbi Yochanan ben Zakkai said that Rabbi Elazar ben Arach's words are better, because they include all that the others said.

One must cling to his rebbi

THIS WAS SUCH A WONDERFUL COMMENDATION BY THE *GADOL hador*, but what happened to Rabbi Elazar ben Arach? We don't find him in the pages of the Gemara; and the reason is that he didn't cling to the Sages. After his rebbi died and all the *chaveirim* went to Yavneh, he didn't go along with them, because his wife said it was comfortable where they were. "If they want to learn," she said, "let them come to you." So he remained behind and he forgot his learning. He fulfilled the first half of Rabbi Yochanan's words, *tze'u ure'u eizohi derech tovah*, but he forgot about *sheyidbak bah ha'adam*, to cling to it.

A man must be loyal to his wife

THE FIRST TIME IN THE TORAH THAT WE FIND THE SUBJECT OF clinging and being loyal and persistent is *vedavak be'ishto*.[16] A man has to cling to his wife; he has to be loyal to his wife; when he marries he should intend for it to be for the next ten million years. That is why it says "*al kein*, therefore a man forsakes his father and mother and clings to his wife"; Hakadosh Baruch Hu created Chavah not as a separate being originally — He created her from Adam, as a symbol that

---

16. *Bereishis* 2:24

they have to be together. The word *davak* is the symbol of loyalty, a symbol of clinging to Hakadosh Baruch Hu, a symbol of perfection of character. Exercising one's free will, one's option to choose to be loyal forever, is one of the great functions of a man's *neshamah*.

In *Masechta Sotah* the Gemara[17] says, "*Ish ve'ishah zachu, Shechinah beineihem,*[18] if a man and a woman are worthy, Hashem's Presence is between them." The Gemara (*Kiddushin*)[19] says, "*Sheloshah shutafim yeish ba'adam,*" in the creation of a man there are three partners: *aviv*, his father, *imo*, his mother, and Hakadosh Baruch Hu. Of course, we need the *nifla'os haBorei* in order to create a living being; without the agency of the *Borei's* hashgachah, such a miracle as a new human being would never take place.

If two parents eat potatoes and drink a little milk, they are capable of producing a human being, which means that this human being is nothing but the components of milk and potatoes. These are recombined in different, marvelous combinations and out comes a living, sentient, feeling and thinking human being.

The miracle of milk

WHAT IS MILK, AFTER ALL? A COW DOESN'T DRINK MILK IN ORDER to produce milk; it eats grass, which comes from rain and snow combined with the elements of the air, amino acids from the nitrogen and carbon dioxide and other traces of gases in the air, and they combine to make grass. And the grass turns into milk and into meat. So when a human being is finally born, it is a bundle of nitrogen from the air and oxygen from the air and carbon dioxide from the air. Only they are recombined in such staggeringly complicated chemical combinations that it is a *neis*.

But this is not what the *ma'amar*, *Sheloshah shutafim yeish ba'adam*, is telling us, because you could say the very same things about a rabbit. This *ma'amar* means something entirely different. It is telling us that although the miracles in the creation of *every* living thing are beyond the ability of the human mind to fathom, a human being is something far greater than that; he is a miracle that is far beyond the miracle of life. It is a special manifestation of the Presence of Hakadosh Baruch Hu that makes this miracle happen.

---

17. *Sotah* 17a
18. See *The Beginning* p. 80 (224), *Career of Happiness* p. 98
19. *Kiddushin* 30b

At the time of chuppah the Shechinah comes down and stands there with them

WHEN DOES THE SHECHINAH COME DOWN AND JOIN THE corporation? It happens at the time of marriage, when a man and woman are standing under the chuppah, and they are being bonded together. *Zachu*, if they are worthy, *Shechinah beineihem*, the Shechinah comes down and stands there with them.[20]

We are like moles that are born blind and spend their lives underground in darkness, and we never can see the truth. All our lives we are unaware of what is really happening with us. But if we cannot feel it with a sensory perception, let us at least realize with an intellectual awareness that when people get married, Hakadosh Baruch Hu is standing under the chuppah. As amazing and impossible as that is to comprehend, it is crucial that we understand it.

And so, when the Torah says *"vedavak be'ishto,"* it is not referring merely to a bond that is created between two physical entities but to a bond with of Hakadosh Baruch Hu Himself. *Shechinah beineihem* means that Hakadosh Baruch Hu is standing not off to one side; He is *between* them. He *is* the bond of marriage.

There is such a sublimity in a Torah marriage that we have to learn in order to elevate our minds to our concept

THERE IS SUCH SUBLIMITY IN A TORAH MARRIAGE THAT WE HAVE TO learn and learn in order to elevate our minds to that concept.[21] When a young couple approaches the chuppah, their heads may be full of everything but this; as with most other things, they are living with superficialities, unaware of the great variety in life. He is thinking of how much the whiskey will cost him; she is wondering whether the flowers on her veil are well arranged; the father of the kallah is thinking how much the caterer's bill will be; the mother is thinking about how beautiful her daughter looks tonight; or they are praying that they will have a happy future together. But whatever they are thinking does not even approximate the truth, which is far beyond their ability to understand. The Shechinah is here now, and they are being bonded together with the One Who is between them.

---

20. See *Awake My Glory* p. 190 (648)
21. See *Career of Happiness* p. 112

When it says *vedavak be'ishto*, it is like *uvo sidbak* — you have to cling to Hakadosh Baruch Hu; don't let go of His Hand. He is holding his hand in one Hand and her hand in the other. That is *vedavak*. It is a symbol of our attitudes toward Hakadosh Baruch Hu; it is a symbol of our persistence in adhering to the Torah, of all our idealism.

Shir Hashirim is a mashal,[22] a parable for the love between Hakadosh Baruch Hu and His people *Knesses Yisrael*. We should never make any error and yield to the foolishness of shallow, ignorant people who try to interpret *Shir Hashirim* otherwise. The fact that in the parable Am Yisrael is portrayed as the bride and Hakadosh Baruch Hu as the groom is very significant as it relates to an actual chassan and kallah. It means that when you see a chassan and a kallah, the chassan is a mashal of Hakadosh Baruch Hu, and the kallah represents all of Am Yisrael. Even people who have been married for a long time should realize that they symbolize this great lesson.

A wife should accept the idealism and Torah her husband brings home from the beis medrash

THE HUSBAND SYMBOLIZES HAKADOSH BARUCH HU — FOR WHAT purpose? Not so that he should behave like Hakadosh Baruch Hu, but so that his wife should look up to him and accept his teachings. She accepts the idealism and the Torah he brings home from the beis medrash, just like the Jewish people accepted the Torah from Hakadosh Baruch Hu, and like Sarah accepted the teachings of Avraham Avinu. It says *VeSarah shoma'as pesach ha'ohel*.[23] Sarah's minhag was that whenever Avraham was talking she would stand behind the flap of the tent, and she was listening. *VeSarah shoma'as*, she always listened. She didn't want to lose the opportunity of hearing Avraham speak. That is the picture of Sarah's way of life; she listened because Avraham had a lot to say. Sarah herself had a lot to say — she was like an experienced Beis Yaakov Seminary teacher; she has taught many girls for years and years, but it is *because* she is an expert teacher that she never loses the opportunity to learn more. *Sarah megayeres es hanashim*, she preached to women, and because of that Sarah had a taste for learning, for understanding and hearing. *VeSarah shoma'as*,

22. See *Career of Happiness* p. 113
23. *Bereishis* 18:10

she would listen whenever she could.[24] She heard every word that Avraham spoke to wayfarers who were visiting.

And so the wife tries to get all the Torah she can from her husband, who symbolizes Hakadosh Baruch Hu. The Jewish wife symbolizes *Knesses Yisrael*, which means the husband has the welfare of his wife always in his heart, like Hakadosh Baruch Hu *oheiv amo Yisrael*. Hashem loves them not only in order to give them His Torah, but also to supervise them, to provide all of their needs. The Gemara[25] says about a husband, *sheheim teluyim becha, ve'atah talui bemi she'amar vehayah ha'olam* — your wife and children depend on you, and you depend on Hakadosh Baruch Hu.

You have to feel responsible for the happiness of your wife and children

WHY SHOULDN'T IT SAY YOUR WIFE AND YOU ALL DEPEND ON Hakadosh Baruch Hu? *Sheheim teluyim becha* means that you have to feel responsible for them like Hashem feels responsible for Am Yisrael. You have to feel responsible for the happiness of your wife and children, not merely for bringing home the money. Of course some woman might tell her husband that this means that you have to take me out; you have to spend time talking with me; you have to see that I am happy. But she should remember the first part of the mashal: a husband has to bring the Torah down to her. If he won't sit and learn or go to the *batei medrash*, he will have nothing to bring down to her.

Of course a husband shouldn't neglect his wife. There was a man who never wanted to talk to his wife — not because he was such a big *masmid*. He used to come home from work, she would serve him supper, and he would bury himself in the pages of the Jewish newspaper. Whenever she wanted to talk to him, to tell him the news of the day, he would say, "Don't bother me. I'm busy now." But one night she died, and the doctor and the ambulance came and they wanted to take her away, but the husband said, "No, she will spend the night here." All night he sat near her bed holding her dead hand and talking to her, trying to make up for what he had missed. Your job is to make people in your family happy. *Sheheim teluyim becha*, they depend on you, just like you depend on Hakadosh Baruch Hu.

---

24. See *The Beginning* p. 306 (18:10)
25. *Chullin* 84b

A marriage has a great kedushah

BECAUSE A BRIDE AND GROOM IS *SHIR HASHIRIM'S* METAPHOR, representing the relationship between Hakadosh Baruch Hu and Klal Yisrael, we can understand what great *kedushah* a marriage has. That is why the Sages called it *kiddushin* — a name of *kedushah*. According to the Torah, "*Ki yikach ish ishah*, a man *takes* a wife";[26] *ki yikchah* — *kinyan*; it is a way of acquiring, a *kinyan*. But you have to know that Hakadosh Baruch Hu was *koneh*, He acquired us, when He took us out of *Mitzrayim*.

People might not understand and might think, on a materialistic level, that *ki yikach ish ishah* is like buying a house. So the Sages stepped in and changed the words. When a man stands under the chuppah with his kallah, he doesn't say *Harei at lekuchah li betaba'as zu*, although that would be just as valid — "You are acquired to me through this." But the Sages didn't encourage that phrasing, because it could make people misunderstand what it means. In the days of Moshe Rabbeinu, when people were on a higher, more noble level, everyone understood what it meant, so they said *harei at lekuchah li*. In the same way, "*Velakachti eschem li la'am*" referred to the hallowed relationship between Hakadosh Baruch Hu and Am Yisroel.

But later, in the generations that were further and further away from *yetzi'as Mitzrayim* and *Har Sinai*, when people began to fall under the influence of the *umos ha'olam*, marriage began to be seen from more of a materialistic focus. The Sages then stepped in and told Am Yisrael to say, "*Harei at mekudeshes li*," so that they should understand the *kedushah* that is in the marriage. It was not the Sages who instituted the *kedushah*; on the contrary, the *kedushah* had been even greater before.

The Torah provides us with many details of the conduct of Avraham and Sarah as a model; Avraham and Sarah created the model for the Mishkan and the *Beis Hamikdash*. The Mishkan was actually an echo, a replica of the house of Avraham and Sarah; and when the Kohen Gadol offered up a *par ben bakar* on Yom Kippur, the Sages tell us that it was an echo of the *par*, the ox that Avraham slaughtered for each one of his visitors when he wanted to give them a sumptuous repast. The *ugos* that Sarah baked were the fore-

---

26. *Devarim* 22:13

runners of the *lechem hapanim* that they put on the *Shulchan*, the golden table in the Mishkan.[27]

The Beis Hamikdash as an echo
of the tent of Avraham and Sarah

THE *KEDUSHAH*, THE EXCEPTIONAL SANCTITY OF THE *BEIS Hamikdash*, was nothing but an echo of what Avraham and Sarah achieved in their little tent. They didn't have a big house — it couldn't have been big, because they were nomads. Their home was just big enough to put on a camel's back to move on further. In that little tent, however, they created something that became immortal in this world and that is eternal in the World to Come. *Ma'asei avos siman lebanim* — it is there to serve as a model for everyone who marries to strive to emulate as much as possible; *chayav adam lomar: masai yagi'u ma'asai lema'asei avosai*[28] — when will my deeds approach the deeds of our forefathers? We understand from *Shir Hashirim* that that is what Hakadosh Baruch Hu Himself sees when He views a Jewish marriage, because otherwise He wouldn't have chosen such a metaphor for his relationship with Am Yisrael.[29]

Therefore, when we speak about the words *vedavak be'ishto*, we understand that it means to cling to his wife and his wife to him with a loyalty that is a semblance of the *deveikus baHashem*. It doesn't mean that a man should be thinking about his wife all the time or she about him — they are both thinking about Hakadosh Baruch Hu all the time; that is what Avraham and Sarah did.

Marriage on the basis of romance
is a recipe for disappointment

ANYONE WHO MARRIES ON THE BASIS OF ROMANCE[30] IS GOING TO be bitterly disappointed, because in married life there is no romance. There is loyalty; there can be nobility and *kedushah* — these are concepts that are real and true. But when people marry for unreal and imaginary purposes, then they are bound to be disappointed. A

---

27. See *Awake My Glory* p. 343 (1102)
28. *Tanna DeVei Eliyahu Rabbah* 25
29. See *Awake My Glory* p. 118 (404)
30. See *Career of Happiness* p. 116

marriage may turn out to be unhappy because it never was what they hoped it would be.[31]

When people marry they should be ready for hard knocks

WHEN PEOPLE MARRY THEY SHOULD BE READY FOR HARD knocks — there is no such thing as a smooth marriage. The definition of marriage is friction. It involves two personalities, each with rough edges; there is no question that there will be tests and ordeals ahead. When Hakadosh Baruch Hu was preparing the plan for marriage, He said "*E'eseh lo eizer kenegdo*[32] — I will make a help opposite him." An *eizer* does not mean a "yes-person" — whatever he says she will say yes, or whatever she says he will say yes. That doesn't help the person; in fact it corrupts the character if one has nothing but agreement. No one can succeed in his ambition to smooth out the rough spots in his nature in this way.

Kenegdo means opposite him, different from what he is. There are differences in human nature between a man and a woman. I spoke with a man recently who was divorced once and was thinking of getting a second divorce, because his second wife was also trouble. I told him that all women are troublesome. All women are a little bit meshuga and all men are a little bit meshuga. That is human nature. The Rambam gives us a very important word of caution: he says that one of the foundations of the Torah is *lo sikom velo sitor* — you shouldn't take revenge and you shouldn't carry a grudge. The Rambam considers this admonition to be the foundation of human society.

People must learn to forgive and forget. Even after the worst quarrel when one side makes the slightest attempt at reconciliation the other side should immediately accept it

IN MARRIAGE THERE HAVE TO BE TIMES WHEN THERE IS SOME FRICTION, but success can be achieved when people learn to accept and forgive and forget; anyone who has a good memory is going to be head-

31. See *The Beginning* p. 74 (2:18), *Career of Happiness* p. 21
32. *Bereishis* 2:18

ing for the divorce court. If a woman brings up what her husband did twenty years ago, and if he remembers what she did once, and they keep on recounting these things over the years, sometimes it grows in the retelling.[33]

People who can forget are the only ones who can live successfully. But this itself involves a process of character improvement. *Mishlei* says about the wife, "*Gemalas'hu tov velo ra kol yemei chayeha*[34] — she bestowed upon him good and no evil all the days of her life." This is not referring to a real human wife; it is a mashal and is speaking about the Torah; the Torah bestows nothing but good. We are wedded to the Torah. It is our wife and it will never do us any harm; but a human wife just cannot be that way. Every man and every woman has to expect some rough riding, but always to keep in mind this great principle of *lo sikom velo sitor*[35] — you don't try to get even and you don't try to remember. Even after the worst quarrel, when one side makes the slightest attempt at reconciliation, the other should immediately accept it, wipe out the past and start this minute with a new slate. Erasing all the old fixations is erasing stains from the neshamah.

This is what is meant by *vedavak be'ishto* — he is loyal to his wife and she is loyal to him. No matter what he said or did, they are loyal to each other, and at the first opportunity they try to erase from their memories whatever took place.

It is disloyalty to remember. If you meet your mother or your sister and you recount what your husband did to you, it is disloyalty; if a man tells anyone what his wife did, it is disloyalty; even after the spouse has died, if the survivor tells the children, "Your mother was a good woman, but she caused me a lot of trouble," it is disloyalty. In life and in death there has to be *vedavak*, loyalty forever, which means to overlook everything.

Sometimes it seems that Hakadosh Baruch Hu is dealing us something that we don't like, but we know that it is actually good for us, because *kol darchei Hashem chessed ve'emes*,[36] His ways are all kindliness and truth, and we are loyal to Him. In the same way, *vedavak be'ishto* requires that a person should always consider his spouse loyal to him and should respond with loyalty, by forgetting. No one is perfect; you search and search, and in the end

33. See *Career to Happiness* p. 129
34. *Mishlei* 31:12
35. *Vayikra* 19:18
36. *Tehillim* 25:6

you find somebody who will step on your toes all the time, because it cannot be otherwise.

In order to achieve perfection we have to learn to live with other people's qualities

THE GEMARA[37] SAYS: "*KESHEIM SHE'EIN PARTZUFEIHEM DOMOS ZO lezo* — just like two faces are not alike*,*" you don't have two faces among all mankind that are alike, and the reason for that is to test man. Can you get along with someone who has a nose you don't like? Of course you have a right to choose a wife whose nose satisfies you, but once you have her and then you become aware of the nose, you just have to make up your mind that it is forever — that is the nose you like. Just like the noses are not the same, "... *kach ein dei'oseihem shavos zo lezo*, people have different minds. What seems to you petty or silly or foolish could be important to another person. No two minds in the world are alike, the Gemara says, and you have to accept a person's mind, emotions, and interests. Of course everything has to be *al pi Torah*. Certainly people have to improve; a wife has to listen to her husband who comes from the beis medrash and brings back instruction, the Torah and mussar that he has heard. But each one has his basic nature, and in order to achieve *sheleimus*, perfection, we have to learn to live with other people's qualities.

We may think that it only our hard luck that we married a woman who has this idiosyncrasy or that queer habit or this way of thinking or behaving. But we have to realize that when the first woman made her appearance in the world, she was already very different. If Adam would have made a woman, she would have been a replica of himself and they would never have married; it would have been an end to marriage. Hakadosh Baruch Hu knows it is the difference that is important. The mere fact that they have distinctive characteristics, that they are different, is what forms the bond of marriage and causes it to be successful.

The Torah says, "*vayevi'eha el ha'adam.*"[38] Hashem could have made Adam wake up from his sleep and find Chavah waiting for him, but then Adam wouldn't have appreciated her, so Hakadosh Baruch Hu packaged her. You have to package anything that you want to be appreciated. When a chassan brings a ring to his kallah, he doesn't bring it

---

37. *Berachos* 58a
38. *Bereishis* 2:22

in a paper bag, he packages it in a leather box with a blue velvet lining, and the packaging tells you how important the contents are. That is why the kallah is delivered to the chassan with *untefirers* (chaperones) with candles, to give the appearance that he is getting something special. She is wrapped up in silk and tulle and ornaments and flowers.

That is why it says *vayevi'eha*, Hakadosh Baruch Hu brought her to Adam. The Gemara[39] says: *melamed sheHakadosh Baruch Hu na'asah shushbin*, Hakadosh Baruch Hu became her *untefirer*. She didn't have any parents to be her *untefirers*, so Hakadosh Baruch Hu did the job, and He did it well. He had *malachim* shining and the Shechinah came shining in front of Chavah and there was Heavenly music. Adam saw that he was getting something special — a beautiful wife. But that was only the packaging. In fact, he was getting someone who was different from him, with whom he would have to live, someone who would test him. She caused him a lot of trouble; she said "Eat from the fruit of this tree." I don't believe she told him that briefly; I think she cajoled him, begged him, urged him, nagged him, and finally, he ate of the fruit of the tree and that caused the biggest trouble the world ever saw. She was created in order to cause trouble, and his job was to refuse it. If he had refused, then the world would have been saved. He had to cause her trouble, too. The Torah only tells us the sparsest details, but they were there to test each other.

Don't get the idea that you should go ahead and test people and vex people in order to sandpaper their character and smooth them out.[40] What about your character? If you are going to be rough and be sandpaper, then try as she will, your wife will become sandpaper too, because that is human nature, and in the process these two people are going to become as perfect as they were intended to be. That is what Hakadosh Baruch Hu meant by *e'eseh lo ezer*, I will make a help .... The help is for you to achieve the purpose of life, which means to become the very best that you can become in this world.

When a chassan and a kallah stand under the chuppah, we say a berachah, *kesameichacha yetzirecha beGan Eden mikedem* — just like you caused joy to your creations, Adam and Chavah, in Gan Eden of old, so it caused them joy as well. What does this mean? When Hakadosh Baruch Hu gives you something that you need, He gives it chocolate coated. For instance, you need fuel for energy, otherwise

39. *Berachos* 61a
40. See *Career of Happiness* p. 118

you can't work or live, so He gives you fuel. Apples could grow on trees containing the elements you need to regenerate your worn-out tissues, to give you energy, but it could grow without flavor or color and you wouldn't enjoy it. But instead Hakadosh Baruch Hu gave apples that are red or gold, and they taste good and have a pleasant aroma, because He wants you to have simchah. It is nothing but fuel, but He is sugarcoating that fuel. Hakadosh Baruch Hu wraps it in a pleasant wrapper.

A wife should make you perfect

A WIFE IS FOR THE PURPOSE OF MAKING YOU PERFECT. A WIFE IS A lot of sugar, a lot of honey. Of course the honey sometimes develops into a bee sting, too. But the purpose is the sting; the purpose is the *eizer kenegdo*, to make you reach perfection through living with someone else. But "*kesameichacha yetzirecha*," — Hakadosh Baruch Hu put it in a beautiful wrapper and He brought her to Adam. The husband loves his wife and appreciates her to no end, especially when she is brought to him with such *untefirers* like Hakadosh Baruch Hu. Therefore, *kesameichaha*, just like you brought this perfection to Adam in such a wrapping that caused him to appreciate it, so give this couple success that they should live together and become great in their perfection of character.

They should be sweet to each other, because sweet sandpaper is also sandpaper. It just can't be helped; marriage is always sandpapering. If anyone becomes discouraged because of the abrasion on his nerves or on his dignity, it cannot be helped — that is how married life is. There must be some minor conflict, some kind of test all the time. The man who understands this great principle and *vedavak be'ishto*, clings to his wife, is clinging to Hakadosh Baruch Hu, because Hakadosh Baruch Hu is there, in the middle of both of them. He will achieve as much perfection as people can achieve by clinging directly to Hashem.

A JEWISH HOUSE 12

N ORDER TO BUILD A HOUSE, THOUSANDS OF DETAILS MUST be planned in advance, from the foundations to the supporting girders to the beams … until gradually it takes the shape of a house. It requires *chochmah*, wisdom, and a variety of skills, to produce such a product. Shlomo Hamelech said about building a Jewish home, "*Chachmos nashim bansah beisah*,[1] it is the wisdom of women that builds a house. This pasuk in *Mishlei* isn't speaking about only women; it is telling us that wisdom is needed to build a house.

What is the holy house, the ideal house, and how does one go about making such a house? These things should be planned ahead as much as possible and should be carried out when opportunity presents itself.

Hashem loves us more than anything else

IT IS IMPORTANT TO EMPHASIZE IN THE HOUSE THE PRINCIPLE OF *oheiv amo Yisrael*, to teach everyone, including yourself, to love Am Yisrael. The Sages reported that a chacham said that if one had to choose

---

1. *Mishlei* 14:1

which is more important, to love Torah or to love Am Yisrael, it would be to love Am Yisrael. Rabbi Shimon bar Yochai was so happy when he heard this that he kissed the man on his head. But why is it that love of Am Yisrael is more important? It is because that is who Hakadosh Baruch Hu Himself loves. The Torah states, "*Ki cheilek Hashem amo, Yaakov chevel nachalaso.*"[2] What does *cheilek Hashem* mean? Out of the whole *beri'ah*, Hashem can choose anything, but what He wants most is His people. Of the whole universe, of things millions of light years away, out of trillions of stars, Hakadosh Baruch Hu said: It is My people that I desire, and *Yaakov chevel nachalaso*, Bnei Yisrael is My inheritance. Hakadosh Baruch Hu is saying there is nothing in the universe that He is interested in more and that He loves more than Am Yisrael.[3]

And, the Torah tells us, "*Hein laHashem Elokecha hashamayim ushemei hashamayim,*[4] behold to Hashem belong the heavens and the heavens above the heavens [meaning all space], *ha'aretz vechol asher bah*, everything belongs to Him; *rak ba'avosecha chashak* Hashem, but only in your forefathers did Hashem delight [*chashak* means He was attached to them], *le'ahava osam*, to love them, *vayivchar bezaram achareihem*, He chose their seed after them, *bachem ... kayom hazeh*," whenever the Torah is read, it is speaking about you; Hakadosh Baruch Hu loves His people more than anything in the universe, with a *cheishek*, a powerful attachment to them.[5]

We should love the Jewish people

HASHEM IS THE CREATOR OF OTHER NATIONS, BUT HE IS NOT THEIR Father. *Banim atem*,[6] you are the children of Hashem; *Ko amar Hashem, beni bechori Yisrael.*[7] This is one of the most basic principles of the Torah, and it has to be made most prominent in the Jewish home. You must know that Am Yisrael is beloved by Hashem, and the more you love Am Yisrael, the more Hashem loves you. The first thing we know about Moshe Rabbeinu is that *vayeitzei el echav,*[8] he went out to his brothers; and Hashem said: That is My man.[9]

---

2. *Devarim* 32:9
3. See *Fortunate Nation* p. 377 (32:9)
4. *Devarim* 10:14-15
5. See *Fortunate Nation*, pp. 152-154, *Awake My Glory* p. 109 (366-367)
6. *Devarim* 14:1
7. *Shemos* 4:22
8. *Shemos* 2:11
9. See *A Nation Is Born* p. 26 (2:11)

Wherever there are frum Jews, love them; as much as you love them, it is never excessive, it will never even faintly resemble the tremendous love that Hashem has for them. In the Jewish home the atmosphere must be saturated with patriotism, with love of our people. Of course our people means Torah people. We love the tzaddikim, the frum men, the frum women, the frum boys and girls, we love all the *doros* that went before us who were *shomrei mitzvos*,[10] and we love all those who are alive today. Hakadosh Baruch Hu is waiting to see if we are going to perform that great obligation of "You should love My people." In the house that you are building, one of the essential elements is to introduce our powerful feeling of love for your nation.

Don't think this is a substitute or competition for love of Hashem. But Hashem has made us so great that He told the *malachim* to be our servants. *Ki malachav yetzaveh lach lishmorcha*,[11] He tells the *malachim* to guard you. This means that we are more important than the *malachim*. The *malachim* don't say *shirah* until they hear Bnei Yisrael say *shirah* first. Hashem wants our *shirah* first; the *shirah* of the *malachim* is only a model for us; but it is only because of us that they are spoken about at all.

In bringing up children, one of the most important points is to emphasize how great is a Jew, how great is Hashem's love for us. *Kol Yisrael benei malachim heim*[12] — we are considered princes. The son of a king is a prince. Hashem is our Father and we are His sons. We are His inheritance, *cheilek Hashem*.

The Jewish nation will always exist

A SECOND ELEMENT THAT MUST BE INTRODUCED INTO THE BUILDING of a Jewish home is the confidence that we are the *Am Olam*, we will be here forever. No other nation is guaranteed eternal existence, but the *Navi* Yeshaya said, "*Ki heharim yamushu*,[13] the mountains will move away, *vehageva'os temusena*, all the hills will disappear, *vechasdi mei'iteich lo yamush*, but My loving-kindness will never disappear from you." This means that Am Yisrael will continue as long as the world will exist, and even when there is no more world — *Kol Yisrael yeish lahem cheilek la'Olam Haba*. The tzaddikim are

10. See *Awake My Glory* p. 354 (1126), p. 352 (1120)
11. See *The Beginning* p. 403 (25:26)
12. *Tehillim* 91:11
13. *Yeshaya* 54:6

in the Next World right now, but you must know, there is a condition — they have to believe in Hashem *Elokei Yisrael*; if not, they will not be *zocheh* to *Olam Haba*. No matter what happens, the tzaddikim knew — even when they were being burned in the gas chambers in Europe — that forever and ever they will continue to exist; their children, their relatives ... Am Yisrael will never disappear no matter what.

Tremendous nations have already disappeared — it is a fact of history. People never dreamed that Rome would be written off the map. The legions of Rome were all over the habitable world; all Europe was under Roman rule. Romans built bridges and buildings everywhere. Roman law was introduced everywhere. Then Rome disappeared entirely, except in historical and archeological interest. But there is no longer a nation that continues to exist; and all other nations are the same. They would have laughed at you in the days of Yirmiyahu Hanavi if you would have said that Bavel would someday disappear. Bavel was the most powerful nation, famous for its great cities and huge buildings. Today nothing at all remains of Bavel. If you want to know Bavel, you have to go underground with bulldozers and dig it out from underneath. But Am Yisrael is promised to exist on this earth, to walk on this soil forever. This confidence must be implanted in all Jewish children and in us. You have to speak about it always and let them know that we are going to endure forever.

Once a person feels that his people are forever, you cannot be depressed

THE NAME YAAKOV TELLS US THAT THE JEWISH PEOPLE WILL COME AT the end. *Yaakov* is from the word *eikev*, heel.[14] Yaakov came *after* Esav. The name Yitzchak means that he, not Yishmael, is the one who will laugh. In the end Am Yisrael will rejoice and will endure forever. Once a person feels that his people are forever, it gives him a different confidence. You cannot be depressed, because when you know that your cause, your ideals, and your family will exist forever, you cannot be discouraged. We should speak about this all the time, to remind ourselves and our children that Hakadosh Baruch Hu promised it to us and that He is demonstrating it. We have lived for thousands of years without a country, without a land, and we are still here, and we are increasing and multiplying. Torah communities are spreading out everywhere,

---

14. See *The Beginning* p. 403 (25:26)

all over America, Australia, England, Russia … the world will always have Torah communities.

Another element that should be introduced in the building of the Jewish home is the principle that the home is a *makom kadosh*. A Jewish house is a holy house. The Shechinah is in *every* Jewish home; this is not a mashal. Where else would Hakadosh Baruch Hu come if not in a place where His word is obeyed constantly? Milchig dishes, fleishig dishes, pareve dishes … everything is done kehalachah; Shabbos, kashrus, davening, mitzvos — at all times the Torah is being practiced in a Jewish home. The Gemara[15] tells us that two sages once passed by the ruins of an old Jewish home where tzaddikim once lived. One sage bent over and sighed in sadness. He was mourning the *churban* (destruction) of that wonderful house. The other sage told him: *Asid Hakadosh Baruch Hu lehachaziram lanu*, someday Hashem will rebuild the Jewish houses again — just like the Jewish body. When a person passes away, you put the body in the earth. But someday, *vene'eman Atah lehachayos meisim*, we will arise once more and we will wear flesh upon our bones. In the same way, the house will one day arise again. A house is *kadosh*, and *kedushah* lasts forever; it won't disappear.

The house is a holy place

TEACH THE FAMILY THAT THIS HOUSE OF OURS IS A HOLY PLACE, AND we have to know how to treat it as if it is holy. For instance, don't let children sit on a table. A table is a *mizbei'ach* (altar),[16] a *makom kadosh*. We put kosher food on the table. We put a siddur on the table. We make berachos at the table. A child sitting on the table is profaning a holy thing. An entire Jewish home is *kadosh*. It is a place where tzaddikim began their lives. Imagine if you could find the house where the Chafetz Chaim was born, or the Vilna Gaon or Rabbi Akiva — that house deserves to be protected forever. Every house where Jewish children were brought up and became adults who were *ovdei Hashem* is *kodesh kodashim*.

That has to be emphasized to children. When they come into the house they should come in with derech eretz. Know the Shechinah is here. It is not a bus stop or, *lehavdil*, a library. A Jewish house is a place where Hakadosh Baruch Hu finds *nachas ruach*, where He sees His Torah being obeyed implicitly, in every detail. If a child wants to

---

15. *Berachos* 58b
16. See *Awake My Glory* p. 348 (1112)

eat something he has to think, Am I still fleishig? Can I eat ice cream? Even the child watches the clock; everyone keeps the Torah carefully. For so many days they guard themselves against any *issur* of eating chametz or anything that is connected with chametz. All day Shabbos, *muktzeh* is avoided. Everyone is observing hundreds and hundreds of details. The house is *kadosh* and we have to teach it to ourselves and to our children and repeat it constantly, so they should understand what they are doing there, and they can participate in making it more *kadosh*. Tell them that every time they do something good in this house, they are making it even more *kadosh*. Every time you learn Torah in the house, every time you daven, every time you say *Birkas Hamazon* or any berachah, the house is becoming more and more *kadosh*.

Among all the best nations in the world, nothing even remotely resembles the Jewish house. *Oheiv Hashem sha'arei Tziyon mikol mishkenos Yaakov*, Hashem loves the *sha'arei Tzion* most, but he loves *mishkenos Yaakov*. When Bila'am took a look at the Jewish tents, he became so enthusiastic and said, *Ma tovu ohalecha Yaakov*[17] — how beautiful are your tents Yaakov — *mishkenosecha Yisrael*. He compared them to streams (or, some say, to aloe trees). The influence of a Jewish home on the people who live there will continue forever, like a stream that flows from there, the tradition of *kedushah* flows from the Jewish home from generation to generation.[18]

Do not bring magazines into your house

THEREFORE, *LO SAVI TO'EIVAH EL BEISECHA*[19] — BE CAREFUL WHAT you bring into the house. Teach children that certain things should not come into the house. If you want to read a magazine that you found in the street, look at it before you enter the house — don't take it into the house. A television, *chas veshalom*, doesn't belong in a Jewish house. This principle of the *kedushah* of a Jewish home is very important for us to learn and to remind ourselves whenever we come into the house. When you come back from work, think: This place where I am coming in is *kadosh*. If you are coming from the beis medrash, you are now going into another place that is *kadosh*.[20]

---

17. *Bamidbar* 23:5-6
18. See *Awake My Glory* p. 337 (1098)
19. *Devarim* 7:26
20. See *Awake My Glory* p. 346 (1107)

In case your wife doesn't share with you these great thoughts and ideals, speak about them yourself; and if your wife is the one who is speaking about them, let her speak. The children will listen. Hearing that this is a *makom kadosh* influences everyone in the house and makes them feel they are growing up in an atmosphere of *kedushah*. Hakadosh Baruch Hu said: You are *kedoshim*, holy to Hashem. If *kedoshim* live in a house, that house certainly has *kedushah* because of them alone.

The world is very good

ANOTHER IMPORTANT PRINCIPLE TO IMPLANT IN A JEWISH HOME IS that which Hakadosh Baruch Hu Himself said, *Vayar Elokim es kol asher asah vehinei tov me'od*[21]— everything is very good, and that must be taught, otherwise out of habit people will overlook this tremendous benefit.

Enjoy snow

TEACH THEM HOW GOOD SNOW IS.[22] SNOW IS A GREAT BLESSING. Teach it to children, otherwise they will never hear it. "*Nosen she-leg katzamer* — He gives snow like wool" (*Tehillim* 147). Wool is kinky, and it imprisons the air and insulates the earth against the frost, so the frost doesn't kill the roots and the important insects in the soil. We need those insects. Also, when snow falls it falls in a "kinky" way and imprisons air, and air serves as an insulator to keep out the frost. The snow is white. White repels the sun's rays, so the white snow doesn't melt so quickly. (In countries close to the equator the soldiers dress in white, because white protects them from the heat.) Not only is the consistency of snow like wool, the color is like wool. And snow melts gradually. The earth drinks in more of the water from snow than it does from rain. The Gemara says one snow is better than five rains. Imagine if children learned to enjoy the snow — not to frolic in the snow, but to look through the window to enjoy the snow. Snow is happiness. It is a gift. You have to gain that attitude. The farmers say that in a year when there is not much snow, the crops in the following spring are going to be poor. When there is heavy snow in the wintertime, the crops will be

---

21. *Bereishis* 1:31
22. See *Awake My Glory* pp. 286-287, *Career of Happiness* p. 76, *Sing You Righteous* p. 247 (530), *Praise My Soul* p. 183 (518)

lush in the spring. An abundance of snow means more food will grow the following season.

Enjoy rain

TEACH THEM TO ENJOY RAIN. WHAT A BLESSING RAIN IS! PURE WATER falls![23] The ocean is salty and briny and full of chemicals. But the sun, from 93 million miles away, sends its rays, and in eight minutes light comes from the sun to the surface of the ocean and causes the water to evaporate. And only pure water vaporizes, and it goes up and becomes clouds, and these clouds come over the continents and condense, and they drop only pure water down to the earth to the soil. Those clouds eventually turn into food for us. Apples are mostly water. Even people are mostly water.[24] When it rains, people are coming down; someday they will appear in the form of human beings. The rain will become food and then it will become grass for animals to eat, and animals take the grass and make it into meat, and we'll eat the meat and after a while we will have girls and boys who will develop from these things. They came originally from the water. They are dressed in wool. Wool comes from the grass that the sheep ate. And so the rain is a tremendous blessing. Everything good comes from the rain. And we say in the wintertime: *mashiv haru'ach umorid hageshem*. If we forget to say it, we have to repeat *Shemoneh Esrei*. You have to thank Hakadosh Baruch Hu for that great gift.

Water causes your eyes to sparkle. It is the water that makes you able to see. Water is the most important element of the blood; it causes your blood to be liquid and have the right consistency to flow freely throughout all your blood vessels and bring nourishment to all parts of the body. Water is everything for us. Baruch Hashem for the glass of water.

Enjoy sunshine

YOU HAVE TO TELL THE CHILDREN HOW GOOD IT IS WHEN THE SUN shines. Light is such happiness. If the sun were a little closer, we would be burned to ashes. If it were a little farther away, we would be ice. If it were a little bigger, we would be burned to a crisp. If it were a little smaller, we would be frozen. The sun is exactly the right size and

---

23. See *Awake My Glory* p. 289 (926), p. 368 (1158), *Sing You Righteous* p. 246 (530)
24. See *Awake My Glory* p. 292 (941)

exactly the right distance from us. Don't think this is a small thing. There are millions of adjustments in so many things that are necessary for life to exist on this earth, and these things are not found anywhere else in the universe. Scientists are able to analyze the chemicals on the other planets and stars, and there is nothing like this earth.[25]

Enjoy air

TEACH THEM TO THANK HASHEM FOR AIR. AIR IS A BLESSING. PURE oxygen would make you intoxicated. It is mixed with nitrogen, an inert gas and a little bit of carbon dioxide.[26] And that little bit of carbon dioxide is what the plants breathe in, and they use it to make starch. It makes all the things that we eat that are based on starch. Teach this to your children. The first time they hear it they will just listen mechanically, but don't think they are not hearing it. Their minds are registering it. Someday they are going to be happy with the rain. All their lives they will have a certain feeling of optimism when they see the rain. If they do not learn this, all their lives they will be negative and disappointed when it is raining. If you plant the seed in their minds now, that seed will take root and produce a beautiful tree that will bear the fruit of happiness.

Teach children how good it is to have a warm home. When I was a boy, only one place in the house was warm — the kitchen stove. We used to lie on the floor by the kitchen stove to keep warm. Today everyone has some form of heat, and the whole house is warm and, Baruch Hashem, you walk in and you thank Hashem that it is warm in the house. Hakadosh Baruch Hu put the fuel into the earth right at the beginning, at the time of *beri'as ha'olam*. He put metal and all the other substances into the earth. As soon as the earth was created it had everything it needed.

And there is the happiness of *begadim*, clothing. You have woolen suits. Wool imprisons the air to keep you warm. Wool doesn't warm you, it only keeps you warm; your body produces the warmth. That is the *neis*. We eat food and the body burns it and makes heat, but the heat is taken out of the body because there is air around it that carries off the heat. But when you have a woolen suit that keeps the heat in the body, the heat doesn't go out. It is a miracle that Hashem

25. See *Rejoice O Youth* p. 313 (705), *Awake My Glory*
26. See *Rejoice O Youth* p. 314 (708); *Sing You Righteous* p. 315 (706), p. 289 (930); *Praise My Soul* p. 256 (747)

is doing for us — *al nisecha shebechol yom imanu*, the miracles that are with us *every* day. We have to thank Him and be happy that we have garments. *Baruch Atah Hashem malbish arumim*, how beautiful it is to have buttons, zippers and pockets, and coated fabrics. Once upon a time they didn't have coated fabrics, they had plain fabrics, and if you stuck your hand in, you tore the sleeve hole. Baruch Hashem, today everything is made with so much convenience. Once as I was looking at the cars on Ocean Parkway going back and forth I thought about how, when I was a little boy, only horses and wagons went back and forth. Isn't it a miracle that automobiles go back and forth without horses pulling them?

By implanting this happiness and optimistic outlook in the minds of your family members, you are giving them a gift that will stand them in good stead forever. It is like looking at the world through pink glasses: the world looks rosy to you; and that is what Hakadosh Baruch Hu wanted us to teach our children. Hashem wants us to say these same words always — *tov me'od*, it is a very good world.

Another important principle to teach the children is that the house is a place where you can do many mitzvos more easily. For example, when the mother says to carry the garbage can out to the street, don't say, "Let Chaim do it." *You* should be the one to do it. Doing that is no less a mitzvah than putting on tefillin. *Kibbud av va'eim* is a mitzvah of the Torah no less than any other mitzvah, and there are many opportunities for *kibbud av va'eim* in the house. Not only should these mitzvos not be refused, *chas veshalom*, they should be asked for. You should ask your father to sit down and let you bring him a glass of water. Tell your mother to sit down so you can serve her. Whenever possible, try to take the mitzvah that is available only as long as your parents are alive, because after your parents pass away the opportunity won't be the same. *Mechabdo bechayav u'mechabdo bemisaso*[27] — you have to honor them even after they die; drop a nickel in the pushke every day in memory of your father and your mother, to give them the *zechus*. It is too late, however, to do the real mitzvah. The real mitzvah is as long as they are alive.[28] A father or mother is a *cheifetz* — an object — of a mitzvah, a tremendous opportunity. The children should realize that this opportunity will not last forever. Someday they will be sorry that they lost it. They could have gained thousands of mitzvos in that house.

---

27. *Kiddushin* 31b
28. See *Awake My Glory* p. 370 (1165)

In addition, a Jewish home is a place for mitzvos *bein adam lachaveiro*. Utilize your brothers and your sisters. If you speak to them kindly — what an important *chessed* that is. *Me'oded anavim Hashem*,[29] Hashem wants people to be encouraged — speak words of encouragement. Sometimes brothers and sister hurt each other's feelings and ridicule each other. This is a terrible misuse of opportunity. Someday you will scatter and each one will look back on the days when the brothers and sisters were together; by then the opportunity will be gone. There are so many opportunities to gain a tremendous mitzvah by saying a few kind words.[30]

The Gemara says that by giving tzedakah to a poor man — *hanosein perutah le'ani nisbareich sheish berachos*[31] — you gain six berachos. *Vehamefayeso*, if you speak kind words to him, *misbarech yud-alef* — you will get eleven more berachos for those kind words. Say *shalom aleichem* to a poor man when you give him a dollar. "How are you, my friend? I wish you well. Be well. *Schep* nachas" — he will be surprised to hear it. Hakadosh Baruch Hu said for this you are getting eleven berachos besides the six berachos you are getting for the money you gave him. Even if your brother and sister don't need money from you, they still need good words; everyone needs encouragement. Even wealthy people need encouragement. This mitzvah of encouraging our fellow man is a neglected mitzvah that is waiting for us. Our fellow men were created in order for us to utilize them and to gain the great *zechus* of saying kindly words, to give *chizuk* to them. Brother and sister provide the best opportunities for this; they are always available in the house. They are among the sources of *ma'asim tovim* if they understand this great opportunity of encouraging each other.

Of course it is a very big thing to learn in the house. A person should learn Torah any place he is. If you open a *sefer* in your house, you are making the house *kadosh*, a *bayis shenishma bo divrei Torah baleilos*, a house in which you hear words of Torah. The house will be made holy and elevated by the words of the Torah you are learning there. It is a place where people are doing good things. You have many mitzvos in the house: all the mitzvos of Shabbos, the mitzvos of berachos, all the mitzvos connected with *netilas*

---

29. *Tehillim* 147:10
30. See *Awake My Glory* p. 376 (1189)
31. *Bava Basra* 9b

yadayim ... countless mitzvos are accomplished in the house. It is a place where you can say *asher kidshanu bemitzvosav vetzivanu al netilas yadayim*. Hashem commanded you to obey the Sages, and by doing the mitzvah of washing your hands you are making the house *kadosh*; but you have to think what you are saying. Train your children to recognize that the house is becoming elevated by means of mitzvos. The more they are able to behave, the more they make each other happy, the more they can honor their father and mother, the more they can open a *sefer*, the more they can serve Hashem in the house — the more they can make the house holy, and the house is blessed. It is a different kind of a house when it is utilized for the purpose of serving Hashem.[32]

Every room in a Jewish house has a mezuzah on the doorpost. Some people kiss mezuzos, but that is not enough. The mezuzah reminds you that Hashem is One, and that you should love Hashem. That is what is written on the mezuzah. It tells us to love Him with all our heart, with all our thoughts, with all our desires. To love Hashem is a subject that is not spoken about enough. When you sit in your house — not only when you walk through the door — look at the mezuzah and love Hashem.[33] It is a mitzvah you can do immediately. Even though you are not head over heels in love with Hashem yet, even if it is an "artificial" love, do it anyway. If you just say it with your mouth, it is even better. Say, "I love You, Hashem." If you did that once in your life, you are an exception. After 120 years, you will wish you could come back to this world for even one minute to say it, but it will be too late then. Hashem will say: I gave you plenty of time when you were on earth, but you didn't utilize your life.

Say, I love You, Hashem

SO DO IT RIGHT NOW. NO ONE HAS TO LISTEN. SAY, "I LOVE YOU, Hashem." What an achievement that is! You are making the house *kadosh* by utilizing the mezuzos, which remind you that Hashem is *Echad*, Hashem is One. He is everything in the world to us. Everything that you can desire, all your ambitions, are in Hashem. We may be far away from the ideal, but at least think about it and strive to come closer to it, and create some superficial resemblance to the love of Hashem.

32. See *Awake My Glory* p. 350 (1115)
33. See *Awake My Glory* p. 377 (1191)

Little by little it will become more and more sincere. As you continue to repeat it, it will come to mean something to you.

So when you are sitting in your house, look at the mezuzos from time to time. Remind yourself that Hashem is there and is waiting to hear the words "I love you, Hashem," *bechol levavecha*, with all your thoughts. You may not do it with *all* your thoughts, but at least love Him a little bit. Teach your children to say, "I love You, Hashem." Let all the children say it in chorus. You will plant a seed in their minds forever. They will be different people. Once you say, "I love You, Hashem," you are transformed entirely. The mezuzos are there for the purpose of reminding us always of the most important things in the world. Hashem thinks about us more than anything else in the world, and we should think about Him more than anything else in the world. He loves us so much, let us think about Him a little bit once in a while. The mezuzah is a grand opportunity to be reminded of Him.

Speak about great people by your table

ANOTHER IMPORTANT POINT TO BRING UP IS TABLE TALK. WHENEVER you are sitting at the table eating, with your wife alone or with your wife and children, you should know that it is an opportunity to be a propagandist for the great truths of the Torah. Before you come to the table, take a minute to think about what you are going to do at the table, how can you best utilize the opportunity. For instance, one day you decide to talk about the Roshei Yeshivos, and you sit at the table with your children and say, "Children, the Roshei Yeshivos are our leaders." The children are busy eating; they are hardly listening, but say it anyway: They are our leaders, the teachers of our people. We should always love the Roshei Yeshivos and speak about them. They are great, holy men; they are devoted to the study of the Torah; they are bringing up our nation's youth in the ways of the Torah. We should appreciate them and praise them as much as we can.[34]

Rabbeinu Yonah says in *Sha'arei Teshuvah* that when you take out time to praise righteous people, you will gain such merit that it will go all the way up to the Heavens. Praise not only Roshei Yeshivos, but also all frum Jews and frum institutions. Praise Bais

---

34. See *Awake My Glory* p. 379 (1197), *Career of Happiness* pp. 56, 64

Yaakov or Bais Rochel for teaching girls the way of the Torah. There are crowds of frum girls, all of them idealistic, who will become mothers of big families. What a wonderful thing they are doing. Praise all the *yeshivos ketanos*, the *mesivtas*, the *kollelim*. Praise all the houses that have big mezuzos on them. Praise all the good things. But you should think about all these things beforehand. Plan your action before you come to the table. Plan in advance what you will talk about today.

Speak about yetzi'as Mitzrayim by your table

PLAN THAT TODAY YOU ARE GOING TO TALK ABOUT THE GREAT SUBJECT of *yetzi'as Mitzrayim*. Speak about it briefly at the table. Another day, do what the Rambam says: *Rak hishamer lecha ushmor nafshecha me'od, pen tishkach es hadevarim asher ra'u einecha, yom asher amadta lifnei Hashem Elokecha beChorev*, never forget the greatest day in history, when we all stood around *Har Sinai* and heard the words of Hashem. The children won't know that it was planned. They'll think you got inspired and just happened to mention it. It is a wonderful idea: every time you go to the table, plan what you are going to speak about today, especially at the Shabbos table. There shouldn't be just chatter, incidental talk coming out by accident. Think beforehand, and guide the conversation in that direction, and you will see tremendous benefits — you are shaping the minds of your family and yourself forever. Table talk is extremely important in a holy Jewish house. Of course there will be some ordinary talk too — they are human beings, after all. But at least if the table is utilized with some noble purpose, then some great idea was introduced at the table this time, and next time there will be another great idea. There are so many important ideas that we have to talk about that are not being spoken about at all.

Speak about David Hamelech by your table

TALK, FOR EXAMPLE, ABOUT THE GREATNESS OF DAVID HAMELECH'S accomplishment in writing *sefer Tehillim*. David made a revolution in the world when he made *Tehillim*. To this day, the whole Jewish nation is reciting David's words every day. Even the gentiles are saying David's words constantly. When David came along with this chiddush of speaking the praises of Hashem, don't think everyone accepted it; he had opposition. Some said not to waste time on that. Talk about Torah, halachos, specific *dinim*, they said, but David persisted in singing to Hashem. He sang to Hashem — *barchi nafshi es Hashem, Hashem Elokai gadalta me'od, hod vehadar lavashta*, You wore the splendor and the majesty. He spoke about the greatness of Hashem and all the great things that Hashem does for the world. And little by little, the world began to accept David's' praises, to the point that the Gemara says two shepherds arose from our nation who had no equal. One shepherd was Moshe Rabbeinu and one was David Hamelech. What David accomplished was almost unequaled.

Speak out the greatness of *Tehillim*. This doesn't mean that you are telling your children to say *Tehillim*. Let them appreciate the tremendous achievement that was made for our nation. We breathe the spirit of David that enters our *neshamos* every day; *Ashrei yoshvei veisecha* — what a beautiful, inspiring point! Anyone who says *Ashrei* three times a day is promised *Olam Haba*. The benefits of saying it are so great and the inspiration elevates you so much that you deserve *Olam Haba*. That is to the credit of that great man who introduced to the Jewish nation the tremendous procedure of speaking the praises of Hashem.

Make all Yomim Tovim joyous occasions

ANOTHER IMPORTANT ELEMENT IN THE JEWISH HOME IS GOOD TIMES, celebration. You should fill your home with celebrations, and not only on Shabbos[35] — sing *zemiros* for Shabbos, make it a joyous occasion — but make every Yom Tov joyous, too. Make Chanukah a joyous time in your home. Make Purim a tremendous day. Make it a house of joy and exhilaration, so that it should be remembered forever. The songs of Purim should ring in you family's ears[36] throughout the entire year. Even on Tu BiShvat, bring in various samples of new fruits that you ordinarily don't have in the house, and let everyone taste the fruit and make a berachah and thank Hakadosh Baruch Hu for the great blessing of fruit. Fruit of the trees is one of the greatest demonstrations of Hashem's kindliness. Fruit is a delicacy, wrapped in beautiful wrappers that Hashem provided. It tastes wonderful and it is healthful too. In Gan Eden, when Adam Harishon saw the fruit he became elevated and appreciated the greatness of Hashem.

---

35. See *Awake My Glory* p. 352 (1121)
36. See *Awake My Glory* p. 354 (1124)

Look at the beautiful apple

AS IT SAYS, "*NECHMAD HA'EITZ LEHASKIL*[37] — THE TREE WAS DESIRABLE to make wise." Look at the beautiful apple and see the redness of the apple.[38] Inside there are seeds, and each seed is more important than the greatest machine you could ever develop by human ingenuity, because one apple seed has millions of bits of data that are necessary to produce an apple tree. Put the seed in the ground, and it gets busy. Without asking for your advice or help it produces a tree with branches and leaves and blossoms and nectar to attract the bees, and it produces apples with seeds in them. And so each seed in an apple should be kept in your pocket always. Look at it from time to time and remind yourself that this seed is more powerful than any computer you could buy. No computer contains as much data as this little seed does. When you eat fruits on Tu BiShvat, it is a glorious opportunity to recognize the kindliness and wisdom of Hashem, the Creator.

The home should be remembered always with great longing

MAKE *MELAVEH MALKAHS* JOYOUS OCCASIONS, TOO. DON'T JUST SIT down *motza'ei Shabbos* and eat. Make a little ceremony there, maybe sing some special, beautiful *zemiros* for the *melaveh malkah*. Whenever you have an occasion to make joyous occasions in the house, always utilize it. The house should be a place to be remembered.

Don't go to a hotel for the seder. Make a seder in the house, and the children will always remember it. Even poets and artists remember the seders they had when they were young. The pictures of the seder are among the most beautiful pictures you will find. At every occasion when you can elevate the mind by some holy happiness, simchah should be introduced into the house. The home should be remembered always with great longing, home sweet home. That is where we had so many good times — in our home.[39]

Encourage your children

ALSO, THE PARENTS CAN MAKE THE HOUSE A PLACE OF SIMCHAH BY encouraging children. As much as possible, when you see something

---

37. *Bereishis* 3:6
38. See *The Beginning* p. 88 (3:6)
39. See *Awake My Glory* p. 371 (1169)

good being done by a child, praise that child. Don't take it for granted. For anything that he does properly, praise him and encourage him. If a child helps a little bit, don't just take it for granted; speak up and be excited about it. What a good boy or good girl this one is! Little by little the child gets to feel: This is the place where I am going to earn encouragement; and he tries his best to be better and better. And children will always remember how happy it was when they were young, when their parents encouraged them and strengthened their spirits with their words. Say words that always make them feel good. "You are a smart boy!" "You are a smart girl!" "You are a good boy!" "You are a good girl." "We like you very much." "We know you are doing very well." "You are behaving very well." Say that, even if it's not true. Keep on praising the children; let them feel that they are getting from you what they want — and they want you to praise them.

Practice saying all berachos out loud

ANOTHER POINT IS MAKING BERACHOS IN THE HOUSE. ALL FRUM JEWS make berachos, but it is made under their breath; you can hardly hear what they are saying. Make your family practice to say all berachos out loud. If you are giving a child a nosh, make him say *shehakol nihyeh bidvaro* aloud. And tell them: When you are saying these words, you should know that you are gaining a very great mitzvah. *Chayav adam levarech me'ah berachos bechol yom*,[40] you have to say a hundred *berachos* every day.[41] But whenever you say them, say them with a little bit of thought. *Baruch*, we bend our knees to You, Hashem, *Atah*, only to You, *Hashem Elokeinu*, You are the *Melech ha'olam*, Who gave me such and such thing. *Borei peri ha'eitz*, You gave me this pear, or this apple; and say the berachah aloud, with feeling, and train your family to say berachos aloud constantly. By saying berachos out loud they will gain the habit of thanking Hashem not only for the food that they eat but for other things, too.

There is so much to thank Hashem for. There are so many things in this world that Hashem is doing for us. Did you thank Hashem that you can walk? There are so many people who cannot walk. They are sitting in wheelchairs, and you stride by with sturdy legs. You make a berachah in the morning *hameichin mitzadei gaver*, You establish the footsteps of man. How many people don't have eyesight? You go out with your two good eyes; you could see and enjoy anything. Your

---

40. *Menachos* 43b
41. See *Awake My Glory* p. 348 (1112)

eyes are two beautiful cameras taking color photographs constantly. You are enjoying life. *Baruch Atah Hashem pokei'ach ivrim*, He opens the eyes of the blind.

Thank Hashem you can sleep

SOME PEOPLE ARE NOT ABLE TO SLEEP. YOU PUT YOUR HEAD ON THE pillow and you immediately fall into a deep sleep. You have to make a berachah before you go to sleep at night. *Hamapil chevlei sheinah*, thank You, Hashem, for putting sleep on my eyes. Are you thanking Hashem for the ability to sleep? Some people lose their ability to sleep in their old age. They are broken. They never get rest anymore. Young, healthy people should thank Hashem that they can sleep. You need happiness to sleep well. When you get up in the morning you are a new personality, you are refreshed. Sleep is more important than food. Get in the habit of thanking Hashem.

Many times some people are unable to relieve themselves, and they don't know what to do. They are desperate. Sometimes they even harm themselves by using artificial means. But you relieve yourself easily. You should feel what a great kindness Hashem has done. What a relief! *Rofeh chol basar*, You heal all flesh. You should be so happy that you can perform your needs so easily. Learn the practice of saying berachos, *rofeh chol basar*, thank You, Hashem, for giving me good health. There are hundreds of things to thank Hashem for. Even if there is no standard berachah to say for many of these things, thank Hashem for them.

You have teeth. Many people have only false teeth, and they are not the same as your own teeth. What a pleasure to eat with your own teeth! Do you thank Hashem for your teeth?

And so we are full of all kinds of gifts that Hashem has given us, and we should learn to thank Hashem for these things. By doing that, we are introducing into our homes a spirit of gratitude to Hashem. Hashem says: That is a house that I have chosen, and that house will live forever. If the house will be knocked down by a builder, even after a hundred years the house is not lost. Someday the house will rise again, in *techiyas hameisim*. All the glory of the Jewish home will someday be created. So *chochmas nashim*, wise women build homes. They try their best, and wise men build the home with all the complements that are necessary to build this structure; and Hakadosh Baruch Hu will bless them with great happiness forever, and the *zechus* of the house will stand by them.

TEN EASY STEPS TO GREATNESS 13

"*B*E'DERECH SHE'ADAM ROTZEH LEILEICH BAH MOLICHIN *oso*[1] — In the way a man chooses to go, he is led." This means that if someone makes an attempt to do something — even on a small scale — he is promised by Hakadosh Baruch Hu that his attempt will produce results greater than the effort he put into it. This is in line with the well-known principle, "*Haba litaher mesayin oso*"[2] — If a person comes to purify himself [meaning to improve himself], Hashem will open up the channels and make it easier for him. Or, as our Sages tell us, Hakadosh Baruch Hu says, "*Pischu Li pesach kepischo shel machat ...*"[3] — Open for Me an opening as big as the eye of a needle, and I will open a doorway for you as wide as the gateway to the *Beis Hamikdash*! For a small effort, we are promised great rewards.

We will discuss ten easy ways of accomplishing great results, but you must realize that, first, although they are easy, they are very

---

1. *Makkos* 10b
2. *Shabbos* 104a
3. *Midrash Shir Hashirim* 5:3

important, because they will lead to great results; and second, they are effective only if you do them, and doing means you must do them again and again — then, *min haShamayim*, you are assured of great results.

The first step:

Hashem performs wonders in order for us to remember them

WE LISTEN TO THE ADVICE OF DAVID HAMELECH, WHO TELLS US "*Zichru nifle'osav asher asah*[4] — remember the wonders that He performed." The question arises: If they are *nifle'osav*, His wonders, isn't it superfluous to say that He performed them? This comes to tell us that He performed them *in order* for you to remember them.[5]

He gives us some examples of these wonders in *Tehillim, perek* 105. We can choose to think every day for a whole minute — sixty seconds — about that great miracle never equaled before or after, that a nation of two million people ate food that fell from the sky — not for one day, but for forty years. The *meshorer* is urging us: *zichru*, remember, *nifle'osav*, His wonders. Talk about it and think about it often. *Bakshu panav tamid*,[6] You, Hashem, did such great things for our forefathers, and in the merit of our remembering it, we ask You to do things for us today.

It is the *zichru* that we are emphasizing. Stop for a minute and think about the fact that the nation had no source of livelihood, no fields to till, no trees, no orchards, no vineyards. Although they didn't plow, they survived for forty years in the wilderness.[7] Today, we still have a memorial to the mann — every Shabbos we put two loaves on the table and cover them with a white cloth, in memory of the double portion that fell erev Shabbos — one portion for Friday and one for Shabbos. It fell between two sheets — the mann fell onto a sheet of dew on the ground, and then a sheet of dew fell on top of the mann. It was packed untouched by human hands, and it was nourishing. It was just as good as eating meat and bread and vitamins. *Zichru nifle'osav*, remember that!

---

4. *Tehillim* 105:5
5. See *Praise My Soul* p. 40 (112)
6. *Tehillim* 105:4
7. See *Praise My Soul* p. 38 (106)

Talk about the great miracle of the mann

THIS *NEIS* WAS MADE ONLY FOR THE PURPOSE OF REMEMBERING; IT wasn't made because it was necessary. Hakadosh Baruch Hu could have supplied them with food in other ways. When they went out of Mitzrayim they were loaded down with wealth — *Venitzaltem es Mitzrayim*,[8] they emptied out Egypt. They could have had a brisk trade with caravans that passed by; they could have bought whatever they wanted. Hakadosh Baruch Hu has many ways of feeding even the greatest multitudes: *Hayad Hashem tiktzar*,[9] Hashem's Hand never falls short. But He gave us mann *lemishmeres ledoroseichem*[10] — so that we should always talk about it. Yet even people who have *lechem mishneh* at the table on Shabbos don't stop to think about it, and that means that, as far as they are concerned, the mann came down for nothing. The reason the mann came down is so that they should tell it to their children, and those children to their children; and we have to tell it to ourselves.[11]

If we spend one whole minute every day fulfilling *zichru nifla'osav asher asah* about the mann, then we are going to have a great deal of *siyata diShmaya*, because Hakadosh Baruch Hu made the mann in order to teach the world *de'ah*. *Veyadata hayom vehasheivosa el levavecha*[12] — the purpose of all these great events was to teach us awareness of Hashem.

Many people talk about Hakadosh Baruch Hu in such an ambiguous way, because He is really very far from their hearts. "*Karov Atah befihem verachok mikilyoseihem*[13] — You are close in their mouths, but You are far away from their insides." They don't feel the nearness of Hashem, although there are *nissim* that were made for the purpose of giving us an awareness of Hakadosh Baruch Hu!

Talk about the splitting of the Red Sea between customers, or on the train

THERE ARE OTHER *NISSIM* YOU CAN FOCUS ON. YOU COULD TALK about *keri'as Yam Suf*: If you are riding in the subway and you

---

8. *Shemos* 12:36
9. *Bamidbar* 11:23
10. *Shemos* 16:32
11. See *A Nation is Born* p. 221 (16:32)
12. *Devarim* 4:39
13. *Yirmiyahu* 12:2

think, "I want to fulfill one of the ten steps to greatness, I want to accomplish something today," then while you hold onto the strap, think of that great spectacle, *bokei'a yam lifnei Moshe*, the sea opened up before Moshe, and Bnei Yisrael walked on dry land in the midst of the sea. Then, when they gained the other side, and a huge army of chariots and horsemen armed to the teeth were chasing after them and entered into the sea, suddenly the two great walls of water collapsed and they went down like stones to the bottom of the sea. There was an earthquake and the bottom of the sea opened up. *Tivla'eimo aretz*,[14] and they were swallowed up.

Imagine what our forefathers experienced on that day. Hakadosh Baruch Hu didn't need that; He could have made Pharaoh get pneumonia that day and put off the chase, and in the meantime, Bnei Yisrael could have escaped without any miracles. But it was done for a purpose — *Az yashir Moshe uVnei Yisrael*,[15] that they should sing forever, as we still do. If you come to davening in time for *pesukei dezimrah*, you could say the *shiras hayam*, but even then, you might be napping while you're saying it; you might be taking a trip to, say, South Africa while you say these words, and you might come back only when you are saying *Yishtabach*, and you missed the whole point. In that case, you could make up for it on the subway, by thinking about that grand spectacle — *vaya'aminu baHashem u'veMoshe avdo*,[16] they believed in Hashem forever as a result of that. That *neis* gave us a push, and the Jewish nation is still running today with the force of that great event; it is dynamite inside of us. It will recharge your batteries when you are holding onto the strap on the subway, or when you are standing behind the counter of your store. Between customers, say, "I want to fulfill that one function of our ten steps to greatness," and you will think about *keri'as Yam Suf* in your own terms, describing it better than I am now.

Think about Matan Torah

Y OU CAN ALSO THINK AND TALK ABOUT *MATAN TORAH*, THAT MOST important event in history, *yom asher amadta lifnei Hashem Elokecha beChoreiv*,[17] when the whole Jewish nation was assembled

---

14. *Shemos* 15:12
15. *Shemos* 15:1
16. *Shemos* 14:31
17. *Devarim* 4:10

together, and the grand Voice spoke from on top of the mountain. They didn't have loudspeakers in those days. It was a voice that thundered from *Har Sinai*, and everyone heard "*Anochi Hashem Elokecha*," and as one man they shouted, "*na'aseh venishma*, we will do and we will learn." The event was so overwhelming that they fainted from ecstasy, *nafshi yatza bedabero*[18] — they more than fainted; they had to be revived. A *tal shel techiyah*, a revivifyng dew, was an event unequaled. No one else even dared to invent such a story for another religion.

Think for one minute, and you can change

IF YOU WILL THINK ABOUT THESE THINGS FOR ONE MINUTE A DAY, YOU can change, and Hakadosh Baruch Hu will say: This man is trying, and I am going to help him more and more. He is going to gain that great attribute of *yiras Hashem* — *Reishis chochmah yiras Hashem*,[19] believing in Hashem implicitly. The purpose of the miracles was to implant the seed of *emunah* in our hearts, and it will grow more and more as the years go by. That little thought of one minute that you invest now is not going to stop; it is going to start sending out roots and a stem and branches. It will bear fruit, and the fruit will fall on fertile soil, and more trees and eventually an orchard will grow. A whole vineyard of *emunah* will develop in your mind if you will plant these seeds as we described them today.

That is one of the easy steps that anyone who wishes to approach greatness and find favor in the eyes of Hashem can fulfill, every day for at least one minute, and *kol hamosif mosifim lo* — if you want to add another minute, even better — you will get a double impetus *min haShamayim*. It is a pitiful waste of our lives if we don't do this every day!

The second step:

"*Vaya'as Hashem Elokim le'Adam ulishto kosnos ohr vayalbisheim*[20] — Hashem made for Adam and his wife tunics, and He clothed them." There are two ways of explaining this pasuk. One is that Hakadosh Baruch Hu fashioned garments; He wanted Adam and his wife to realize who they were. Adam and his wife had already sewed leaves of a fig tree to cover their nakedness, but Hakadosh

---

18. *Shir Hashirim* 5:6
19. *Tehillim* 111:10
20. *Bereishis* 3:21

Baruch Hu said: You are underestimating yourselves; you think the purpose is only to cover your nakedness, but you must demonstrate how great man is. Man is next to Hashem in stature in the universe. His mind and his soul are infinite; the greatness of humankind is beyond our ability to fathom. How could Hashem demonstrate that man is the grand purpose of all creation? He did it by putting garments on them.

Garments give us dignity

NOTHING IN THE WORLD WEARS GARMENTS. PUT MONKEYS IN A college laboratory and dress them with clothes, and within a few days the clothing will become rags and will tear into pieces. Monkeys will never learn to wear clothing like a human being, because it doesn't belong on them; it is superfluous. A monkey has a shaggy coat that grows on him naturally, and he is happy with it. But Hakadosh Baruch Hu gave Adam a nature capable of wearing garments, and the purpose is not merely to keep him warm or to protect him from the heat, but to demonstrate the greatness of mankind. Like Rabbi Yochanan said, *manei mechabdusei*, the garments give us dignity.

Clothing demonstrates that we have a soul

SO AS YOU PUT ON YOUR COAT, YOUR SHIRT, AND YOUR SHOES, KNOW that it is for the purpose of demonstrating that you have a neshamah,[21] a soul within you, and your neshamah has nothing to do with any animal. A human mind could never develop by chance from molecules that united to form proteins and accidentally, randomly, made electric circuits, hundreds of thousands of such circuits in the mind working together, more complicated than any machine man could ever devise! *Adam yetzir kapav shel Hakadosh Baruch Hu*, man is a masterpiece fashioned by Hashem's Hand.

You have no idea
what wisdom went into making a seed

THE TRUTH IS, EVERYTHING IS A MASTERPIECE — EVEN AN ANT; EVEN A seed. You have no idea what wisdom and cunning went into making a seed. But man is the purpose of creation, and our job is to show

---

21. See *The Beginning* p. 104 (3:21)

the world that truth. We have to demonstrate that a man is not an animal. He can't walk in the street half naked, even though it is hot. Clothing is your dignity at all times, to demonstrate to yourself that you and your donkey are two different worlds.

Isn't it fun to have pockets?

THERE IS NOTHING LIKE YOU. EVEN ANGELS CANNOT COMPARE TO YOU; that is our tradition. In order to know what a gift Hashem gave us by creating us as humans, it is imperative that we utilize the garments. Every morning, if you think, "I want to fulfill one of the ten steps to perfection — it is not so difficult, and I want Hakadosh Baruch Hu to say: This man is trying, and I am going to give him a lot of success," then when you put on any garment, choose one element of the garment and think what a gift that is. Do monkeys or elephants wear stockings? Any garment that you wear is a demonstration of the greatness of mankind. Spend one whole minute on that great exercise. Yesterday you were happy with your coat or your dress, which declared that you are a *tzelem Elokim*. Today, think about the fact that it has pockets — an added convenience. Isn't it fun to have pockets? If you didn't have any pockets in any of your garments, you would have to carry a handbag, and someone could snatch it from you if you walked in certain neighborhoods. Pockets are a blessing!

The miracle of wool

THE SECOND WAY OF UNDERSTANDING THE PASUK OF *VAYA'AS HASHEM Elokim le'adam ulishto kosnos ohr*[22] is, as Rav Saadia Gaon explains, that He supplied them with natural fibers. Hashem caused cotton to grow. It is not made for animals to eat — no one can eat cotton, or linen or wool. Nothing in the world uses those fibers except human beings. Think about the miracle of these fibers: A sheep is born almost naked, but he drinks his mother's milk and becomes a big sheep, and then he starts eating grass. He is nothing but grass and water. A sheep does not eat wool, yet year after year he produces a thick coat of wool. Where does wool come from? The sheep is such a technician; he has laboratories all over his skin that are capable of taking the grass and water and breaking them down into simple components and recombining them in such a marvelous combination that becomes wool, which

---

22. See *The Beginning* p. 103 (?3:21)

shoves itself through the pores in its hide. That is the suit that you are wearing. Who made this miracle? Hashem *Elokim* — *Vaya'as Hashem Elokim le'Adam u'lishto!*

You have a long life ahead of you, I hope, so every day you can utilize that minute to think about this. You may be sitting at your meal and have nothing to do but eat; if you think while you are eating, or while you are walking in the street, take out one minute of the millions of minutes of your life, and live for a purpose. That is called living. Don't waste your life! Spend time thinking about your garments and appreciate them. After all, we say every day, "*Baruch Atah Hashem malbish arumim,* You clothe the naked." I know a man who was kidnapped by gangsters, and they let him out without clothes, outside of New York, and it was cold. Suppose someone would come around just at the right moment and offer him a suit — it would be a lifesaver!

Garments are made to make you aware of Hashem's plan for you

THAT IS WHAT HASHEM DOES EVERY DAY. HE IS A LIFESAVER TO US. WE have nothing — we are naked children, and we ask Hashem: Ribbono Shel Olam, give us our garments for today, and He gives you your garments. He lends them to you again and again. The time will come when He won't lend them to you anymore — they don't put a suit on a dead man; there are different garments for him. Once I was watching a dead man being clothed with his final garments, and I was thinking: He will never put on shoes again; he will never wear a hat again. How lucky we are that we can look forward to the great opportunity every day to make something of ourselves. Garments are not to clothe yourself but to make you aware of Hakadosh Baruch Hu's plan for you.

So when you say *malbish arumin* every day, give the words a little thought; and if you will add to that one minute of thinking about this every day, that is a step toward greatness that will give you endless reward. You will have great success in this world, because Hakadosh Baruch Hu has opened up your eyes, and you will begin to see things no one else saw. So far you've seen something that no one sees — that wool comes from grass. Can any huge, innovative chemical company today take grass and change it into wool? It is much too complicated a project for them to do.

We can utilize that minute to marvel at the purpose and the miracles and the benefits of the garments. Just think how your clothes have a slippery lining, so your hand can go into the sleeve easily. In the olden days they had rough linings, and you had to push and shove for your hand to get into the sleeve. It is a pleasure now. You put your hand in the sleeve and it slides in as if it were greased. You have to appreciate every detail of your garments.

When a man opens up the doorway *kepischo shel machat*, even as tiny as a hole in a needle, in this way, then Hakadosh Baruch Hu says: That is the opening for Me — I will give you as a reward, a very great opportunity, *kepischo shel ulam*, as wide as the entranceway to the *Beis Hamikdash*.

The third step:

When you are standing at the threshold of your house, look ahead

"EIZEHU CHACHAM HARO'EH ES HANOLAD[23] — WHO IS A WISE MAN? He who foresees the future." This is speaking not only about looking ahead ten years into the future. If you can foresee five minutes from now, you are a big chacham. As you come home and you are standing at the threshold of your house, look ahead to the first welcome you will get from your wife. Will she say, "How are you, Chaim, how was business today?" — or will she say, "Look how late he comes! I was by myself fighting with the kids all day, and here comes this big shot and I have to make supper for him!"? You have to be prepared for everything; even the best wife or the best husband sometimes loses patience and flies off the handle.

So as you stand at the doorway and think, "I want to accomplish number three on Rabbi Miller's list of steps to greatness and be *haro'eh es hanolad*," then think about what is going to happen on the other side of the door. If you are assailed by a storm of abuse, you can think, "I will be a servant of Hashem." Every day we say, "*venafshi ke'afar lakol tihyeh*," my soul should be like dust for everyone to step on. You could fulfill it at least once. When your wife meets you angrily, you could smile to her and say, "Chana, the house looks beautiful! You look beautiful! The children look beautiful!" Even if she says, "Stop fooling me," you have succeeded; you have come one step closer to greatness, and as a result, Hakadosh Baruch Hu is going to pour a full measure of perfection into you.

---

23. *Tamid* 32b

Spend one minute a day planning ahead

THIS ABILITY TO LOOK AHEAD IS EXTREMELY VALUABLE. ONCE A DAY, spend one minute planning ahead. Think about what is going to happen in your life in the next ten minutes. You can't know what is going to happen, but picture what could happen, and what should be your reaction to any eventuality. Before you enter the beis medrash, for example, as you are walking, think about what lies ahead: Am I going to come late? Then I will have to deal with the problem of how to catch up. If I am too early, what will I do with an extra few minutes so that I don't just waste them? Maybe I will take a Gemara and learn for three or four minutes before davening — a big accomplishment! Maybe I will find that somebody there has a bad cold — I should choose a seat where he won't sneeze on me. Watching out for colds is also *ro'eh es hanolad!* Maybe there is someone there who likes to talk in the beis medrash — make sure not to sit near him.

Think ahead. If you are going to your place of business, or to see a customer to sell him your goods, think about what your customer will say when you display your merchandise, and think about what you can answer him. I am not talking about how to succeed in business or as a salesman; I am talking about success in the practice of looking ahead.

If you are making a wedding for your son or daughter, and you have met the parents of the chassan or kallah, but now you are going to meet the whole family — look ahead and think how you will react: There is a tough old man there in your wife's family who doesn't want a *mechitzah*, and he comes over to you with anger. What if you become frightened, and in your desperation you think you have to stop this man and push him to the floor? You may lose yourself, *chas veshalom*. There are all kinds of lunatics in families, and you can't tell what is going to happen at the chasunah, when everyone may be angry and excited. *Leis kesubah d'lo rami bei tigra*, there isn't a chasunah without someone being offended. You have to be prepared.

Practice thinking ahead before you enter any place

PRACTICE THINKING AHEAD BEFORE YOU ENTER ANY PLACE: ON THE threshold of your customer's place of business; on the threshold of your home; on the threshold of the beis medrash or shul; as you enter the bus — if you can, choose a good seat and sit near the bus driver. It is safer up front. Whatever you do, think a minute as you are walking toward the bus. Get into the habit of being a wise man, *haro'eh es hanolad*, who looks ahead. A little bit of practice will get you started on a career of having foresight. Maybe someday you will be able to think thirty days ahead. When the secretary of state has to make a statement about a certain country, he calls in all those who know the language of that country, and they have to formulate the language, and he talks to diplomats to find out what their reaction will be. Then he calls in the Pentagon people to consult about whether we are prepared to defend ourselves in case they attack our forces there. Before the secretary of state makes any decision, he goes to all the experts, and finally he comes up with a statement that includes as much as possible all the looking ahead that he could do. To be anybody in this world, you must have the ability to be *haro'eh es hanolad*.

The *Tanna'im* looked ahead and ahead and ahead, and they saw what would be the result of this deed all our days and in the Word to Come. If you do things for the ultimate goal, that is a real *ro'eh es hanolad*, but it is good to start out by spending one minute thinking ahead to the next ten minutes, and then Hakadosh Baruch Hu will say, "If you start in that direction, I will give you a good push and you will become somebody."

The fourth step:

Shmuel Hanavi's father Elkanah went up every year to the Mishkan of Shilo for Yom Tov with three purposes in mind: to bring his Yom Tov offerings in the Mishkan; to take council of the Kohanim Chofni and Pinchas, who were great men; and *lehishtachavos laHashem*, to bow down to Hashem.

To bow down to Hashem is extremely important — "*vehishtachavu laHashem behadras kodesh*,"[24] to bow down to Hashem with the glory of holiness. When you bend over at the beginning of *Shemoneh Esrei*, you should know — *da* — *lifnei Mi atah omeid*,[25] before Whom you are standing. Bowing down is a great form of avodas Hashem. *Romemu Hashem Elokeinu vehishtachavu*,[26] bow down to Him — utilize the opportunity.

---

24. *Tehillim* 29:2
25. *Berachos* 25b
26. *Tehillim* 99:9

It is fundamentally important for a man to realize that he is nothing at all

THE WORD *HISHTACHAVEH* IS A REFLEXIVE FORM OF THE WORD *shachah*, to be low, and it means to make yourself low. It is fundamentally important for a man to realize that he is nothing at all — people are born and they die and nothing is remembered of them; we are *afar va'eifer*, dust and ashes. When Moshe Rabbeinu said, "*Venachnu mah*," it was not merely an expression of humility, but the truth.[27]

The soul is extremely important

THE NESHAMAH, ON THE OTHER HAND, IS EXTREMELY IMPORTANT — IT is a *cheilek* of Hashem, breathed into man, but no one becomes arrogant because of the neshamah. All human pride is based on physical things — the looks or the size of a person's body, his strength or money or power.... It is extremely important to know that all physical and worldly qualities are nothing; you cannot do a thing to help yourself. *Hakol bidei Shamayim*, everything is in the hands of Heaven, and we are *kechomer beyad hayotzeir*,[28] like a piece of clay in Hashem's Hands.

David Hamelech said, "*Yadrich anavim bamishpat ...*"[29] — Hashem leads the humble with judgment, and He teaches the humble His way." Hashem chooses the humble ones; Moshe Rabbeinu was *anav mikol adam*, the most humble of men. This attribute of humility makes you beloved in the eyes of Hashem. All the wicked are proud and arrogant, and all our great men are humble people. *Kesher tefillin herah le'anav*[30] — Hashem showed Moshe the *kesher* of His tefillin because Moshe was an *anav*.

We must work on humility; humility is a form of *yiras Hashem*. You cannot be afraid of Hashem when you consider yourself important, when you are proud and arrogant and overbearing. How valuable is the accomplishment of a man who is able to lower himself before Hashem. This doesn't mean to lower yourself before *resha'im*. We lower ourselves before Hashem because that is the truth.

---

27. See *The Beginning* p. 56 (176)
28. *Yirmiyahu* 18:6
29. *Tehillim* 25:9
30. *Berachos* 7a

To succeed in life,
you must have humility

IF YOU WANT TO SUCCEED IN LIFE, YOU MUST HAVE HUMILITY. IN A BANK, who is sitting behind the desk of the vice president? It is a man who has humility — or at least he tries to show humility. When you come to complain to him, he listens to you politely. If you go outside and complain to the man who is sweeping the bank, he will answer you with anger. He gets angry, and that is why he is a janitor. If you want to be somebody, you have to have humility.

True humility is even better. It helps you in this world and in the Next World. If you want to remain married, you have to have humility. Sometimes husbands and wives fight only because they each want to lead the house. If both are humble, then she says, "Chaim, you take the lead," and he says, "Sarah, I will take the lead if you tell me to, but you are smarter than I am." (He should take the lead, by the way.)

When you bow down, tell Hashem,
I am humbling myself before You

HUMILITY IS A GIFT. *MAH SHE'ASESA ANAVAH EIKEV LESULYASAH asesah chochmah ateres leroshah. Eikev anavah yiras Hashem,*[31] "The heel of humility is *yiras Hashem*." *Yiras Hashem* is a great thing, but it is only the bottom of *anavah*. The heel of humility is *yiras Hashem*, but *reishis chochmah yiras Hashem*, the head of wisdom is *yiras Hashem*. *Yiras Hashem* is the top of wisdom, but when you get there, you start to climb another ladder. The ladder of *yiras Hashem* goes to *anavah*, which is the greatest of all attributes. When you bow down, it pays to utilize the opportunity to tell Hashem, "I am humbling myself before You."

When you bow down,
think about the greatness of Hashem

THE OTHER CHARACTERISTIC OF *HISHTACHAVEH* IS TO REALIZE THE greatness of Hakadosh Baruch Hu, Who is *Melech malchei hamelachim*, the King of the universe — He rules the entire universe. *Ligdulaso ein cheiker,*[32] there is no fathoming His greatness; this

31. *Midrash Shir Hashirim* 1:9
32. *Tehillim* 145:3

means we have to continue all our lives to think how great Hashem is. *Gadelu laHashem iti*,[33] attribute greatness to Hashem, and here is an opportunity, when you bow down before the greatness of the King of the universe. So you have these two elements that you could accomplish through the great *avodah* of *hishtachavu*. You can do this anytime during the day. When no one is looking, just bow down once to Hashem in order to fulfill this item on our agenda, and that will be an opening for Hashem to give you success to go further and further in greatness of *da'as* and character traits.

The fifth step:

When you say shalom aleichem, think what you are saying

IF YOU MEET SOMEONE ON THE STREET, AND HE SAYS "*SHALOM ALEICHEM*," he may not be thinking what he is saying, but when you answer him "*Shalom aleichem*," you should think what you are saying, because it makes a very big difference. Someone else may say *shalom aleichem* as a formality, but when you say it, you mean to say "I want you to have peace." Peace means success. He should have happiness. Everything should go well with him. That is what shalom means. In order to make sure that you are sincere in your greeting, as you walk away from him, repeat this blessing again, even if he doesn't hear it.

Anyone who blesses a Jew is going to get a berachah

HE MIGHT SAY "GOOD SHABBOS" OR "*MAZEL TOV*" OR ANY OTHER blessing but it is a formality. You could listen and then walk away, but if you repeat "Mazel tov" or "*Berachah vehatzlachah* to you," and you mean it, then you are a great man. When you do this, you are giving a berachah to yourself. Anyone who blesses a fellow Jew is going to get a berachah. Hakadosh Baruch Hu promised Avraham Avinu, "*va'avarechah mevaruchecha*[34] — I shall bless those who bless you." People think this means that if gentiles bless Jews they will get a berachah; what about Jews who bless Jews? The Gemara says that they will also get a berachah.[35]

---

33. *Tehillim* 34:4
34. *Bereishis* 12:3
35. See *The Beginning* p. 207 (12:3)

The Kohanim bless you with the words "*Yevarechecha ...,*" but who is blessing the Kohanim? "*Vesamu es Shemi al Bnei Yisrael va'ani avarecheim*[36] — they put My Name on Bnei Yisrael, and I will bless them." Who will I bless? There are two ways of interpreting this pasuk. One way is that if the Kohanim bless Bnei Yisrael, then I, Hashem, will bless Bnei Yisrael as a result. The other way is that if they bless the Bnei Yisrael, I, Hashem, will bless the Kohanim as a result.[37]

If you interpret the pasuk in the first way —they put My Name on Bnei Yisrael and I will bless Bnei Yisrael, then who blesses the Kohanim? The Gemara answers, *va'avarechah mevarachecha*, I will bless those who bless you. So we see that if you bless a fellow Jew, you will get a blessing from Hashem.

One morning, the Alter of Slobodka walked by a house with another yeshivah man and the Alter said to the house, "Good morning." The young man with him asked who hears his "good morning." The Alter answered, "They have to hear it?!" That is greatness: He said good morning not because he wants the man to hear it, but because he wants the man to have a good morning.

If you walk down a Jewish street, say good morning

IF YOU WALK DOWN A JEWISH STREET, SAY GOOD MORNING. GOOD morning means that they should have a good breakfast, that husband and wife should live in harmony, they should have nachas from their children, they should have a lot of parnasah, no colds today, no trouble in business. Good morning means everything. He should digest his food well, everything should work out perfectly ....

If you want to get a berachah from Hashem, then as you pass by a Jewish store, you bless the owner, even when he doesn't hear, that he should have a lot of big business today, that his wife shouldn't bother him, that the customers should all pay on time, that the merchandise delivered should have no blemishes ... that his daughters should get married quickly. As you pass by the store, it doesn't cost anything to do that, but it is big investment, because *va'avarechah mevarachecha*, I will bless those who bless you.

---

36. *Bamidbar* 6:27
37. See *Journey To Greatness* p. 74 (6:27)

When you say yasher koach, mean what you say

IF THE GABBAI GIVES YOU AN *ALIYAH*, SAY *"YASHER KOACH"* FOR THE *aliyah* — it doesn't mean a thing. But suppose the real phrase, *"yeyasher kochacha,"* is translated to mean "your strength should increase," you want that the gabbai to live longer because he gave you an *aliyah*; he called you up to the Torah. Think about the meaning of the words. All this may seem very silly; if you go outside and tell this to people, they will laugh at us, and we will laugh back. Yitzchak means he is the one who laughs last!

So every day, at least once, give a sincere blessing to a fellow Jew, whether it is "Good morning" or "Good Shabbos." Whatever it is you can think of to include in that blessing, bless a *Yisrael* every day.

The sixth step:

Do you know what is the longest berachah in the siddur? It is the berachah we say about the sunlight. Isn't it a tragedy that people don't know that? After *Barechu*, we say *yotzer ohr*, and it ends with *Baruch Atah Hashem Yotzer hame'oros* — it is the berachah for light. What a tragedy it is how people waste their lives: every day, so much time is occupied with that berachah, and the *malachim* testify, "*me'orei ohr she'asisah* — because of the luminaries of light, *yefa'arucha selah* — they praise You forever." The whole *kedushah* of *yotzer* is only to illustrate the greatness of the light.

Once a day say, Hashem, I am grateful for light

ASK A MAN, "DID YOU THANK HASHEM FOR THE LIGHT TODAY?" HE will scratch his head; he doesn't remember. But since you've enlisted in this endeavor, *bli neder*, to fulfill this item on the agenda, then once a day, not during davening, take a look at the light and say "*Baruch Atah* ... [without Hashem's Name] ... *Yotzeir hame'oros* — how grateful I am to You, Hashem, for the light." What a great kindness light is! *Le'oseh orim gedolim, ki le'olam chasdo*, His kindliness is forever. I know people never think about that, and they will laugh at you — so don't tell it to them! *Yihiyu lecha levadecha ve'ein lezarim itach*,[38] *Mishlei* says. Keep it to yourself, and don't share it with strangers. If you share it with strangers, it will turn into ashes, because they will laugh. Keep it a secret.

---

38. *Mishlei* 5:17

The miracle of sunlight

SUNLIGHT IS A MIRACLE OF MIRACLES.[39] THE SUN IS VERY FAR AWAY from here. The light travels 186,000 miles a second. Nothing in the world travels that fast. It takes over eight minutes for the sunlight to get from the sun to us. So when you are walking in the sunshine, think: Eight minutes ago that sunlight was on the sun. And Hakadosh Baruch Hu is delivering it to you with all the benefits.

Sunlight is not one thing, it is violet light, purple light, red light, green light ... a variety of colors. When you put them together, they become sunlight. When you take a prism, you can break up sunlight into different colors, and each color has a different purpose. Sunlight gives you vitamins as it hits the skin. If children live in areas where there is no sunlight, their bones don't develop properly. You have to take bitter-tasting oils and vitamins to make up for the lack of sunlight. Sunlight makes you healthy. It creates food — when the sun shines on the chlorophyll, it creates starch, and starch is food. Animals eat the grass, which is starch, and they make meat. Everything starts with sunlight — sunlight is the source of food.

If you hear me talking on a tape recorder, that battery has been recharged by sunlight. The sunlight gives me the strength to talk. This is not exaggerated. The sunlight has put power into the food, I put the food into myself, that food gives me strength, and I am talking and thinking by means of the sunlight. This is only the beginning of a discussion on the miracle of sunlight — we have to recognize that miracle.

Isn't it a pity, when such a big berachah is assigned to that subject, to ignore it, day after day? We have to thank Hashem forever and ever. It doesn't penetrate the first time you hear it, so you have to say it to yourself again and again. Every day, say "*Baruch Atah Yotzeir hame'oros*," and after a while, *haba litaheir mesayin oso* — Hashem will help you to improve further. Little by little your mind opens up, and you begin to appreciate that happiness. One side benefit you get from this is that when you see light, after a while you become happy. Light cheers you up. *LaYehudim haysah orah vesimchah*[40] — light is happiness.

---

39. See *Praise My Soul* p. 266 (770)
40. *Esther* 8:16

Sunlight creates happiness in you

RABBEINU YONAH, IN *SHA'AREI TESHUVAH*,[41] TALKS ABOUT OLD people. An old man needs simchah. Without simchah, you cannot be *ovdei* Hashem, so he asks, what can an old man do to get simchah? He should get simchah from sunshine, Rabbeinu Yonah tells us. He quotes a pasuk: "*umasok ha'ohr* — how sweet is the light, *vetov la'einayim liros es Hashemesh* — how good it is for the eyes to see the sunlight." Sunlight is beautiful, and it creates happiness in you. After a while, happiness will be your natural reaction from looking at light. Light is supposed to do that, only our hearts and minds are hardened, and we don't think. We walk like robots. So now, wake up and start living, and start enjoying life. After a while you will understand what you are saying when you daven — *Baruch Atah Hashem Yotzeir hame'oros.*

The seventh step:

Learn to enjoy your ears

LEARN TO ENJOY YOUR EARS. HOW LUCKY YOU ARE THAT YOU HAVE two earphones attached to your head, in the right places. The *Chovos Halevavos* in *Sha'ar Habechinah* speaks about the necessity of spending time on *to'eless ha'eivarim*, the benefit of the various limbs. As you walk the streets, even if a driver doesn't honk his horn, you hear the rushing, oncoming car and that sound saves your life.

The sense of hearing is essential for successful living. If you have a hearing aid, you still should be grateful for your ears, because you can't put your hearing aid on your legs, only in your ears. In fact, it is not the ears themselves that are hearing. Ears are wonderfully fashioned. They collect the sound waves in the air — that is why they are shaped like shells. They concentrate the waves, and as the sound waves hit your eardrum, the eardrum vibrates. There are three remarkable bones behind the eardrum that are connected to each other. They exaggerate the vibration of the eardrum and make a bigger vibration, which then comes into a nerve; the nerve goes into your brain and you hear in the brain.

The brain is a computer that can sort out the sounds

THE BRAIN IS A COMPUTER THAT CAN SORT OUT THE SOUNDS, AND YOU recognize the sounds right away; it is a wonderful way of recogniz-

---

41. *Sha'ar Sheini os* 9

ing people. There are millions of people in the world, and no two people have the same voice. Even in the dark, you can recognize a voice. And sound travels extremely rapidly; so if you stand here, and you speak to someone at the end of the hall, the sound waves travel through air, bobbing up and down like waves on the ocean. Air that is pushed by your voice comes back again, but in the meantime another sound wave is pushed and comes back, and then another, until a wave hits the other side where the person's eardrum is. Did you ever see the wind blowing a field of grain? It looks like a wave is traveling across the field, but the grain is not traveling across the field at all. One stalk pushes and hits the next stalk and comes back again. The next stalk pushes the stalk after it, and so on, and there are waves. That is how the sound waves travel until they finally hit the ear. It is a miracle of miracles!

So this wonderful device that Hakadosh Baruch Hu supplied us with, which functions so well, deserves a little bit of enjoyment on our part. Yes, learn how to enjoy your ears. Eventually, you will come to be happy that you possessed ears, and then you can transfer your attention to some other function of the body.

Enjoy your fingernails

ENJOY YOUR FINGERNAILS. HAVE YOU EVER TRIED TO PICK UP A NEEDLE after you cut your nails short? Who know how many forms of craftsmanship are impossible without fingernails? Fingernails are blessings. They are used to fashion things. Just think of the wonder: this keratin that grows under the fingernails is not bone, hair or flesh. It is a special material — where does it come from?! Every week you cut your fingernails and they keep on growing. They come from the bread you eat and the milk you drink. Bread and milk can make fingernails — that is miraculous — and we have to learn how to appreciate them. We have to learn how to appreciate our feet, our fingers, our noses.

What a wonderful gift a nose is

WHAT A WONDERFUL GIFT A NOSE IS — AND NOT ONLY TO SUPPORT the glasses! It is important for a nose to be in that position. When there is a blow to the face, the nose intercepts the blow and it saves your eyes. That is why the nose projects. Also, when you are asleep and the pillow falls on your face, you are not suffocated, because the nose projects and forms a little cave, allowing the air to enter the space between the pillow and your cheeks and chin. For so many reasons, a nose is a wonderful gift.

Learn how to appreciate your limbs

LEARN HOW TO APPRECIATE ONE OF YOUR LIMBS. SPEND TIME ON it, and after a while you will be happy, because each one of your limbs supplies you with opportunities to enjoy life. So you will enjoy your ears, your fingernails, your feet, the muscles in your arms ... you will begin to enjoy everything in your body, and then you will be able to say with honesty, "*kol atzmosai tomarnah, Hashem mi chamocha*! All of my parts say 'Hashem, who is like You?' " All the parts of your body will sing to Hashem, even your ears and your fingernails — otherwise you are not speaking sincerely when you say that all your parts will sing; otherwise, even your mind doesn't sing to Hashem, because you are falling asleep. But once someone appreciates every part of his body, every organ sings to Hashem. That is literally what it means.

The eighth step:

Pose for a picture. You have to realize that in this world you are being photographed, and someday the film will be played back, and you will see yourself as you really are. So for one minute, imagine that the camera is focused on you. If you are sitting at a wedding, and a man with a camera is passing your table where you have a full cheek, you tell him, "Wait till I swallow. Don't photograph me with a cheek full of food." You swallow, then you are ready. That is the picture that will remain in the album forever.

A person is always being photographed by Hashem

HASHEM HAS AN ALBUM. REALIZE THAT YOU ARE BEING photographed, because you are, every minute. It is hard to pose always, but sometime during the day, pose for a little while, just to practice. Have a pleasant face; be calm. By the way, your mind too is being photographed. Be aware that Hashem is looking at you: *Da mah lema'alah mimcha, ayin ro'ah* — Hashem is photographing you, and it is for ever and ever. You will never be able to erase that picture.

So isn't it better if, say, when your husband comes home, you put on a nice face? You want to pose for eternity. You husband will take a picture when he comes into the house and he will hang it up. Will the picture be of a sad, gloomy face — depressed, or scolding? When your husband comes in, at least for that moment, put on a nice face and give a greeting; ask, "How was your day?" At least then you have fulfilled for one moment that function of *emunah*, of realizing that the way we are living now is forever. Every moment in this world is being put on record, and the tape is going to be played back again and again. In the next world, among the things we will do is that we will see the picture of our lives played back again. Won't you be happy if you have some moments when you look like a hero instead of like a silly fellow? Of course it is not enough to pose for one minute, but at least you make the attempt. *Haba litaheir mesayin oso*, if you come to do something to perfect yourself, Hakadosh Baruch Hu is going to help you.

The ninth step:

"*Im yesh malach meilitz echad mini elef*[42] — If a man has someone to defend him on the day of judgment ...." A man is called before the Great Tribunal, and Hakadosh Baruch Hu calls in the witnesses. Who can say anything about this man? If nine hundred and ninety-nine people accuse him, but one man speaks up for him, Hakadosh Baruch Hu says, "I will listen to that one man": *Im yesh malach meilitz echad mini elef*, if one man will speak up for you, *vayomer peda'eihu meiredes shachas*, and says: Redeem him so he shouldn't go down to the pit, *matzasi kofer*, I have found a redemption. That is how important it is to have one man who thinks well of you. If that is the case, how important it is to find at least one man with whom you will make a hit. Women should find one woman. Go all out. Show your best side to that individual.

Try to make a good impression on people

CHOOSE ONE PERSON, AND DO AS MUCH AS YOU CAN — SHOW HIM your best side, and make that person think well of you. I once spoke to a great man many years ago, and he said that it is important to do that, because your perfect behavior toward this one man will spread to others after a while. *Haba litaheir mesayin oso*. Once you are decent and very good to one man, Hakadosh Baruch Hu will help you succeed with everyone else. Think of ways and means of impressing one man so he will think that you are a kindly fellow, that you are

---

42. *Iyov* 33:27

an honest man, a decent man. Go out of your way to be helpful to him. Encourage him. Smile when you see him and let him think you are the best fellow in the world.

I know it may be a kind of deceit, but from that deceit you will be rewarded. Hashem says, "*matzasi kofer*," I found someone who speaks up for you. When everyone came to accuse you, this one man will come to defend you. Hakadosh Baruch Hu says: I found a *kofer*, I found redemption. That is how important it is to find one man who thinks well of you. And therefore *al tehi baz l'chol adam*, don't scorn any human being. Don't step on anyone. This could be the one man who might save you, the one man on whom you had an opportunity to make an impression — don't spoil it.

The tenth step:

Always ask Hashem for success

ASK FOR SUCCESS — THAT IS AN EXTREMELY IMPORTANT PART OF THE agenda of achieving success. Whatever you are going to do, if you want to be a member of our club here, get into the habit of asking Hashem for success. If, *chalilah*, you have a cut in your finger, don't postpone — put something on it, like an antibiotic ointment, but while you are doing it, say *yehi ratzon milfanecha sheyehei eisek zeh li lirefu'ah*, that this should heal me. Don't rely on the chemist. *Al tivtechu ...* — don't depend on a human being. Ask Hashem for help.

If you are starting up your car, ask Hashem to give you success on this trip, even if you are not going out of town and you won't say *tefillas haderech*. Believe me, in town you need a lot of *siyata diShmaya*, a lot of help from Hakadosh Baruch Hu. So ask Hashem, without a berachah, for success.

If you are going to see a customer, before you walk in, say, "*Yehi ratzon milfanecha shetatzlicheini* — Hashem, please help me." Before you give a lecture, ask Hashem to help you deliver your lecture. Whatever you do, ask Hakadosh Baruch Hu to give you success — it is a very important step. Don't say, "I won't bother Hashem, I will take care of myself this time."

And in your place of business, when a customer walks in, say a quick tefillah that the customer should buy from you and pay the right price and not complain. That is the way to succeed. Hakadosh Baruch Hu will say: I see you are trusting in Me. *Baruch hagever asher yivtach baHashem*, blessed is the man who puts his trust in Hashem; and therefore, *vehayah Hashem mivtacho*, Hashem will reward him by becoming his trust. This applies to everything you do. If you are walking down to the chuppah, about to get married, the kallah sometimes has sense enough to take a little siddur and say a tefillah under the chuppah. But the chassan needs a lot of success; marriage is a very complicated business, and you need a great deal of help. Why don't you ask for success?

When you walk in the street, ask Hashem for a successful walk

WHEN YOU WALK OUT IN THE STREET, ASK HAKADOSH BARUCH HU for a successful walk. One man was standing on the corner waiting for the light to change, and a woman lost control of her car and ran up on the sidewalk. Her car knocked him against the fence, and he became a cripple. Years later, he is still in the hospital. Everyone has to realize that we need success constantly, even for a simple walk down the street.

From time to time, at least once a day — in order to belong to this *chaburah* of *sheleimim*, of those who want to become somebody in this world and not waste their lives — say a tefillah before you do something.

A statement in the Gemara sums up all this. The Torah says: *vehiskadishtem vihyisem kedoshim*, make yourself holy and you will become holy. The Gemara says, *Adam mekadesh atzmo me'at, mekadshim oso harbeh*, a man makes himself a little bit holy, then Hakadosh Baruch Hu will make him very holy. And so it is not silly at all to do these small things. It is a very wise step. The Gemara explains that down here you make yourself *kadosh* in a small way, and Up There they will make you *kadosh* in a big way.

Hakadosh Baruch Hu will see that you are closing in on ten fronts. It is like a little wave, but that wave travels. No energy is lost — that is a law of nature. Some bits of energy get so diffused by the time they reach faraway points that you don't notice them anymore, but they are never lost. Hakadosh Baruch Hu keeps everything in mind, and He will carry out His promise to you: If you open up for Me *kepischo shel machat*, like the opening of a needle, I will open wide for you *kepischo shel heichal*, like the entrance to the *Beis Hamikdash*!

And so it pays to take the first step in the right direction, because Hakadosh Baruch Hu will be with you and help you take many steps to the success for which your soul yearns, and you will gain perfection.

QUESTIONS FOR RABBI MILLER 14

The Sages *teach us that Hashem tested Avraham Avinu ten times. Yet in the* sefer Mesillas Yesharim *we are taught that* "kol inyanei ha'olam…nisyonos heim le'adam — all *the affairs of the world are trials to a* man. If so, it would appear that Avraham Avinu must have been tested far more than ten times. How, then, did the ten *nisyonos enumerated by the sages differ from the rest of the trials that Avraham faced throughout his life?*

While it is most certainly true that "all the affairs of the world…are trials to a man," it is very important to realize that these trials vary in their degree of difficulty depending on whom it is that is being tested. The purpose of a test is to bring out the best in an individual and to give him an opportunity to earn perfection in his service of Hashem. Therefore, the greater a person is spiritually, the more difficult his tests are going to be. As the sages tell us, "*Kol hagadol me'chavero, yitzro gadol heimenu* — one who is greater than his friend, his *yetzer hara* is also greater." Being that a *tzaddik's yetzer hara* is far more powerful than that of the average man, it stands that his tests will be that much more difficult to pass. Hashem would not present a person on a low spiritual level with a difficult trial; rather, to him he offers much less challenging tests. We are now in a position to understand that Avraham's tests must have been excruciatingly difficult, and as he grew spiritually the level of difficulty certainly increased. The ten tests enumerated by the sages were the ones that Avraham endured at the heights of his service of Hashem, and they were therefore the most challenging. The Midrash compares this idea to different types of linen: In days gone by, when one wanted to make his linen white and soft, he would beat it with a stick. If the linen was of superior quality, says the Midrash, then one could continuously beat it until it gained a fine appearance. But you could never do that with linen of poor quality; hit it one too many times and it you will have destroyed it.

Q&A *Should a parent allow a young child to drink soda?*

The answer is yes — if it's Shabbos. Giving your child soda on Shabbos will bring him to enjoy and savor Shabbos, and this is a mitzvah. Of course, one should first try to offer a child water. When the thirsty young man reaches for the soda bottle, tell him to wait a moment. Explain to him the benefits accrued by drinking water, and what a magnificent creation water is. If after drinking, let's say, two large glasses of water, he still wants soda — then let him have it. You will have enabled him to experience joy on Shabbos, and this is a mitzvah.

Q&A *Is there anything wrong with listening to a non-Jewish radio talk show host that has a conservative and right-wing perspective on life?*

Let's put it this way: it's certainly better than listening to a liberal. However, it is important to know that even a non-Jew of sterling character does not possess an outlook on life that is in anyway compatible with a proper Torah perspective. He makes light of that which we deem sacred and his values are foreign to our own. The truth is, the less association that you have with non-Jews, the better off you will be. While it is true that on occasion we must show that we are in agreement with the policies of the more upstanding non-Jews in society, for the most part we must hold fast to the principle of *"Hen am le'vadad yishkon* — it is a nation that dwells in solitude." This is how Balaam described the Jewish nation, and it is worthwhile for us to try and live up to that description. The Jewish people must exist separately from our non-Jewish counterparts. We must know, however, that it is not only from the non-Jews that we must isolate ourselves; unfortunately there are many "upper-class" Jews in today's world that would serve as very great stumbling blocks for us, should we not veer far away from their influence. As a rule, the more time one spends alone, the better off he will be. Of course, if one can spend time with tzaddikim then he will certainly be well off, as there is no greater company than a tzaddik. Otherwise, however, one should attempt to live a life of solitude, and to do so is a very great achievement.

In our day and age, this idea is no longer appreciated. But take my word for it — it's as true today as it ever was. Savor the moments that you find yourself alone, not in anyone's company but your own. You'll find that these moments present very real opportunities for growth and character development. For experience testifies to the fact that the more time one spends in the company of others, the more likely he is to fall under their influence. You'll begin to act like they act and eventually think like they do as well. It is of utmost importance to give yourself a chance to grow on your own, not being weighed down by the travails and the chains of your environment.

Q&A *How physically attracted does a man have to be to a woman in order for a shidduch to be a successful one?*

The Gemara tells us "*assur le'adam she'yikadesh es ha'ishah ad she'yirenah,*" it is forbidden for a man to marry a woman until he has looked at her. Now, the Sages haven't told us that a man must be *infatuated* with her physical appearance. He simply has to look at her and not be repulsed by what he sees. The same thing applies to a woman: she must simply not be disgusted by the man's physical appearance. It is important to realize that when the Sages tell us that one must look at a potential spouse, they are not referring to looking only at one's physical appearance. He must "look" at her personality as well. Very often, an attractive woman can fall under the category of what the Sages describe as "*nezem zahav be'af chazir,*" a gold nose ring in the nose of a pig. This description can be applied to a woman with a very fine appearance, but lacking intelligence. The truth is that there are many beautiful women who simply do not possess very much intellect.

Therefore, when a man looks for a potential wife, make sure that she is an intelligent person. A man should also look for a girl who is on the quiet side and not loud and vivacious. Make sure that she is a girl who won't want very much, and that she will go along with your wishes and ideas. A man must make sure to clarify whether or not a potential spouse wants to have a large family. In addition, find out whether or not she is the type of person who will allow you to have space when you need it and time to yourself if you so desire. Be careful to clarify each and every one of these issues and don't make any mistakes! If a girl meets all of these requirements, then don't spend too much time looking her in the face. As long as you are not repulsed, go ahead and get married, and Hakadosh Baruch Hu will grant you much hatzlachah.

Q&A *How can a yeshivah student expect to be able to earn a living, without making the necessary preparations or taking the necessary measures?*

This is a very serious question. The answer to your question is one word — *bitachon*, putting one's trust in Hashem. If an individual lives with *bitachon* then he will be provided for. But it must be stressed that the *bitachon* of which we speak is *true bitachon*. Simply paying lip service to the idea will in no way assure a person of a livelihood.

How a yeshivah student should prepare for the day when it becomes necessary to earn a livelihood is a matter that I will not discuss; for each person is different and is therefore required to take different steps to support his family than someone else. But I must tell you that it is a question which requires our attention and deserves to be pondered. I have my own opinion on the matter, but I will not state it in a public forum. I will tell you, however, that there are a lot of men out there who are not fulfilling what they promised to fulfill. When a man gets married he makes an official transaction binding him to the stipulations recorded in the *kesubah*. Among those stipulations are "*ana izun ve'eflach*," I will work and support my wife, as well as "*ve'okir*," I will honor my wife, "*ke'hilchos guvrin Yehudi'in*," as is required of Jewish males. A husband commits himself by means of a binding transaction to support his wife! If a woman chooses to forgo the stipulations in her *kesubah* and work all of her life to support her husband while he's learning, then she has waived her right to have the *kesubah's* conditions fulfilled. However, if she does not wish to grant her permission to allow her husband to learn while she plays the role of breadwinner, then he has absolutely no right to do so. So how does a yeshivah student prepare himself for this eventuality? It's a question that I won't answer, but it is certainly a pressing issue.

Q & A How great a mitzvah is donating blood to religious Jews in need?

Giving blood is the greatest form of *bikur cholim* that there is. People are under the impression that one fulfills the mitzvah of *bikur cholim* only by visiting the sick. This is incorrect! If when visiting them, you tend to their needs and provide for them, then you have performed an even greater level of *bikur cholim*. Can anyone imagine a greater way to provide for an ill person who needs it than by donating blood? There's no question, it's certainly a very great mitzvah.

Q & A What is meant by our Sages expression "Sonei matanos yichyeh," that one who hates gifts will live?

This expression means the following: Hashem placed us in this world for the express purpose of utilizing our *bechirah*, our free will. However, when a person receives gifts from another, he ultimately becomes enslaved to that person. He begins to do things simply to please the one who bestowed gifts upon him, and eventually yields to his influence. This prevents him from exercising his free will, negating the reason for which he was placed in the world to begin with. However, when a person refrains from accepting gifts, he is free to serve Hashem as he pleases. The Sages tell us that Hakadosh Baruch Hu stated, "*Ve'halach zeh ve'kanah adon le'atzmo,*" this one went and acquired a master for himself? "*Ki li Bnei Yisrael heim,*" the Jewish people are My servants, "*Ve'lo avadim le'avadim,*" and not servants of other servants. Hakadosh Baruch Hu wants us to be enslaved to him and to none other.

Therefore, when an individual accepts gifts from other people, he should know that he will no longer be considered to be among the living. After all, if the entire purpose of our coming to the world was to utilize our *bechirah*, then, what reason remains for such an individual to continue living? He has no more *bechirah* to speak of, having accepted gifts from others and now only saying what they want him to say and do what they want him to do.

The Gemara relates that there was a certain individual who wished to give a gift to a talmid chacham. The talmid chacham refused to accept it, exclaiming, "Nicha licha de'achi lo? — Do you not want me to live?" We see therefore that the acceptance of gifts results in the shortening of one's life.

How can one come to rectify the trait of speaking too much, if it is in his nature to do so?

Now we come to one of the greatest achievements that a man can achieve in his life — the achievement of learning how to keep quiet. The Rambam said the following: "le'olam yarbeh adam be'shtikah," a person should always produce a great deal of silence. To produce silence is a wonderful achievement! A certain maggid once lectured in Radin, the town of the Chafetz Chaim, for three hours. When the maggid concluded his drashah, the Chafetz Chaim remarked that this maggid is the finest of men, and he deserves to be compensated accordingly. When queried as to why this was so, the Chafetz Chaim replied that it was not so much for what the maggid had said, but that he managed to keep his audience totally quiet for three whole hours! What an achievement! If it had been up to the Chafetz Chaim, the maggid would have spoken for longer than three hours!

We are taught that "al kol rega ve'rega she'adam chosem piv," for every moment that a person muzzles his mouth, "zocheh le'ohr haganuz," he merits to bask in the hidden light of Olam Haba, "sheh'ain kol malach u'biryah yicholim le'sha'eir," which accrues a joy that neither malach nor any one of Hashem's creations can measure. Now, that glorious light is earned by keeping silent for just one moment — can anyone imagine how much reward can be earned by remaining quiet for two moments? This should give us an idea of just how important it is to remain silent.

The Rambam tells us that one of the criteria by which a person's life is evaluated is to what extant he was "marbeh be'shtikah," a producer of silence. So let us begin to produce some silence! The question is, however, how one whose nature it is to be verbose can begin to exercise some control over his manner of speech. Here's an idea: The next time you are about to open your mouth, imagine that it will cost you a large sum of money if you do so. Think of how many mitzvos you stand to lose by doing so; think of how much of your life you are giving away. Shlomo Hamelech states in Koheles, "Ki HaElokim

ba'shamayim ve'atah al ha'aretz al cain yihiyu devarecha me'atim,"
For *Elokim* is in *Shamayim*, and you are down on the earth — by keeping this in mind we will fulfill the end of the pasuk — therefore your words will be few. Think about it for a moment: If you were standing in the presence of a great man, would you dare open your mouth? Certainly not! How much more so, when we arrive at the realization that we are forever standing in front of Hakadosh Baruch Hu — will we have any problem whatsoever remaining silent?

Remember what I have just told you, for it is of inestimable importance. Now I am going to say something which might bother some people: The telephone, yes the telephone, is one of the greatest *nisyonos* and obstacles in the way of practicing proper *shemiras halashon*. For we must realize that *shemiras halashon* is not only comprised of refraining from uttering forbidden speech, it even includes refraining from speaking *devarim beteilim*, words that will serve no real purpose to have been spoken. *Shemiras halashon* means that one makes as much effort as possible to avoid talking. Of course, there are times when one must speak. For example, when a husband comes home from work and is greeted by his wife who was home all day long battling with the kids, it is more than likely that she will wish to speak with him. He should sit down with her — but let her do all the talking. All he has to do is listen. Over the course of the conversation she might ask him, "Are you listening, Chaim?"

"Of course I'm listening," he'll answer. Meanwhile, he'll be looking into a Gemara, or have started eating supper! Let him do just as our Rabbis have instructed, "*Ya'aseh atzmo ke'ileim,*" he should make himself like a mute. There is no need to say anything at all — just listen.

As we mentioned, the Sages teach us, "*mah umnaso shel adam be'olam hazeh?*" what should be man's profession in this world? "*Ya'aseh atzmo ke'ileim,*" he should make himself similar to a mute. The Sages continue, "*yachol ha'kol,*" I would think that this applies to all forms of speech, "*talmud lomar, tzedek tidaber,*" speak words that pertain to righteousness. Speak words of Torah, and say a few kind words here and there. But realize that speaking properly and knowing when to speak is an *umnus*, a trade that must be learnt and studied.

The Chafetz Chaim added an additional insight into the Sages' statement. Said the Chafetz Chaim, the Sages are not instructing us to actually be an *ileim*, a mute; after all, there are times when it is necessary for a person to speak. Rather, the Sages have told us to be *ke'ileim, similar* to an *ileim*. This means, said the Chafetz Chaim, that even when one is forced to say something, he must make himself like a mute when it comes to speaking words that are forbidden by the Torah. Let's say, for example, that somebody approaches you and begins to speak *lashon hara* about someone else. What's worse is that he wants you to add your two cents as well. What should you do? Speak if you have to, but speak like an *ileim*. Don't say one word about the topic that he has brought up. Rather, speak about the weather or about how much it costs to buy a suit in today's world. By avoiding the subject that he wanted to speak about, you've made yourself like an *ileim*.

The Chafetz Chaim was once traveling on a train with several businessmen. Fearing that his companions were likely to strike up a conversation that involved *lashon hara*, he posed a question about Belgian horses. The businessmen quickly began to speak about Belgian horses. The Chafetz Chaim was not finished, however. He began to stoke the flames, as he wanted the conversation to continue, and started to criticize Belgian horses. The conversation became a heated one, and one of the men actually reprimanded the Chafetz Chaim for speaking *lashon hara* about horses! Eventually, the men got tired of discussing Belgian horses, and the conversation soon died down. The Chafetz Chaim, once again fearing that the next conversation would be one of a forbidden nature, quickly brought up another subject — English horses. Once again, the Chafetz Chaim attempted to lengthen the conversation by throwing in a few negative remarks about English horses. It worked, and the men argued about English horses until they arrived in Vilna. When the Chafetz Chaim got off the train, he was quite pleased, as he had prevented his companions from speaking *lashon hara* about people, through cleverly speaking *lashon hara* about horses. He had spoken, but he had spoken like an *ileim*.

In short, sometimes we must speak, but we must remember to be careful about what we say. Learning to speaking properly is an *umnus*, and it's one *umnus* that we are all required to learn.

Q&A *Are we going to be held accountable for feelings of depression? Is it truly someone's fault if they are depressed?*

I want to tell you something, *Rabbosai*. The Sages tell us that "*be'derech she'adam rotzeh leileich bah molichin oso,*" in the way a person wants to go, in that way he will be led. If a person desires to be sad, he will certainly succeed in doing so.

But, let me tell you, Hakadosh Baruch Hu is not going to reward anybody for bring depressed in this world. You'd like to be depressed about the *churban Beis HaMikdash*, the destruction of the *Beis HaMikdash* — fine. You'd like to be depressed over your sins — fine. But for a person to be sad for no reason at all? This is what the Sages have termed *bechiah shel chinam*, grieving for no reason whatsoever — and it is a very grave sin, indeed. Do you know why we go through a Tishah B'Av, year after year? Because Tishah B'Av was the night that a Jewish nation sojourning through the desert wept for no reason. *Va'yivku ha'am ba'lalah ha'hu*, the Jewish nation cried on that night, and they cried for nothing. What did they have to cry for — they were on their way to Eretz Yisrael! *Eretz zavas chalav u'd'vash!* You're crying? says Hashem, "*biglal zeh yivku banai*," now the Jewish people are going to cry — but with good reason — for many years to come. We see, therefore, that weeping for nothing is a very big sin. Quite frequently, I get phone calls from people who are sad for no reason. So I ask them, "What are you sad about? Is your husband working?" They answer, yes. "Does he give you money?" Yes. "Does he ever hit you?" No. "Do you have children?" Yes. "Do you have a house?" Yes. "So what are you so sad about? Are you sick?" No, they answer, I'm just sad. "I see," I tell them. "It sounds to me like you are looking for trouble," I say. "If you're looking for trouble, believe me, you're going to find it."

When someone gets sad over nothing, Hakadosh Baruch Hu says, "So you are looking for sadness; that's the path on which you'd like to go? I'll help you become even sadder." So after a while, this sadness evolves into full-blown depression, and then there's Prozac, medicines, doctors, psychologists, and all types of *tzaros*. Therefore, it is a person's own fault if he allows himself to sink into such a low depressed state. Let a person think *Shabbosdik* thoughts, as much as possible: how the world is a good place, about how he, Baruch Hashem, has enough to eat; Baruch Hashem his house is warm in the wintertime; Baruch Hashem, he has electric lights; Baruch Hashem, he's not living on the streets, he's not homeless, he has a roof over his head, he can lock the door at night — Baruch Hashem, he has everything. If a person thinks in such a manner, he won't become depressed.

Now when Hakadosh Baruch Hu sees that you're looking for happiness, he says, "So you're looking for happiness? I'm going to make you even happier." Sing in this world and you'll sing in the Next World too.

Q&A *Is there a difference between the neshamah of a man and a woman?*

When it comes to the actual makeup of the neshamah there's no difference, whatsoever. But when it comes to a person's role in perfecting that neshamah, Hakadosh Baruch Hu has given each individual a different way and opportunity to go about doing so. For example, when a woman gets married and dedicates her life to her family, to someone other than herself, she is transforming her very nature. If a mother would retain her selfishness, it would be impossible for her to function successfully in her role. She has her children to worry about; sometimes they may not be feeling well, and it is she who will be responsible for tending to them. She has to prepare food for her family, and they rely upon her for many other things as well. She has to carry a child within her and eventually nurse that child. In short, she has dedicated her life to others.

But in order for a mother to be able to perfect her neshamah, she mustn't merely do "acts of kindness" like the gentiles do. Rather, her *chessed* should be with the intention of serving Hashem! This brings Hakadosh Baruch Hu a great amount of satisfaction, and He therefore exclaims, "By assisting others, you are helping My people and serving Me in a form that is most desirous." Imagine what a great accomplishment it is to bring up future servants of Hashem! This is what Chavah exclaimed when she bore Kayin, "*Kanisi ish es Hashem*," I have acquired a man — a son — not alone, but with Hashem! Giving birth to children and then raising them so that they will one day be servants of Hashem is an extremely important achievement for her neshamah, and it goes a long way in earning it the perfection that it needs. A woman is not expected to devote her hours to Torah learning, nor is she expected to meditate upon Torah ideas. She can certainly do so if she wishes, but her main area of achievement will be in transforming her neshamah through acts of *chessed* intended to benefit Hashem's people.

A man, however, has to perfect his neshamah in a different way. While a man neither gives birth to children nor nurses babies, there are still multitudes of ways through which he can earn perfection. A man must go to work to earn a living, and there are very many *nisyonos* that he will encounter throughout his day. An entire section of *Shulchan Aruch* was written to deal with the laws that apply when one has to compete with another for a livelihood! There's a very great perfection a man can acquire when out making a living! Of course a man is also required to dedicate a part of his day to Torah learning, and other mitzvos that a woman wouldn't have time to perform because of her day to day responsibilities. We see, therefore, that a man and woman secure perfection for their respective neshamahs in different ways.

Q&A *What was the purpose in* Hakadosh Baruch Hu's *telling Avraham Avinu* "Ki ger yihiyeh zaracha be'eretz lo lahem," *that his children would one day experience* galus *at the hands of the Egyptians?*

Honestly, this is not a very difficult question at all. Let me begin by posing the following question: Why did Hakadosh Baruch Hu *ever* inform Avraham Avinu as to what lay in store for him in the future? For example, in several places, the Torah relates that Hashem told Avraham that he was destined to be the forebear of a great progeny. Why was it necessary to inform Avraham of this fact? One reason is because "*Hashem beirach Avraham ba'kol,*" Hashem blessed Avraham with everything. This blessing, of course, included Avraham's being the father of a very large offspring, and this was a fact that Hakadosh Baruch Hu wished to share with Avraham. There, however, is something more.

We are taught that "*me'odeid anavim Hashem,*" Hashem offers constant encouragement to those people who deserve it. Why did Hashem tell Avraham that he was to be the father of a great posterity? Because He wanted to encourage him. This is not to say, of course, that Avraham Avinu needed very much encouragement. The chances of Avraham — who as a child growing up in Ur Casdim was able to hold firm to the faith that only he knew to be true — growing discouraged were very slim. The Sages teach us, however, "*Be'derech she'adam rotzeh leileich bah molichin oso,*" that Hashem leads a person down whichever path he chooses for himself. Therefore, Hashem decided, as it were, to provide Avraham with adequate encouragement, by promising him many generations of offspring.

But there is an even more important reason. Do you know what Avraham's greatest desire was? Do you know what he wanted the most? To fill the world with knowledge of Hashem's existence. Therefore, wherever Avraham went, "*vayikra be'sheim Hashem* — he proclaimed the Name of Hashem." Avraham knew, however, that the most effective way to reveal the truth of Hashem's presence to the world would be through an Am Yisrael. Specifically through a nation of individuals who would be faithful to those ideals that he preached would the world be enriched with those same ideals. For the primary function of a Jew is to speak of the greatness of Hashem at all times. As the pasuk states, "*Am zu yatzarti li*," these people that I created for Me, "*tehilasi yisapeiru*," they should relate My praise. This, indeed, was what Avraham yearned for the most — a nation that would constantly sing the praises of Hashem. Hakadosh Baruch Hu therefore told him, that he would, in fact, succeed in his mission; the world would one day be populated by a nation of Hashem, who would declare His Omnipotence every day by reciting the *Shema*. The truth is that until recent years, the Jewish nation did just that. It was not so long ago that each and every Jew kept the Torah, to a greater or lesser degree. You were able to eat in almost any Jewish home, without any concerns whatsoever, and it is our hope that one day this greatness of the Jewish people will be restored. Baruch Hashem, even today there are many Jews who are *shomrei Torah*, and we must know that Hakadosh Baruch Hu delights in that; *im yirtzeh Hashem* there will be many more such Jews. It brought Avraham Avinu tremendous joy to know that the glorious Name of Hashem would one day be promulgated throughout the world by means of his children, and that's why Hashem continued to inform him about his future descendants again and again.

Now why did Hakadosh Baruch Hu have to tell Avraham about what was going to befall his children in Egypt? He did this in order that Avraham would become aware of the great success that was to be the lot of the Jewish nation, which only came about because of their bondage in Egypt. *Shibud Mitzrayim*, the Jewish people's period of slavery in Egypt, was absolutely necessary. Oh yes. For it was only due to the Egyptian oppression that the Jews became so enthused about the redemption that Hashem brought about. Only because of their having been slaves to Pharaoh did the Jews so eagerly accept the Torah. Their gratitude at having been freed from Egypt generated such an overwhelming love for Hashem that they declared "*Na'aseh v'nishma*." We must also understand that the Jews accomplished great things in Egypt. Their years as slaves taught them about the plight of the downtrodden. Why must we take pity on *gerim*? Says the Torah, "*Ki gerim hayisem be'Eretz Mitzrayim*," for we, too, were strangers in the land of Egypt. We are commanded to show mercy to slaves. Why? "*Ki eved ha'yisem be'Eretz Mitzrayim*," for you were slaves in Egypt. There were many other notable achievements as well: Despite everything that we endured in Egypt, despite all the oppression and hardship, we refused to change our Jewish names. Our language remained the same, as did our style of dress — it remained purely Jewish. We fought back against the environment, refusing to give in to the prevailing cultures. These are very great accomplishments! Therefore, the tidings of his descendants' future slavery in Egypt were not necessarily bad ones to Avraham, as he knew what was to be the eventual outcome. He was well aware of the success that lay beneath the surface of that *galus*, namely the eventual "*asher hotzeisi eschem me'Eretz Mitzrayim lei'hiyos lachem lei'Elokim*," the redemption wrought by Hakadosh Baruch Hu for the express purpose of taking us as His nation. It is for this reason that Hashem informed Avraham about what was going to happen to his descendants, in order to encourage him by letting him know that his children will ultimately form a perfect nation that will be chosen to accept the Torah.

Q&A *Being that* Olam Haba *is a benefit that is enjoyed to the extent that one has perfected his mind in this world, is there any share at all for a* shomer Shabbos *Jew who did not accomplish very much in the area of Torah study?*

If a person did not gain *sheleimus ha'da'as*, perfection of knowledge, in this world, is there something waiting for him in Gan Eden? The answer is, yes, because it is not possible to observe *Yiddishkeit* and not perfect your mind to a certain extent. Take your average, everyday, Jewish simpleton, for example. Suppose this Jew is walking past a store that has treife provisions in the window. Now this Jew is hungry, but he refuses to enter the store and buy food, as he won't eat anything treife. This is a tremendous achievement for the mind! Simply knowing that as a Jew he has obligations and restrictions is an achievement of mental perfection. Of course, there are much greater degrees of mental achievement, but that in itself is great as well. If a Jew passes by a movie theatre showing a filthy movie — all the movies inside are filthy — but decides against going inside, rather, he just keeps on walking, he has achieved something quite significant. For he has demonstrated a purity of soul that will accompany him to the Next World.

But you must know that not everyone has an equal share in *Olam Haba*. Each tzaddik has his "*chupah le'fi kevodo*," his own canopy of diamonds depending on to what extent he excelled in Torah and mitzvos in this world. In some places there will be an abundance of diamonds, yet in other places there will be far less. In this world, if you have a comfortable home, and then your neighbor from across the street builds himself a palace, it may bother you a little bit. Ultimately, you tell yourself that it doesn't matter very much anyhow; this is only *olam hazeh*, and before long everybody winds up in the cemetery anyhow. So all in all, it doesn't make a big difference. In *Olam Haba*, however, it makes an enormous difference, because it is for all eternity! It will therefore be extremely painful when you see other people who will have achieved more than you — but by then it will be far too late to do anything about it. The *Olam Haba* of a person who tried harder in this world and perfected himself by doing more than others will be far different than the *Olam Haba* that will be received by those who achieved less. It is for this reason that although there will be a place for *every shomer mitzvos* in *Olam Haba* — everyone will have his appropriate share — there is a world of difference that separates between a regular *shomer mitzvos* and someone who has attained a higher degree of *da'as*. People don't have any comprehension of what this means. They'll say, "As long as I get a back seat in *Olam Haba*, I'll be happy." What a mistake! Let's say that you would be given a back seat in a shul. Would you be happy? Not at all! You'd be outright insulted! Why should this guy sit up front and I'm stuck here in the back? But after a while, shul comes to an end and you go home; you aren't stuck in the back forever. In *Olam Haba*, however, there is no going home. You're there for all eternity, and a back seat there will cause you much suffering. You'll be full of *charatah*, regret, and it will be a nagging worry forever and ever. For such people, *Olam Haba* will be mixed with a certain amount of sadness, as they will be plagued by the lost opportunities that were so attainable in this world.

> *We are all aware of the great principle of* tzelem Elokim, *that every individual is created in the Divine image. Being that this is so, how could Avraham Avinu ignore this principle and refer to himself as* afar ve'efer, *dust and ash?*

This is not a particularly difficult question to answer. Avraham Avinu was certainly aware of the excellence that Hashem bestowed upon mankind. Of this there is no question. He understood that which we are taught by the Sages, "*Chaviv adam she'nivra b'tzelem*," that man, who has been created with a *tzelem Elokim*, is beloved by Hashem. On the other hand, however, he realized that this beauty, this *tzelem Elokim*, will one day rot away beneath the earth.

Avraham understood that the *tzelem Elokim* is a gift that Hashem granted him, and it is a gift that He will one day take back. Therefore, he declared, "*Anochi afar ve'efer*," I am but dust and ash, as he realized just how temporary the body's existence truly is.

But we must know that it is of the utmost importance to properly maintain our *tzelem Elokim* by washing our faces each and every day. Don't think that I am making this up, because the Gemara states this explicitly! Imagine if a king gave you a portrait of himself as a gift, says the Gemara. If you would neglect that portrait and allow it to gather cobwebs and dust, it would be a very great insult to the king! Therefore, we must wash our faces every day, because we were created in the image of Hashem. Washing our faces for any other reason is a sin, but if we wash our faces because we want to maintain our *tzelem Elokim* it is a mitzvah. This is also a wonderful lesson to teach our children. When your child washes his face, tell him, "Go and wash your *tzelem Elokim*! Wash that picture of Hashem!" Make him understand that his face is the image of Hashem — the portrait of the king, as the Gemara taught us — and that by keeping it clean, one is honoring Hashem. What a fine lesson to give over to our children!

Do not forget, however, that one day this marvelous *tzelem Elokim* will decompose and be devoured by worms. It's very important to think about that. It is for this reason that Avraham said that he was *afar ve'efer*, as he did not wish to forget the end that awaited him and become arrogant. For *ga'avah*, pride, is the root of all sins, because when man becomes haughty, he thinks only of himself — and that is what ultimately leads to sin. We see, therefore, that Avraham was able to keep both of these lofty concepts in mind simultaneously, viewing himself as both a *tzelem Elokim* and *afar ve'efer*. This is the hallmark of a great man. *Resha'im*, wicked people, do not think this way; "*I'm a tzelem Elokim* and *you* are *afar ve'efer*," is the way they think! But Avraham Avinu was far beyond such a way of thinking. In everybody's face, he saw *tzelem Elokim*; wherever he looked, *tzelem Elokim*. Yet at the very same time, he realized that he was no more than *afar ve'efer*, dust and ash. For great men are well acquainted with life's ultimate truth. They know that they have been placed in this world for the express purpose of earning a share in *Olam Haba*. As the Sages teach us, this world is but a *prozdor*, a corridor, leading to the great palace that is the World to Come. Now, even though this world is nothing more than a *prozdor*, they do not take this world lightly;

rather, they live with the utmost caution, lest they come to transgress any one of the Torah's commandments. So while they may be singing Hashem's praises and thanking Him for His kindness *every* moment of their lives, they still possess a tremendous amount of *yiras Hashem*, as well. Does that sound contradictory? Well, I'm going to let you in on a very fundamental principle of Torah knowledge. That is, when it comes to *da'as Torah*, you will often come across two contradictory principles regarding a certain idea, yet each one must be kept in mind and maintained. Let me give you an example: Everybody knows that it is impossible to make Hashem happy or sad. As we are taught, "*Im tzadakta ma titen*," even if you are a tzaddik, what are you truly giving to Him? You are not giving Him anything whatsoever, and you can bring Him no true happiness. This is both true and very logical. Yet we also learn, "*Eizehu chassid, oseh nachas ruach be'borei osei ha'machasid bahem*," that one has to act as though Hashem derives nachas from you like a father or mother has nachas from a child. These ideas certainly seem to contradict each other, yet we are required to keep both of them in mind. If someone believes that he is able to make Hashem happy, then he is a *min*, a heretic, for you can't make Hashem happy. Hashem is far too noble and exalted to possess emotions such as joy or sadness. However, we are required to act as if He enjoys and receives gratification from our deeds, as the pasuk states, "*Yehi kevod Hashem le'olam yismach Hashem be'ma'asav*." We see, for example, that the tzaddikim believe that Hashem is *nisgav bimromam*, above any physical attributes whatsoever, yet on the other hand, we find Hashem described as an *ish milchamah*, a man of war, or a *zakein yosheiv be'yeshivah*, an elderly man sitting in yeshivah. Each thought is contradictory, but each one is essential to learn and contemplate. So while we must act as if we accord Hashem nachas when we act properly and do what's right and vice versa, in our *seichel*, our intellect, we must be aware of the fact that Hakadosh Baruch Hu is *nisgav u'meromam* and above all of these things.

Q&A *Is it possible to receive the reward for one's mitzvos in this world?*

It is certainly possible, but believe me, you don't want it. It is a very big *onesh*, a terrible punishment to receive one's eternal reward for a mitzvah in the form of a million dollars! The worst possible thing is to get paid back in this world! A mitzvah deserves compensation that is *le'ad u'lenetzach nitzachim*, eternal joy in the World to Come. If someone has deserved to receive such a horrible punishment as getting his eternal reward for mitzvos in this world, it is called *nekamah gedolah*, a truly terrible retribution.

Q&A *Did the* Dor Hamidbar *utilize all of the miracles that Hashem performed for them in the wilderness?*

They most certainly did, and don't make any mistake about it. Listen carefully; it was worth it for you to come here tonight just to hear this. My rebbi used to say that there was never a generation which was as righteous and had as deep a recognition of Hakadosh Baruch Hu as the *Dor Hamidbar*. But we must understand, if they were indeed so pious a generation, then why were they punished as severely as they were? Let me explain with a mashal: Let's say you have a son who is a tzaddik; he learns well and he acts properly. One day, however, he decides to spend some time with the derelicts who waste their time hanging around the streets. He spends about an hour of his time with them, and then returns home. When he enters the house, you greet him with a big *potch*. Shocked, your son asks, "Why are you *potching me* for? I'm a good boy! Why don't you *potch* the other boys?" So you answer him, "I don't care about those other boys; it is you that I care about and you whom I focus my attention on. It is only because you are truly such a good boy that you are getting *potched*." Perhaps now it will be somewhat easier to answer our question. We must realize that Hashem doesn't give *potches* to the goyim — what does He care about the goyim? The *Dor Hamidbar*, however, witnessed the giving of the Torah; they were the talmidim of Moshe Rabbeinu! Hashem expects a great deal from individuals on such a lofty *madreigah*, such a lofty level of spirituality. They knew the ways of Hashem, no question. No other generation ever knew Hashem's ways like they knew! Yet as the *Kuzari* explains, they came under criticism because Hashem expected more from them. But were they affected and did they utilize the miracles that they experienced? No question about it! If we were alive in their generation, we wouldn't have benefited from the miracles nearly as much as they did! The *Dor Hamidbar* absorbed the effects of Hashem's nissim in the same manner that a sponge absorbs water! They became different people as a result of the nissim. In *Navi* we learn that after the generation of Yehoshua, there no longer existed a generation "*asher yadu es Hashem*," that knew Hashem. What a queer statement; how are we to understand it? It means that the generation that entered Eretz Yisrael, and all subsequent generations thereafter, did not know Hashem like the generations of old. We can't even imagine the level of the *Dor Hamidbar*! Just getting a glimpse of Moshe Rabbeinu was enough to change you forever! It was a generation that consisted of a Moshe Rabbeinu, an Aharon Hakohen, and a Miriam! But don't think that they were the only one's who were great! *All* of the Jews who died in the *midbar* and didn't enter Eretz Yisrael were very, very great! What an extraordinary generation it must have been! We are taught that Rabbi Akiva stated, "*Dor Hamidbar ein lahem chelek be'Olam Haba*," that the *Dor Hamidbar* has no share in *Olam Haba*, as they didn't fulfill that which was expected of them. But he came under criticism for saying so, as Rabbi Ezra countered, "*Shavke Rabbi Akiva le'chassidusa*," Rabbi Akiva forsook his *frumkeit* by saying such a thing! Rabbi Eliezer HaGadol added, "*Aleihem hakasuv omer*," about the *Dor Hamidbar* it is stated, "*ish hu le'chasidah*," gather to Me in *Olam Haba* all of My pious ones, "*kol ha'brisi al eizeh*," those that entered into a covenant with Me on *Har Sinai*. The *Dor Hamidbar*, indeed, were the pious ones; there was never another generation like them. If the world would had been created just for that generation, it would have been well worth it, as they possessed more *emunah*, love for Hashem, and fire in their Divine service than any other generation ever did. It's a very great pity that people are not aware of this. It's truly amazing to note that murder is not found among the sins of that generation. Just think about it for a second. For forty years, at least two million people lived crowded together and not one case of *shefichas damim*, not a single case of murder! That is not a small thing. No, we will never truly grasp the greatness of the *Dor Hamidbar*, but at the very least we should know that they were the greatest generation that has ever existed.

Q&A *What should be the thoughts of somebody who wins a large sum of money?*

The best thing to do is to think in advance, *before* you win any money. Don't wait for the moment that you become an overnight millionaire to begin thinking, because by then you won't be able to think, and it will be too late. You must

understand that wealth is a very great test and an enormous responsibility. You may be surprised to hear this, but there are many people
who have become wealthy unexpectedly. I can tell you many stories
about individuals who suddenly found themselves wealthy, even in
today's day and age. Whether it was through the death of a rich uncle,
or by making a lot of money in an auto accident, these people
became rich in a flash — and it most cases it ruined them. The key is
to plan in advance. If you understand what the purpose of money is,
then you just might be able to manage if you do happen to win that
lottery. Even though I've never been in such a situation, I'm going to
give you some sound advice and tell you what you should do.

The first thing you should do is immediately put your money in the
bank and let it sit there. Don't do a thing. Try as hard as you can to conceal your good fortune from the world. If the newspapers publish your
name then take a vacation for a few weeks and disappear from the scene.
The main thing is to keep the news of your wealth quiet. Once word gets
out you will be mobbed by *meshulachim*, by charity collectors, and
countless organizations will call you up for money. The best thing to do
is to disappear for a few weeks and think over what you are going to do.

Of course, you must give a certain amount to tzedakah right away,
but the remainder of the money requires great planning to decide
what to do with it. You may want to change your lifestyle. Perhaps
you've worked for many years, and now you wish to retire and sit and
learn Torah. Full-time Torah learning is a wonderful thing, but before
you make such a drastic change in your life, give it a decent amount
of thought. Perhaps learning all day is not the best thing for you at
this time, and you would be better off continuing with your job.

Being that unexpected wealth can cause such drastic tidal waves on
the surface of one's normal life, it can very often lead to divorce as well.
Therefore, you ought to engage in a great deal of circumspection before
you begin to spend your newfound fortune. I must tell you that many of
the individuals who I know that became rich in a short time were in very
great debt a year later. Many of them later said they were sorry that they
had won the money in the first place. You should just know that if one
acts wisely it is possible to succeed with or without money.

Jews who are both righteous and rich have a very important place
in Torah life. A wealthy frum Jew is a blessing for the entire world!
Wealthy Jews have opportunities to earn mitzvos that others with less
money don't have. They have to know where to put their money in

order to earn the most mitzvos, but if they do, they can earn very great merit. Whether a Jew gets rich suddenly or after an extended period of time, it is of the utmost importance to have Torah advisers who will be able to guide him in spending his money.

Q&A *In one of the recent* shiurim, *the Rav suggested that one should maintain an "illusion" in one's marriage for as long as he possibly can. Doesn't such a masquerade detract from the truthfulness of marriage and limit any opportunity for a strong, close, and helpful relationship?*

Absolutely not. Truthfulness is only beneficial when it is used as a medium to achieve a good purpose. But if truthfulness is misused it can be a very harmful medium, indeed. Therefore, I reiterate — Don't tell the truth about yourself, nor reveal the "true you" to your spouse. A woman came to me recently, outraged over something that her husband had done. I asked her what he could have done that would evoke such a response, and she responded by telling me that she had discovered that her husband had gone against her advice on a certain matter twelve years ago. Here we have a husband — a talmid chacham no less — who had committed what his wife had considered to be a cardinal sin — he had used his own mind. Now his wife was literally fuming, and she told me that she wanted to go and speak to a counselor. I simply told her that just because her husband didn't tell her that he was considering using his own brain to solve a certain issue, in no way that branded him a disloyal spouse. Spouses do not have to reveal everything to each other. Her husband is a talmid chacham and he has his own way of thinking. If he chooses to act according to his own intuition then so be it. A woman has her own secrets as well. Does she have a mitzvah to tell him about each and every course that she failed when she was in high school? If she doesn't, does it mean that she is hiding things from him? Such silliness! A woman doesn't have to nor is she required to tell her husband anything detrimental about her family. Why should she have to tell him such a thing? As a rule, a spouse should not tell the other spouse anything about himself that will not build up his image in the eyes of the spouse. On the contrary, you should try your hardest to be perceived in a certain image, even if it is entirely illusory. Of course, if you put on an act that can be easily seen through, then you're sure to fail. But if you're capable of masquerading your entire life — then, by all means, continue to do so. If you put on a quality performance throughout your stay in this world, then at the very end Hakadosh Baruch Hu will remove the curtain and give you a big round of applause.

This subject of acting is an important principle of human behavior. A person should never show what he truly is. When you get married, make up your mind that you are going to deceive your wife into thinking that you are actually a nice fellow. I'm not saying that it's easy, but try to the best of your ability. If you can't convince your wife, at least let her parents think that you are a nice person. Being that you only see them from time to time, this shouldn't prove to be too difficult. Maybe get your brother-in-law to think that you are a quality human being. Or better yet, if you want an interesting project, choose one member of your wife's family and go all out to impress upon him that you are actually a nice person. I myself did this once, not to my brother-in-law, but to a different member of my wife's family. Do this long enough and you will notice a very interesting result: Once you have succeeded in convincing this person that you are a decent fellow, you will be motivated to try it with other people as well. I remember well the words of a certain tzaddik. People once approached him and told him that his talmidim are deceiving the world by acting frumer than they really were. Do you want to know what his response was? He replied, "May they keep on deceiving others until they finally deceive themselves." Just wait and see, once you see that others consider you a nice fellow, you will begin to see yourself as a nice fellow as well. It is very good advice for one to hone his acting skills, because after a while you become absorbed into your role and identify with whom you are supposed to be playing. You never know, this just might be your greatest success in life.

Q&A *If a child performs mitzvos that his parents weren't responsible for teaching him, do they still receive a reward?*

Of course they do. But the more they contributed to his ability to perform that mitzvah, the more reward they will have earned. However, even if they have contributed nothing at all to his ability to perform the mitzvah they still get rewarded, as they are responsible for bringing this child into the world. Therefore *b'ra mezakeh abba*, a son accrues merit for his parents, even in such a case.

Q&A Why don't rabbanim spend more time lecturing on the importance of honesty in business?

In truth, a Jew gets taught this lesson each and every day. When a little boy goes off to the yeshivah and learns "*arba avos nezikin* (the opening chapter in *Maseches Bava Kamma*)," he is being taught to be honest in business! After all, the halachos of *nezikin* are all about taking care not to damage another person's property. A certain man once approached me and asked me why his grandson has to spend his time learning law in yeshivah; in all likelihood he won't end up becoming a lawyer anyway. Do you know what this man's grandson was learning? He was learning the halachos of *nezikin*! He was learning *Bava Kamma*, *Bava Basra*, and *Bava Metzia*! So I responded with a statement that I heard in the name of Rabbi Yisrael Salanter. Rabbi Salanter said that unless a person is raised with a sensitivity toward the property of other people, then don't expect this feeling to develop over time. A child must be ingrained with this sensitivity from the earliest age possible! A child must know that if you damage someone else's property you have to pay for it. This is a very big chiddush for a young child. He is used to going into a store, opening up boxes of merchandise, and damaging whatever he can. He doesn't know that is wrong to do such a thing. Therefore, the first lesson that a child is taught in yeshivah is that a *mazik*, one who inflicts damage, is responsible to pay for the damage he has wrought. He also learns that it is forbidden to steal and that he is required to return a lost item to its owner. Jewish children are certainly being taught these lessons, Baruch Hashem! *Mi ki'amcha Yisrael*, who is like the Jewish nation, which teaches its youths from the earliest age possible that it is wrong to damage *mammon acherim*, the property of others? No other nation can be compared to the Jewish people, for only we have *Bava Kamma*, *Bava Metzia*, and *Bava Basra* to ingrain in our children just how important it is to respect the property of others.

Q&A How can one instill children with respect for elders?

Let me ask you a question in return: How does one instill children with respect for Hashem? The answer is that you simply must teach it to them. The same thing applies to respect for one's elders. How does one go about it? I'll explain: The next time you are inspired to implant in your children an appreciation for the words *"mipnei seivah takum v'hadarta p'nei zakein* — in the presence of an old person shall you rise, and you shall honor the presence of a sage," tell them the following: Do you know why Hakadosh Baruch Hu commanded us to respect an older Jew, both man and woman? It is because they have lived a long life together with the Torah. For so many years they lived successfully with the mitzvos of kashrus, Shabbos, and *taharas hamishpachah*. Every day we say the words *"asher kidishanu be'mitzvosav,"* that performing mitzvos adds holiness to our being. This is especially true about the mitzvah of Shabbos, about which it is written *"mekadesh es amo Yisrael,"* that it makes the Jewish nation holy. It is only logical therefore, that elderly people are more *kadosh*, are holier, than younger people, as they have kept more mitzvos and observed more Shabbosos than have younger people. That is the way to teach your children respect for elders, by teaching them that elders are more *kadosh* than they are.

One must not forget, of course, the fundamental principle of *"chanoch la'na'ar al pi darko,"* that one must educate a child according to his way, his nature. Therefore, if a child is filled with a lot of energy and his personality tends to lean in the direction of haughtiness, then one must teach him to be moderate, polite, and humble. But it is important to realize, however, that *"al pi darko"* means that the chinuch, which you are giving over to your child, is a chinuch that is going to train him to walk down the long path of life that awaits him. *Darko* means "his path," and it refers to the highway of life, which we all must travel upon. If someone wants to drive a car, you wouldn't give him the keys without first teaching him the necessary traffic rules — that would be rather dangerous! You must teach your children how to properly function in the world. How to do that is a vast subject, and I won't be able to cover it in the short time that we have tonight.

A child must be taught derech eretz! Teach him not to talk too much. Teach him not to be lazy, and to have an interest in helping others out. Teach him to be friendly to everyone except to those who act immorally and incorrectly. Teach him to avoid *resha'im* at all costs. Teach him to constantly think about Hakadosh Baruch Hu. There are so many things that you have to teach a child! But this is a subject for a different time. The important thing to remember is that when you are teaching your child, you are teaching him to travel down the highway of life.

Q&A How can a person free himself from the negative character traits of sinah, *hatred,* and kinah, *jealousy?*

To accomplish this, I suggest opening a *Mesillas Yesharim* and studying it slowly, like a Tosafos. This will open your mind and enable you to gain an understanding of the issues that face a person in *olam hazeh*. A person must be well aquainted with the challenges he must be looking out for in this world! After doing this for a while, your mind will be filled with *seichel* and *chochmah*, and all the foolish attitudes of this world will automatically be filtered out. There will be no room in your mind for either *sinah* or *kinah*.

Of course, it must be understood that there is always going to be a certain amount of *kinah* remaining in you. You will never be entirely free of it. The *kinah* that I am referring to is called *kinas sofrim*, and it is a jealousy that will be with you forever. What is it? Let's say you are a great tzaddik, and you daven an hour long Shemoneh Esrei. But there is someone next to you in shul, maybe an even greater tzaddik, who davens longer. You instinctively feel a certain amount of jealousy in your heart of that tzaddik. You would also like to be able to daven and serve Hashem with the same intensity that he does. This is *kinas sofrim*, and it is a very good thing, indeed. There will be *kinah* in the next world as well. We are taught, "*Melamed she'kol echad michvo me'chupas chavero,*" that in Gan Eden each person is given his own chuppah to sit under, a beautiful chuppah of diamonds. For every mitzvah a Jew performs, another diamond is added to his chuppah. So let's say that a tzaddik and his wife are sitting beneath their chuppah of diamonds and basking in the pleasures of the next world. Suddenly they turn around, and they see that the chuppah next to theirs has a diamond which theirs does not have. This will be a cause of jealousy for them, as well as one of regret, because they, too, could have had that diamond in their chuppah.

Therefore, when one spends his time learning about the purpose of life, many foolish notions and ideas will leave his head. Like the Rambam says, when an individual learns Torah, his mind is freed from a great amount of the *shtus* of *olam hazeh*.

Q&A What is the best way to honor your parents and grandparents?

The best way to honor one's parents is by becoming a more complete servant of Hashem. Like I said before, take a *Mesillas Yesharim* and learn it like a *Tosafos* — in time it will change you. In order for a person to improve his avodas Hashem, he must have a rebbi. Unfortunately, however, we don't have very many rebbis today. So make the *Mesillas Yesharim* your rebbi; that's a very good rebbi to have! The *Mesillas Yesharim* will open your mind, and after studying it intently, it will show you how to become a bigger tzaddik. Do you think, perhaps, that you have reached the pinnacle of your avodah, and that there is no room for improvement? Let me ask you a question: Do you have the proper *kavanah* each time you recite the berachah of *Magen Avraham* in *Shemoneh Esrei?* You really should, because if you don't, you are not *yotzei* the entire *Shemoneh Esrei!* Your whole *Shemoneh Esrei* is *batel* and void if you don't have *kavanah* during *Magen Avraham!* So maybe there is some work that needs to be done there. Let's move along to the berachah of *mechayei ha'meisim*. Don't think that this area doesn't require extensive avodah as well! The Sages teach us that "*Kol Yisrael yeish la'hem chelek la'Olam Haba*," every Jew has a share in the World to Come. That's assuming, of course, that he doesn't have a weakness in his *emunah* in *techiyas ha'meisim*, the resurrection of the dead. For if he does, he forfeits his share in the World to Come! A person has to work on his belief in *techiyas hameisim*, and *Shemoneh Esrei* gives us that opportunity.

We then come to the berachah of *HaKel Hakadosh*. When we say *Hakadosh*, we are referring to Hashem's unfathomable perfection; it is perfection so sublime and exemplary that we can never finish speaking about it. This is what we mean when we say in the *Kedushah*, "*Ki'shem she'makdishim oso be'shmei marom*," that the *melachim* can not stop speaking about the greatness of Hashem. We, too, should never finish speaking about the unimaginable greatness of Hashem. But before we get to the point where we are able to think about *finishing* to speak about Hashem, we should work on *starting* to speak about Hashem. Let me ask you: How often do you speak about the greatness of Hashem? Do you *ever* think about the greatness of Hashem? Oh, it's a waste of time you'll say? You already know that He is great so why do you have to bother yourself by thinking about it? Oh no! You must constantly think about the greatness of Hashem! "*U'gedulasecha asaprenah*," you must constantly speak about His greatness as well!

But how does one do it? That's a big subject, and it's not for now.

The next berachah is *Atah chonen le'adam da'as*, You, Hashem, have granted us *da'as*. What an important berachah this is. There are so many people out there that have no *seichel* whatsoever. Many of these people are in insane asylums. Many of them are crowding into the offices of psychologists and psychiatrists, just waiting to be pre-scribed medication. These are people with impaired *da'as*. Baruch Hashem, you have a mind that functions normally! *Baruch Atah Hashem chonen hada'as!* Many people lose their minds as they grow older, depression can set in and disturb a person. All kinds of terrible things can befall a person's *da'as!* Are you thinking all of these thoughts when you say "*Baruch Atah Hashem chonen hada'as*"? If you're not, then there is a lot of work that needs to be done. Think about that.

When you say, "*S'lach lanu avinu,*" and ask Hashem for forgive-ness, are you simply banging your chest without any *kavanah*? If you are, think for a moment about the aveiros you transgressed today. You weren't *mechabed*, you didn't honor your parents sufficiently today. Bang. I talked too much today. Bang. I better start guarding my tongue. Each time you say *s'lach lanu* you should give some thought to something that you did wrong that day. There will be plenty of things to think about.

Shemoneh Esrei is truly a very important subject. If you daven *Shemoneh Esrei* properly, you are doing a very great service and pro-viding much benefit to your father, mother, and other ancestors. I just chose *Shemoneh Esrei* as an example, but in addition to *Shemoneh Esrei*, there are a thousand other mitzvos that you can perform and thereby honor your parents.

What steps can be taken to erase bad memories?

I know a person that once picked up a newspaper and saw a piece of *tiflah*, something that was foul and immodest. Needless to say, the image was stuck in his head and he needed a way to rid himself of this memory. What's a per-son supposed to do? What advice can be given to a person who glances at one of these foul billboards hanging high in the air? There are such terrible ideas on billboards and public advertisements! So what do we do? We follow the Rambam's advice and fill our heads with Torah ideas and thoughts of quality. This way there won't be any room left in our heads for thoughts that are vulgar and inappropriate. It's very, very important to have a head that is full of Torah ideas! For instance, are you thinking about how fortunate you are to be a Jew, *she'lo asani goy*? Are you thinking about your tzitzis — *u're'isem oso uzechartem es kol mitzvos Hashem*? When you glance at your tzitzis, does your mind become flooded with thoughts of mitzvos? If it doesn't, it's a pity. From now on, when you look at your tzitzis, get into the habit of thinking about mitzvos! Think about a mezuzah; think about *shemiras halashon* or about learning Torah! There are thousands of quality thoughts to think — all you have to do is think one of them. Let's say you are walking along and you see a mezuzah — what should you think? I'll tell you. Think about the omnipotence of Hashem — *Hashem Echad*. What does *Hashem Echad* mean? It means that He is the only Supreme Being that exists, and He made the world come into existence from nothing. At least that much you should think. I'm not saying that you will be able to think these thoughts each and every time you see a mezuzah, but it should at least remind you of something. Maybe it will remind you about the importance of learning Torah, and you'll get busy and learn. When you are sitting at your Shabbos table and enjoying your Shabbos meal, take a look at the mezuzah — it's watching you. When you are sitting in your house and eating, the mezuzah is watching you. Be careful not to eat what you shouldn't, don't get angry, act politely, and make a berachah with *kavanah*, because you are under constant surveillance. This is what the mezuzah should say to you, and this is how to get bad memories and thoughts out of your head.

Now what should you do about sad thoughts, worries, and concerns which plague you constantly? All you have to do is start worrying about your sins instead. As the pasuk tells us, "*Mah yisoen adam chai gever al chatav*," what does a person have to complain about? His aveiros! Believe me there is plenty to worry about, and once you start worrying about your sins, you won't worry about anything else. In our day and age, who worries about their sins? Most people spend their time worrying about other people hurting their feelings. That is what concerns us. So do you want a remedy for those worrisome thoughts — worry about your aveiros!

Q&A *Should parents mix in if they see their children fighting?*

Absolutely! Children should be taught that fighting is wrong and that they should never do it. Now, I understand that children are constantly fighting, but, nevertheless, it is a parent's responsibility to put an end to it time and time again, if need be. *Hinei mah tov u'mah na'im sheves* **achim** *gam yachad*! Teaching your children to get along in the house will train them for later in life! If you train them how to get along in the house, you will enable them to one day get along with their spouses, *machatanim*, business partners, employers, and just about everybody else. A life of shalom begins in the home! Therefore, make it a point to constantly speak about shalom with your children. Keep speaking about it with your child, and eventually something will sink into his little head.

Q&A *Why is it that the prohibition of taking revenge does not apply to criminals or the wicked?*

If you are interested in hearing the subject explained at length, I refer you to a tape entitled "Kosher Revenge." But for now, let me begin by saying that every instinct in mankind has been placed in man for a purpose. There is no instinct that is inherently wrong, it's just a question of what we do with it. The instinct of taking revenge was put into the world for the express purpose of taking revenge against criminals. We must vent our rage at wrongdoers, not like the liberals who ridicule the idea of the death penalty because they say it is only used in order to relieve our pent-up emotions. Do we have pent-up emotions? Yes. Must they be relieved? Yes. But why? Because Hakadosh Baruch Hu gave us those feelings *in order* that they be relieved! Hashem gave us those feelings in order that wrongdoers and criminals should be punished! Therefore, it was a very great crime when a certain Orthodox organization worked so hard to get the governor, who opposes the death penalty, elected. That Orthodox organization committed a crime against the Jewish people by doing what they did. For restoration of capital punishment is of the utmost necessity for keeping crime in check. Just keep in mind that these people have done a grave disservice to the Jewish people. The instinct of taking revenge is the key to dealing criminals the punishments they deserve. It is only when people have atrophied their natural instincts, and have suppressed the feeling of revenge, that crime flourishes and justice is no longer practiced.

Q&A *Why is the* tochachah *read at such a rapid pace? Would it not be more effective if it was read slowly and with more emphasis?*

The truth is that in our day and age, maybe it wouldn't be such a bad idea to read it that way. But in ancient times, people were well aware of the true meaning of the *tochachah*, and for them it created very great anxiety and depression. When people had a better understanding of the Torah, it sufficed to read the *tochachah* quietly and quickly. No one walked away unimpressed by the lesson the Torah was imparting, because there was a clear understanding of the *tochachah's* message. Sadly, today it is only a formality. It really wouldn't be a bad idea if the *tochachah* were read loudly and slowly, but I am not going to change any customs. The benefit of reading the *tochachah*, however, has been lost. Its purpose is to make us realize that nothing happens without a reason. When misfortune strikes, it is because the Jewish people are forsaking the Torah, and Hakadosh Baruch Hu is not about to sit quietly by and let that happen. But if you don't listen to the words of the *tochachah*, you will never know that lesson.

Q&A *What should be done when in-laws refuse to let their son-in-law study Torah?*

Now, I'm not sure what you mean by studying Torah. If studying Torah means lying in bed all day long and doing nothing, then the in-laws are certainly right. Let him go to work and support his wife! A husband is obligated to work and support his wife, unless he has some alternate way of earning an income. However, if a man has means of bringing in money, then sitting and learning all day is a wonderful thing! But if by studying Torah, you mean going at night to study Torah, or on Sundays or Shabbosos, then the in-laws have nothing at all to say about it, just as they have nothing to say about their son-in-law keeping a kosher home! You have to keep a kosher home no matter how vehemently your in-laws disapprove, and learning Torah is part of keeping a kosher home. Like we say everyday, *ve'dibarta bam*, you must speak about the Torah, *b'shivticha b'veisecha*, when you sit in your house. If you feel that it is necessary for you to learn in a beis medrash, then you are required to do that as well.

Q&A *What should we learn from the recent tragedy of three gedolei Yisrael passing away in such a short period of time?*

The first thing we have to learn is that "*Mi gever yichyeh ve'lo yireh maves* — who is the man that will live and never see death?" Everyone eventually dies, and it is important to have a realistic view on life. A person's life span is limited, and a person must therefore take the utmost care not to waste time. Now, just as a person has to get busy at accomplishing things in life, he also must get busy at learning how to enjoy life. Isn't that a novel idea? Life is short, and you must learn to enjoy it! Included in this is learning how to enjoy marriage. There are very many people who suffer through their marriage instead of utilizing it properly and being happy with it. Hakadosh Baruch Hu has blessed us with lives that are full of happiness, and when He sees that you are lacking recognition of that fact, He asks, "Why are you wasting the precious opportunity that I have given you? Don't you see that life is not forever?" This is one of the lessons that we must learn when we see somebody pass away. Namely, that we must begin to achieve and derive happiness from our lives. Now, I don't know if the passing of three gedolei Yisrael in a short period of time is an exceptional thing or not. But I do know that when any gadol passes away, it is meant to serve to inspire us to achieve all that we can in our lives.

A second lesson we should learn is that we must try to produce gedolei Yisrael by supporting yeshivos and kollelim! If you are a young person, try and become a gadol yourself. It may seem like an impossible task, but don't worry! You don't need a good head to become a gadol, all you need is a good pair of pants. You have to sit and learn. It goes without saying that you must learn in the right way. Learn and review what you have learned until you understand it clearly. Then go over it again and again and persist — eventually you will become a gadol. Therefore, go and utilize your spare time and make up your mind to become a gadol, a talmid chacham, or a talmid of a chacham. The world is today in need of *lomdei Torah*, more than it ever was. In conclusion, the passing of a Torah Jew should spur us to either support Torah institutions or become talmidei chachamim ourselves, or do both.

How can one subordinate his emotions to his intellect?

Q&A Let me draw a scenario for you: Let's say a person loses a large sum of money. Now, intellectually he knows that losing the money was the best thing that could have happened to him, as Hakadosh Baruch Hu only does what is good for a person. However, he nonetheless feels vexed and disturbed by the loss he incurred. How can he put his emotions under the control of his intellect? The answer is that he should realize that he has been granted a golden opportunity to add an element of perfection to himself! Let him think again and again about how this mishap was for his benefit. Yes, the pain of having lost the money might continue to lodge in his mind, but after constantly repeating that it was only for his benefit, the message will eventually sink in a little bit. If you can arrive at such a realization, then you have achieved something very great. It doesn't mean that you have to start singing and dancing over your misfortune, because such a reaction would be unnatural. But if you are able to ingrain this idea into your head, that everything that transpires is for the best and that maybe you are even becoming a better person because of it, then you are already on the road to self-improvement.

Q&A *Why didn't Yosef's brothers, who were tzaddikim, consult the Sages of their generation when they wanted to judge and condemn him as a* navi sheker, *a false prophet?*

Yosef's brothers *were* the Sages of the generation! The only question is why they chose not to consult their father. The answer to that is because he was a *nogei'a be'davar*, an interested party, who would find no fault with his beloved son, Yosef. Why didn't they consult their grandfather, Yitzchak? Because asking a grandfather is tantamount to asking a father. They were both *nogei'a be'davar*, and they would therefore not be consulted. The brothers then went to consult with the next greatest Sages of the generation — themselves. They were also the ones who spent the most time with Yosef, and they believed that they were able to see certain character traits in Yosef that their father simply could not see. It is for these reasons that the brothers took it upon themselves to decide that Yosef was a peril to the family.

Q&A *Should a person be frightened by the prospect of death?*

It depends on what you mean by being frightened. Should a person become depressed because of the prospect of death? By no means. The Jewish people don't dwell on the subject of death, and we try not to emphasize morbidity. It is for this reason that the Torah starts with a *beis*, a letter that is closed on three sides and only opened in the front. This is supposed to teach us to always and *only* look ahead in life. We are not to look toward Gan Eden, Gehinnom, or the day of death — just look ahead. Live for this world, and try to achieve whatever you can in it. Get married and live happily and joyfully! Shabbos should be joyful, as should one's performance of mitzvos! Torah is about achieving simchah! Live life with a zest and accomplish happily. Of course, in the back of your mind you must be aware that life is limited and that you aren't going to live forever, but don't grow depressed and morose because of it! The Torah does not want anyone to fall into depression because of the prospect of death.

Q&A *Does public opinion determine if a person is a mensch, or is that something which can only be determined by a talmid chacham?*

Only an individual who is capable at determining such things should be allowed to decide who is a mensch and who isn't. A talmid chacham is certainly a capable person, and the bigger a talmid chacham he is, the more capable he will be at determining whether a person is a mensch or not. But this is a very delicate subject, and if a person suspects that he is not a mensch, then he very well may not be one, so he better start working on himself!

Q&A *How can one conquer the trait of arrogance?*

Let us first listen to what our Sages have to say. "*Da mei'ayin basa, u'le'an atah holeich, u'lifnei mi atah asid li'tein din ve'cheshbon* — know from where you came, where you are going, and in front of Whom you will be called to give an account." We have three very important principles here. [end of tape]

Q&A *How can a person offer chizuk and encourage someone who is suffering from yisurim and misfortune?*

If the person is capable of understanding such words, speak to him and let him know that the *yisurim* he is enduring are cleansing him from his guilt. We are taught that *yisurim mechaprim*, yisurim achieve atonement for a person and save him from the suffering that he would have had to endure in the Next World. Only, the *yisurim* in the World to Come are worse than then the ones in this world — far worse. Therefore, when people suffer in this world they are receiving a very special gift from Hashem. Hakadosh Baruch Hu, in His kindness, is giving them an opportunity to endure the *yisurim* of *olam hazeh* instead of having to experience much more painful *yisurim* in *Olam Haba*. Tell this person that if he is accepts his *yisurim* lovingly and says, "Hashem, despite the fact that You have given me suffering, I love You," then he will have achieved something very great.

We say in *Shema* every day, "*Ve'ahavta eis Hashem Elokecha be'chol levavecha* — you should love Hashem with all your heart," "*u'vechol nafshecha* — and with all your life." The Sages comment on the pasuk "*u'vechol nafshecha*," "*Afilu be'sha'ah sheneital es nafshecha*," you should love Hashem even if He takes your life. Suppose you are 120 years old, and lying on your deathbed, and you come to the realization that you are about to leave the world. If you are able to say, "I love You, Hashem," despite all of your suffering and sadness, then that is a tremendous achievement. Being *mekabel yisurim be'ahavah*, accepting suffering with love, is an act which will earn you very great merit. Accepting *yisurim* without *ahavah* is also something — after all, it will spare you from worse suffering in *Olam Haba* — but it cannot compare to accepting suffering with love. But don't wait for the *yisurim* to decide to love Hashem; if you are able to love Him without *yisurim* it is a far greater accomplishment!

Let's say you bite into an apple, a delicious dessert, or a piece of cake — it tastes good, doesn't it? So tell Hashem how much you love Him for it! This is even better than being *mekabel yisurim be'a-havah*. For when a person is in the midst of suffering, he doesn't want it to simply pass him by without his having gained anything from it; he therefore thanks Hashem for the *yisurim*. But when a person is experiencing pleasure it is far more difficult to recall his love for Hashem! If he can, nevertheless, bring himself to express his love for Hashem, then he will have done something very great, indeed. So learn how to love Hashem for a piece of cake or a breath of fresh air! Go ahead and inhale right now; feel that beautiful breath entering your lungs and thank Hashem for the air He has given you. Air is very important! Put your head in a bucket for three minutes, and when you come out gasping, you will realize just how important air is!

So take a breath and thank Hashem for it. Go out walking in the street one night and thank Hashem for the nighttime! *Asher bedvaro ma'ariv aravim u'bechachmaso posei'ach shearim u'besevunah meshaneh itim* — nighttime is an incredible *chochmah* and *tevunah*! When you daven Ma'ariv give some thought to what you are saying! You are thanking Hashem for creating nighttime! Nighttime is a gift! Daytime is also a special gift, as we thank Hashem every day for creating the light when we say "*Yotzer ha'meoros.*" If a person learns to thank Hashem sincerely, he will have become one of the wisest of all people.

Q&A *Is it important for a person to know what is going on in the news? If so, how should he go about finding it out?*

Let me tell you how I get the news. I walk in the street and stop by a newsstand. Then I glance at some of the headlines. Do I see anything of quality? Nothing at all! What's in the headlines? The Knicks! Some tall black man with a basketball in his hand is pictured on the front page of the newspaper! Is anyone actually interested in that nonsense? What a crazy world! I wouldn't spend a penny to buy a newspaper. I walk by, read the headlines and continue on my way. But that's it. To spend your money on that silliness and have it pollute your mind is a terrible waste.

Q&A *What should a person do if he wants an attractive wife just to impress his friends?*

If a person wants to marry a woman simply to impress his friends, then he is not a very big chacham. You have to marry a woman with whom you will be able to get along and build a house of holiness.

Usually when a marriage starts off, you arrive at the realization that your wife has deceived you, and you have deceived her. You thought her middos were perfect? You soon find out just how perfect those middos really are. So get ready for reality. Everybody looks nice and speaks nicely when they are dating, but when it comes to living together, you begin to realize that things are not quite as simple as they may have initially seemed. Of course, you should try to choose the best spouse you can, but you will still be deceived. Do you want to have a successful marriage? Let me give you some tips: Keep your mouth closed and never criticize your spouse. Always say "yes" to your spouse and never say "no." Even if you don't intend to listen, say "yes" anyhow. Always be nice to your son-in-law and your father-in-law. Never say anything negative to your son-in-law; don't give him advice, just give him money and *kavod*. The same thing applies to a daughter-in-law — don't offer her any advice. Never, ever, mix into their relationship. Never ask your daughter how she gets along with her husband; the same way she shouldn't inquire about your marriage, you shouldn't inquire about hers — it's really none of your business. What takes place between a husband and wife is their own business, and they shouldn't tell their parents anything. Therefore, while it is very important for a person to look for the very best spouse he can find, it is just as important to make sure that he is being the best person he can be.

Q&A *How much time should a person give up in order to mekarev others?*

It depends on the person. Some people have a lot more to learn before they begin to shoulder the responsibility of teaching others. Such people don't have very much time to give away. Their going out to teach others would be comparable to an impoverished individual giving tzedakah — it's important that he make use of that time to teach himself.

I remember about sixty or more years ago, I and a group of other students were taking a walk with the Rosh Yeshivah of Slabodka. One of the students asked him why we spent so much time in the yeshivah as opposed to going out and doing *kiruv*. The Rosh Yeshivah answered that before we went out to *mekarev* others, it was necessary for us to first ripen on the *eitz ha'da'as*, the Tree of Knowledge. You can't just take a green apple and feed it to people! It first has to develop its taste and its juice; only when it contains something within itself can it be given over to others. The same thing applies to a yeshivah student. A yeshivah bachur must first ripen and mature inside the confines of a yeshivah before he will be able to give over what he has learned. Therefore it is of the utmost importance to first develop and mature in your personality before you can hope to influence others.

Q&A *How are we to utilize our experience of being discriminated against?*

It is important to realize that our being discriminated against is a sign of our aristocracy. *Kol she'ein vehayah le'echol einah mihem*, if a Jew is not afflicted by the goyim, it is a sign that he is not a real Jew. Being Jewish is something noble, something aristocratic. Our being persecuted, therefore, is our badge of aristocracy. So let's say you are walking down the street one day, and a goy calls you a dirty Jew. It should make you very happy! Baruch Hashem, you stem from noble ancestors and you belong to an esteemed race! On the other hand, *"kol haposel be'moomo posel,"* if someone refers to somebody else as dirty and no good, you can bet that *he* is the one who is dirty and no good. I remember walking in the Bowery about seventy years ago. All of a sudden, a goy turns around and calls me a filthy Jew. I took one look at this goy, and it wasn't too difficult to tell who was really the filthy one! He was drunk and staggering and could barely stand on his feet. He was dirty, unsanitary, and reeked so horribly that I couldn't even stand next to him. This is who called me a filthy Jew! Hakadosh Baruch Hu told us that He is going to make us distinctive among the nations of the world, and for that reason we are going to be despised. The wicked will always hate the good, and this is why all of the world's wicked loathe the Jews, because the Jews are the best people in the world. Jews tend to be the most decent, law-abiding, charitable and least violent people in the entire world. Jews have good middos and act with dignity. Most goyim, on the other hand, are devoted to immorality and to acting indecently. Even the goyim of one hundred and fifty years ago were filled with immorality, violence, and every form of indecency! *She'hivdilanu min ha'to'im* — Baruch Hashem, Hakadosh Baruch Hu distinguished us from the goyim, who live their lives in error and confusion. You must know that being a Jew means that you are the very best! You are the aristocrats of humanity! So *"al yipol lev adam me'kiva,"* don't ever feel sad or offended by the insults of the goyim! On the contrary, be happy that Hashem chose you and set you apart from the nations of the world. *"Baruch Hu Elokeinu she'baranu lichvodo v'hivdilanu min hato'im,"* Hashem separated us from all the nations that wander after false gods, embarking off on a direction that leads them straight to Gehinnom. As for Klal Yisrael, *"Kol Yisrael yeish lahem chelek la'Olam Haba"*!

Q&A *Why don't girls wear yarmulkes?*

Let me ask you: Why do men wear yarmulkes? The answer is because Hakadosh Baruch Hu declared, *"Atem tehiyu li mamleches kohanim ve'goy kadosh,"* the Jewish people is to be a nation of exalted Kohanim. As we are well aware, a cap was among the four *begadim* that the

Kohanim were required to wear; it was called a *para hamigvaos*. It is for this reason that we, too, wear yarmulkes and hats on our heads — to remind ourselves that we are a nation of Kohanim. In ancient times, it wasn't necessary to wear a yarmulke, for little time had elapsed since Hashem had uttered His eternal declaration. Each and every Jew identified fully with this concept and viewed himself as a Kohen. But as the generations progressed and hundreds of years passed by, there were some Jews that began to forget their status as Kohanim. On account of this, Jews began to place yarmulkes on their heads as reminders. In the morning, we recite the berachah "*Oter Yisrael be'tifarah*," thanking Hashem for crowning us with splendor. This berachah refers to the head coverings worn by Jewish men. Notice that the words *tifarah* and "*para*" *migvaos* share the same root. This is because the yarmulkes and hats that we don each day are meant to be reminders of our status as Kohanim and servants of Hashem! By wearing a yarmulke we show that we are *yirei Shamayim* and loyal servants of Hakadosh Baruch Hu.

It is important for girls to know that leadership rests in the hands of their husbands. This is a very important lesson! Let us think about this for a moment: As we know, men are commanded to perform *mitzvos asei she'haz'man grama*, time-bound mitzvos. Women, on the other hand, are not required to perform these mitzvos. What is the reason for this difference? The answer is that women have other important obligations to tend to, which exempt her from these commandments. A woman must know that she is a *briah shel chessed*, she has been created for the purpose of performing *chessed*. Being a wife and mother is a very significant role, and it requires her to be selfless and totally dedicated to performing *chessed*! It takes a woman's entire effort to succeed in being an efficient mother and wife. Investing her abilities in raising children is very time consuming but is a tremendous *zechus* for her! The Gemara goes so far as to tell us that the *zechus* of a woman is greater than the *zechus* of a man. Why is that? Because on occasion a man will do a certain mitzvah for the sake of *kavod*, in order to gain prestige. Women, however, don't have any chance to show off, as they are always in their homes and tending to important things. It is for this reason that the *zechus* of a woman is greater than that of a man, and it therefore stands to reason that a man has to work much harder in order to be found *zocheh* in the eyes of Hashem. Now, of course, a woman is considered *kadosh*, holy; *every Jew is a kadosh.* But she has a different role than a man, and she must realize that. Don't try to be an Orthodox feminist and do all of the same things that men do! Your job is to be a kosher Jewish woman who serves Hashem in the way that He intended! You must get married, have children, and raise them in the *derech haTorah* that they should grow to be decent frum Jews! What a tremendous accomplishment that would be! If you do this, you will one day sit on a golden throne in Gan Eden and reap a reward that is no less than any man! Just do it the way a woman is supposed to do it, that's all. Just remember: A man puts on a yarmulke or a hat in order to resemble a Kohen who served Hashem in the *Beis Hamikdash.* A woman also has a *beis hamik-dash* — her home. In that *beis hamikdash*, she needn't wear a yarmulke — her snood is good enough! This is a woman's role in *mamleches kohanim*, and it is Hakadosh Baruch Hu's assurance that if a woman serves Him like she is supposed to, she will receive as great a share in *Olam Haba* as any man.

Why did Hakadosh Baruch Hu create the world?

The Sages teach us that *olam chessed yibaneh,* the world was built on the foundations of kindliness. In other words, the world was created for the purpose of bestowing *chessed.* The Name of Hashem, the one which is spelled *yud-kei-vav-kei,* refers to Hashem's attribute of being a *mehaveh.* What does this mean? Let me explain. Everyday we say the words *Shema Yisrael Hashem Elokeinu.* The Name Hashem over here refers to Hashem's being a *mehaveh* — the One Who has brought everything into existence. The pasuk then continues, *Hashem Echad.* Here, the Name of Hashem refers to a different aspect of His being a *mehaveh;* namely, that not only has He made the world, but He continues to sustain it and will it to exist. This is the greatest act of kindness imaginable! All one has to do is to look at the continuous existence of our world, and he will clearly see how Hashem is nothing but *chessed. Olam chessed yibaneh!* This is the meaning of the pasuk, "*Hodu la'Hashem ki tov ki l'olam chasdo,*" that His world is one of kindliness. That is why Hashem created the world — *ki chafetz chessed hu,* because He desires kindliness. Avraham Avinu sat at the entrance of his tent *ke'chom ha'yom,* when it was excruciatingly hot outside. What was he waiting for? For wayfarers — he wanted to perform acts of kindness for them. It was so hot outside, however, that not even wayfarers were walking around! Avraham said that he couldn't live that way; if he couldn't host guests then he was wasting his life. Avraham understood that his purpose in life was to emulate Hashem! The same way that Hashem was *machnis orchim* by allowing *us* to live in His world, so too, Avraham wished to be *machnis orchim*. He wished to show that he was emulating Hashem every day of his life. Avraham grew so disappointed that Hashem finally sent somebody for him to host. Who did Hashem send? Now, He couldn't send human beings; it was far too hot outside for any man. So Hakadosh Baruch Hu sent *malachim* instead! When Avraham caught sight of the *malachim* he fell down on his face and pleaded with them, "*Al na sa'avor,*" not to pass him by, but rather, to partake of his hospitality. We see, therefore, that Avraham lived to emulate Hashem who is *kulo chessed*. It is for this reason that he so desperately wanted to host guests and tend to their needs.

So why did Hashem create the world? For the purpose of bestowing *chessed* to mankind. But He didn't only intend to bestow the kindness of this world. Oh no. This world was created to give us an opportunity to prepare for the unimaginable *chessed* of *Olam Haba*. By living properly in this world, we will merit partaking of a *chessed* that is so great that not even *malachim* could fathom its greatness. That *chessed* is *bimkomo*, in Hashem's Heavenly abode, and it is a kindness that the tzaddikim are enjoying this very minute, just as Hashem intended when He created the world. Hakadosh Baruch Hu is a *chafetz chessed* and that is why He created the world.

Q&A The Sages *state that Hashem initially offered the Torah to the goyim, yet they refused it. How are we meant to understand this?*

What you're asking is as follows: If the Jewish people were the intended recipients of the Torah, then why did Hashem offer it to the other nations of the world? I'll illustrate the answer by means of an important mashal. From the beginning of time, the world has had great men. Noach was a great man and the father of all the goyim. Chanoch, who came later, was also a very great man. Throughout these generations, Hashem was constantly watching and observing how the nations of the world would respond to these great men, and what he saw was rather disappointing.

Perhaps there were some people who followed their lead and improved themselves, but there were not enough. This was a very great disappointment. So Hashem kept waiting and watching. *Asarah doros me'Adam ve'ad Noach*, there were ten generations from Adam Harishon until Noach, and the results were disappointing to Hashem. Then there were *asarah doros me'Noach ad Avraham* which were also disappointing, that is, until Avraham appeared on the scene. In Avraham, Hashem saw a man whose entire being — mind and emotions alike — were devoted to understanding the greatness and kindliness of Hashem. In addition, he also wanted to spread his knowledge of Hashem and teach others — this is the man that Hashem had been waiting for, and he was therefore chosen to be the father of the Jewish nation. The Sages compare Avraham to a tree blossoming with fresh fruits in the barren wilderness. I found fresh fruits in the wilderness, said Hashem, and I have therefore chosen Avraham and his descendants. Up until Avraham Avinu, the nations of the world had tremendous opportunities! Any one of them could been the chosen people! Avraham wasn't forced to become the *tzaddik* that he became; the world is full of free will and anyone could have stepped up had they chosen to.

When the Sages tell us that Hashem offered the Torah to the different nations of the world, it doesn't mean that he approached each nation with a Chumash, and said to them, "Accept the Torah." We know that the goyim's response was "*Mah k'siv bei*," they wanted to know what is written in the Torah. The *Sifri* tells us that this is all a mashal and such a thing never actually happened. Hashem didn't really show each of the nations a Chumash. Rather, he gave them opportunities to choose the paths to righteousness which are outlined in the Torah. They had opportunities to choose *tznius*, decency, and morality but they failed to do so. It was Avraham who was chosen, and it was his children who said *na'aseh ve'nishma*. Hashem had finally found the people he has been looking for, and this is what it means that the goyim rejected the Torah.

Q&A *How should a person feel when he sees a Reform leader?*

Just rush away! Keep away from *resha'im*, as David Hamelech taught us, "*Ashrei ha'ish*," happy is the man who has nothing to do with *resha'im*. Don't associate with them at all. Any organization that they belong to, you make sure not to belong to. Let me teach you an important lesson: Only associate and spend time with tzaddikim. *Ashrei ha'ish*, happy is the man whose time is spent with tzaddikim who go on the *derech Hashem*. Such a man is surely going to fulfill the lofty purpose for which he was created.

Q&A *Is there an idea that sometimes it is better to speak back to a goy who has instigated a quarrel? Of course, to start up with him is a bad idea. But maybe it is worthwhile to show him that Jews are not shmatas, rags, that can be ridiculed. Shouldn't we demonstrate self-confidence?*

You should realize that it is your *yetzer hara* that is trying to convince you not to be a shmata. Look at what is says in *Mishlei*: "Al teitzei la'riv ma'her," don't be too quick to quarrel. It certainly pays to be a shmata! All of this business about not letting yourself be a shmata is something new and foolish. Next time you find yourself wondering, "How can I let that goy make a shmata out of me?" realize that it is for your benefit! If someone threw a diamond worth $1,000 at you, what would you say? You'd say, "Throw another one at me!" Getting ridiculed is a diamond! This goy is making you a billionaire! Just stand there and listen to his insults, and don't say anything at all. Forget about the incident, and in time you will see who the real winner is. He'll also respect you more for it later.

Q&A *The pasuk states, "Shomer pesa'im Hashem — that Hashem protects fools." That being the case, why doesn't Hashem protect all the foolish people who smoke?*

You must understand that there are two types of *pesa'im*. One kind of *pesi* is a person that doesn't know any better. Let me give you an example: Suppose a person takes ill and goes to a doctor. The doctor examines the man and then goes on to prescribe him the wrong medication. There was a time when all doctors were of the opinion that if a man had a fever, the way to cure him was by melting pearls and pouring them down his throat. That's what the doctors did to Louis XIV! This is foolishness, of course. But the patient isn't at fault; the doctors prescribed this foolishness! In such a case we say *shomer pesa'im Hashem*, Hashem protects *pesa'im*. Forty years ago, when a yeshivah bachur announced his engagement and handed out cigarettes, it was certainly meshugas, nonsense. But in those days, there were no warnings on cigarettes; no one knew how dangerous they were! Therefore, this bachur is a *pesi* who simply didn't know any better. But today, smoking makes you a different kind of *pesi*, because cigarettes have warnings on them. Nowadays, everyone knows that cigarettes cause a variety of illnesses! Therefore, if a bachur gets engaged nowadays and gives out cigarettes, he is far worse than a *pesi*! So there are two kinds of *pesa'im*. The first is a *pesi* who just doesn't know any better. The second, however, is a person who could have taken the necessary steps to avoid the problem but didn't. *That* person is not a *pesi*, but a *poshei'a*, a negligent individual. The Gemara discusses a case where a man marries a *ketanah*, a young girl. There is a dispute between the *Tanna'im* whether or not the couple should have children; being that the girl is yet young, it might be detrimental to her health. The Sages answer that they can indeed have children, because *shomer pesa'im Hashem*, Hashem will protect them. There was a time when people married young girls; this was a natural and normal thing to do. If a risk is being taken in the act of nature, the couple is not blamed and *shomer pesa'im Hashem*. But if people engage in activities which their *seichel* tells them is harmful, then they deserve whatever happens to them.

Q&A *We are taught that the older a talmid chacham gets, the wiser he becomes. However, we see many cases of aged talmidei chachamim who unfortunately lose their wisdom. How are we to explain this contradiction?*

The only time a talmid chacham decreases in knowledge and wisdom is if he loses his mind. But you must realize that when a talmid chacham loses his *seichel* it is as if he is dead. You are no longer looking at the same person. I know of a certain talmid chacham who, sadly, lost his mind at an old age and began to walk around the streets improperly clad. Do you mean to tell me that this is the same person as before? It's not the same person; the talmid chacham has passed away and someone else has taken his place. But if a talmid chacham retains his *seichel* there is no question that he will mature in his wisdom and understanding of Torah. Therefore, there is no contradiction whatsoever. When a talmid chacham ages, he grows in wisdom. That is, of course, unless he becomes senile, in which case he is no longer the same individual.

Q&A It states in halachah that one who is davening should make his requests in lashon hakodesh. *Is the reason for this because the* malachim *that carry our tefillos to Hashem only understand* lashon hakodesh?

Malachim, by the way, understand other languages; they know much more than we do. *Malachim* simply favor a person who speaks *lashon hakodesh*. They want to hear a person speak *lashon hakodesh*, and when he does they intervene on his behalf. But you realize, of course, that Hakadosh Baruch Hu can hear anything, and He doesn't need any emissaries whatsoever. *Binah hagigani*, He can even understand your thoughts! It all depends on whether you daven with *kavanah* or not. A person only needs *malachim* to intervene for him if his davening lacks *kavanah*. But if he davens with the utmost *kavanah* then he doesn't need any *malachim* at all. The problem is that many of our tefillos are not so sincere. We therefore send Hashem a note by way of a *malach*, hoping that He will give it a look and accept our davening. But the *malach* has to want to deliver the note in the first place. If he takes a look at your note and it is composed in *lashon hakodesh*, then you can be pretty confident that it will get delivered. But a note in English? *Malachim* don't like English very much. They only deliver notes in *lashon hakodesh* or Yiddish. Yiddish is the Jewish language, by the way; it is a holy, holy language. You should try to speak more Yiddish! The only reason that I speak English here is because there are many people in attendance who don't understand Yiddish. But you should train yourselves to speak Yiddish in your homes. Train your children to speak Yiddish. If you speak Yiddish, not only will the *malachim* listen to you, but Hakadosh Baruch Hu will give you greater berachos as well. Hashem wants to hear *our* language! By speaking Yiddish, you are walking in the footsteps of Rabbi Akiva Eiger *zt"l*, and all of the other great gedolei Yisrael who for hundreds and hundreds of years spoke and delivered their shiurim only in Yiddish! It is a language of *kedushah*! Yiddish is full of holy words that have their roots in the Gemara. Take the word "*tamar*," for example, which in Yiddish means "maybe." That word is derived from the Gemara's expression "*Ve'im tomar*"! "*Mistama*," which in Yiddish means "likely," is another word that has its roots in the Gemara; as does the word "*a'vada*," which means "certainly." There are so many Gemara words in Yiddish! Yiddish is endowed with the *kedushah* of the Gemara and the *kedushah* of all the gedolei Yisrael and tzaddikim who spoke it.

Lashon hakodesh is also fine — if you are actually speaking *lashon hakodesh*. Modern, newspaper Hebrew is not *lashon hakodesh*; it's a new language, a translation of English. All of the idioms and styles of modern-day newspaper Hebrew are similar to the idioms and styles of the goyish newspapers, and that is not called Hebrew. But if a person speaks true *lashon hakodesh*, like they sometimes speak around the *Sefardi* talmidei chachamim, then that's just fine!

Just remember that our ancestors in *Mitzrayim* merited *geulah* partly because of the fact that they did not change their language. It is of the utmost importance that we follow in their footsteps!

Q *Can the Rav tell us the hespedim that were said after the passing of the Chafetz Chaim?*

A To be honest, it was a very long time ago and I really don't remember. There was certainly a great deal said, however. I could tell you what I thought at the time, though. Like so many others, I had heard stories of the Chafetz Chaim when he was still alive. A friend of mine, who is in the Next World now, went to see the Chafetz Chaim. I wasn't able to go, as I didn't have enough money to travel from Lithuania to Poland. In those days, you couldn't go directly to Poland if you didn't have a legal connection, and you had to travel through Latvia instead. My friend made the trip to Poland and entered the waiting room of the Chafetz Chaim. In the waiting room, my friend noticed an elderly man lying sound asleep on a bench. He thought nothing of it, and he continued to wait. He ended up waiting a very long time. After much time had passed, the old man woke up and noticed my friend sitting next to him. "Young man, how can I help you?" he asked. "I've come to see the Chafetz Chaim," was my friend's reply. "I *am* the Chafetz Chaim," said the old man. My friend was speaking to the Chafetz Chaim, and he hadn't even realized! The Chafetz Chaim began to tell my friend a *vort*: "In America," said the Chafetz Chaim, "people say that time is money and money is time. Money is therefore something very precious. If you waste money, you will have to waste more time earning money. My advice to you is save your money. This way you won't have to work very much, and you could spend the rest of your life sitting and learning. Time is money and money is time. Time, as you know, is life. It therefore stands to say that money is also life. So don't waste any money, and you won't waste your life." That's as much as I can remember about their meeting.

I remember many years ago when the Chafetz Chaim was still a younger man, and had recently published the *Mishnah Berurah*. I was just a boy then, but I recall the day when the *Mishnah Berurah* arrived in the American yeshivos. It was certainly valued, being that it was a new *sefer*, but it didn't command any of the *chashivus* that it commands today. Why was that? Because people never truly appreciated the Chafetz Chaim when he was alive. Many people did not realize just how great he was, and they didn't view him in the way that the later generations do. The Chafetz Chaim did not make himself out to be an important individual; he carried himself simply and was a *pashut* person. There were people who found it difficult to look up to such a *pashut* person! For example, the Chafetz Chaim refused to wear gloves. He believed that wearing gloves was *ga'avadik*, an act of haughtiness, so he kept his hands in his pockets instead. People with a more superficial outlook on life would say, "Reb Yisrael Meir, what a fine ba'alebus, such a fine person." But did they think that he was the *gadol hador*? Hardly. As I've mentioned before, we, too, have to work very hard not to make that same mistake in our generation. There are gedolim and tzaddikim today that deserve far more respect than they receive; we have to make *every* effort to try and appreciate them.

Q&A *If gaining an awareness of Hashem is the most important thing that a Jew can do, then why don't we spend our days learning* Chovos Halevavos *and* Mesillas Yesharim *as opposed to* Bava Kamma, Gittin, *and the other* masechtos *in* Shas?

That is a very good question. Let me explain to you why we learn a *sefer* like *Chovos Halevavos*: When we learn *Chovos Halevavos*, we are learning *how* to live. Learning Gemara, however, is *living*. Without learning Gemara, you are not really alive. As we say everyday, *Ki heim chayeinu* — Gemara is our life! We are taught, "*Lo karas* Hakadosh Baruch Hu *bris im Yisrael ela mishum Torah shebe'al peh*," Hashem entered into a covenant with us only due to the fact that we would learn the *Torah shebe'al peh*! We see, then, that learning the Gemara is very, very important! But when we learn Gemara it is also important for us to have other forms of Torah knowledge as well. This Torah knowledge is referred to as *tzudah*, things that are learnt in addition to the Gemara. This knowledge enhances the Gemara learning and gives it more taste! Let's say that you are eating a piece of meat. The meat, however, was not flavored with salt, onions, or other flavorings. That meat is not going to taste so good! The same thing applies to learning the Gemara; it becomes so much more precious and enjoyable when an understanding of our *sefarim* enhances it! The great *sefarim* awaken our minds and supply us with an insight into *Da'as Hashem, bitachon* in Hashem, and *ma'alos Hashem!* Once you have ingrained some of this knowledge, open up a Gemara and see how it is all expressed in its halachos, and in how we apply these halachos practically. This is so important! Most of our time must be spent learning Gemara; if you have time and desire to learn Mussar, it must be correctly apportioned.

Rav Yisrael Salanter once praised his talmid Rav Simchah Zissel Ziv. Rav Simchah Zissel had approached his rebbi, Rav Yisrael, and had asked him how much time each day he should devote to Mussar study. Rav Yisrael responded, "For you, three hours a day is sufficient." Why did Rav Yisrael instruct Rav Simchah Zissel to learn three hours of Mussar a day? Because he knew that his talmid spent not three hours, but *twelve* hours a day learning in the beis medrash! For such a person, three hours would be enough. But a person must learn a great deal in order to justify three hours of Mussar learning a day. In most European yeshivos, a half-hour Mussar seder was the norm. But believe me, it was truly an experience to witness the way that they learned Mussar in those yeshivos! I arrived in Europe at the end of the great era, but the yeshivos were still on the highest *madreigah.* Everyday there was a half-hour Mussar seder — a very inspiring Mussar seder, I might add! Everyone learned a small section of a Mussar *sefer* at a time and repeated it again and again. At first they read slowly and softly, but as they continued to read, their voices grew louder and louder. By the end of the *seder*, everyone was shouting! The entire yeshivah had erupted, each *bachur* repeating a *ma'amar* over and over again! I remember sitting next to a certain tzaddik who repeated his *ma'amar* so many times that it finally penetrated my ears and made a tremendous impression on me, as well as on everyone else that heard him! All of the bachurim learned Mussar that way, and they were very inspired by it. Mussar is a tremendous subject. But don't think that they only learned Mussar in Slabodka! Oh no, they learned much Torah as well! In the Slabodka Yeshivah, the bachurim waged the *milchemes haTorah*, the war of Torah, all day long! It was like armies battling each other inside the yeshivah! There were great tumults in learning, halachah, and *pilpul chaverim*, discussions and debates among peers, that occupied the days and nights of the bachurim! When it came time for Mussar seder, however, the *pilpul* stopped immediately, and then the Mussar learning began.

In short, although Mussar *sefarim* are valuable and precious, we must never forget *ki heim chayeinu*, that it is *limud haTorah* which sustains us.

Q&A *Can the Rav tell us a little bit about the recently departed, Rabbi Mordechai Gifter zt"l?*

Rabbi Gifter and I knew each other as young boys, and we were friends. He was a very frum boy, idealistic and intelligent even at a very young age. I was the one who advised him to travel to Telshe, Europe and learn in the yeshivah there. When I got married in Europe, Rabbi Gifter was in attendance. I even have a photograph of him at my wedding. He developed a very good head and a very sharp mind, and that is why he deserved to become what he became. He was always a *yirei Shamayim*, a *ba'al derech eretz*, and was constantly engrossed in learning. For a period of time he was a rav in a small town in Massachusetts, after which he traveled to Telshe and eventually married. When Rabbi Elya Meir Bloch passed away, the time came for Rabbi Gifter to be appointed rosh yeshivah of the Telshe Yeshivah in America.

The loss of Rabbi Gifter is a far greater loss than you can imagine. In the last years of his life, he was completely unable to function, as he was very ill. But in his prime, he was a very active personality. He spoke out against national offenses and wicked ideas. When goyim did things that were wrong and corrupt he publicly condemned it. He was a man with a conscience and a real fighter, but was always a ben Torah and a *yirei Shamayim*. Truly a great loss.

Q&A *Is global warming something to be concerned about, or can we rest assured that Hakadosh Baruch Hu will protect the earth?*

Global warming is entirely a concoction of the liberals. You needn't be concerned about it at all.

Q&A *How can one think about* Olam Haba? *Is it possible for us to imagine it?*

We know just as much about *Olam Haba* as a man who was born blind knows about the color red. Just as he has no way of possibly grasping the color red, so do we have no possible way of fathoming the pleasures of *Olam Haba*. We do know, however, that there is no pleasure in this world that can even remotely compare to the bliss of *Olam Haba*. We also know that the bliss of *Olam Haba* increases each and every second that we are there. That is a very important principle. It is also of great importance to know that we have been placed in this world in order to prepare for *Olam Haba*. Singing to Hashem in this world will earn us the right to sing before him in the World to Come. So start learning how to sing to Hashem — it will serve you well in *Olam Haba*!

How do sandstorms benefit the world?

I must admit that I don't have the answer to every question. However, I will tell you what I know. A sandstorm is certainly a very good thing! When sand is removed from a place that it had been resting in for an extended period of time, not only does it prevent bacteria and vermin from developing in those areas, but it also allows the bottom layers of sand to be exposed to the sunlight. Now, sunlight kills germs. Quite often you have germs on your hands that you are not even aware of! What happens to them? In most cases, the sunlight kills them in about twenty minutes or so. So by a sandstorm's coming and revealing the bottom layers of sand, the sun is able to kill the germs and smaller mites which are developing there! Instantaneously, we are provided with a fresh, germ-free desert surface! I am sure that there are additional benefits to a sandstorm as well.

Let me take a moment to discuss the benefits of forest fires. A forest fire is a very great benefit! Rotten old trees that have become havens for bacteria and all kinds of harmful germs are razed to the ground. The forest floor is now cleared and ready to be occupied by fresh, healthy, new trees which contain no bacteria or fungi whatsoever! We must know that every time the earth is disturbed, a certain rejuvenation of the earth's surface takes place. This, in turn, causes a renewal of growth in a healthy way.

But doesn't a forest fire burn healthy trees also?

Yes it does. However, it is of the utmost necessity. For if these trees would not be destroyed, in time they would be been poisoned by the fungi that are already being harbored in the diseased trees. These trees must be sacrificed in order to be able to save the forest and start again. These are not my words; all the books say that a forest fire is a benevolent phenomenon, which causes a fresh new crop of trees.

Q&A *Will families reunite when Mashiach comes? What about husbands and wives?*

The relationships that we see in our lifetime are eternal relationships; they last forever and ever. The pasuk states, "*Hinei mah tov u'mana'im sheves achim gam yachad.*" Do you know why it is so good when brothers live together in harmony? Because if their relationship is one of peace and harmony, then it will last them for all eternity. Each brother will be filled with joy in *Olam Haba*! This is not to say that a person's happiness in *Olam Haba* is dependent on someone else, because it isn't. It means to say that part of the happiness will be a feeling of tremendous affection for those that were close to him. On the other hand, if there is disharmony, then the brothers will not be together in *Olam Haba*, and that joy will be lacking.

Let's say you have children — are you happy with them? Do you derive nachas from them in this world? If you do, then in the World to Come you will take even greater pleasure from the nachas that you feel. You will be tremendously happy with the nachas that your children gave you, and it will be part of your joy in *Olam Haba*! The more unity that exists between people that are closely related, the more politely and pleasantly you act, the happier you will be in *Olam Haba*! If husbands and wives are polite to one another, tolerant and patient with each other, and even willing to take a little bit of scolding in good humor, then there is no way to describe the happiness that will accompany them in the World to Come! There they will be together in sublime joy; it will be a very great nachas for them! It is difficult for us to even imagine the great happiness a husband and wife will feel when they greet one another in Gan Eden. There they will be considered one unit, and they will be forever united. They will have a *chibah*, a love that will continue for all eternity and under the most optimum circumstances. That's the most I can tell you until I get there — then I'll tell you more.

Does this concept apply to friends and neighbors as well?

Every relationship is eternal to a certain extent. The degree to which it is eternal varies depending on the relationship. A good friend is not as eternal a relationship as a husband and wife. A son is also more eternal than a good friend. Certainly, if someone has an extremely cordial relationship with someone else — *chavrusas*, for example, or very friendly neighbors — then they, too, will enjoy each other's company in the World to Come. One will especially benefit if he establishes close ties with a tzaddik in this world. If you are able to develop a relationship with him, then you will maintain a certain connection in *Olam Haba*. I can't get into it now, but there is no question that all relationships in this world are going to be maintained on a much higher level in *Olam Haba*.

But the main principle is that whatever you accomplish now is a *hachanah*, a preparation for *Olam Haba*. The fact that you are thinking about Hakadosh Baruch Hu this moment is a very great achievement, oh yes. In the World to Come you will merit to gaze at the *ziv HaShechinah*, the shine of Hashem's Divine Presence, according to the effort you made to think about Him when you were alive. However, the less a person thinks about Hashem in this world, the less he will be able to enjoy the *ziv HaShechinah*. The Rambam said that, by the way. He said "*tzaddikim yoshvim ve'a-troseihem be'rosheihem*," in *Olam Haba*, tzaddikim sit with crowns on their heads and enjoy the splendor of the Shechinah. What are these "crowns" that the tzaddikim are wearing? They are the *da'as*, the awareness of Hashem that they acquired in this world. To the extent that you've acquired a crown in this world, to that same extent you will merit to derive pleasure from gazing at the Shechinah in *Olam Haba*.

Q&A *We find that the Sages criticized certain eating habits, such as eating bread without porridge. Why did they condemn such a thing?*

If a person had a diet that was harmful to his health, the Sages were quick to criticize it. A person must eat foods that are capable of being digested. He must take care to drink enough water with his bread in order that it should saturate and soften the food in his stomach. If a person doesn't drink enough, he will find it difficult to relieve himself. It's a *sakanah*, a health risk, not to drink enough liquid with your bread. The Sages were critical of people who lived abnormally, and put their health at risk. Putting your health at risk is a sin like any other.

The Rav once stated that a person who attributes his misfortune and unhappiness to his sins is a sinner. Doesn't the Gemara say, however, that if an individual finds himself afflicted by yisurim he should yefashfeish be'ma'asav, examine his deeds?

It all depends. If a person is struck by misfortune he should certainly examine his deeds. That is, unless he will examine his deeds and attribute his *tzaros* to everything but his own carelessness. If he ignores the fact that it was his own negligence which brought suffering upon him and instead searches for other reasons, then he is truly a sinner.

Let me give you an example: A young man once told me that a *meshulach*, a tzedakah collector from Eretz Yisrael, came to his house. The young man very kindly prepared a glass of hot tea, and placed it on the dining room table for the *meshulach*. He then went into the kitchen, leaving the glass of tea on the table, and began to prepare a meal for the *meshulach*. In the meantime, the young man's son approached the table and tipped the steaming hot tea all over himself! The child was scalded and had to be rushed to the hospital. The father later approached me and asked what sin he had done to deserve such a tragedy. I told him the sin of leaving his son alone in a room with a hot glass of tea. That would have been the proper way to be *yefashfesh be'ma'asav!*

There was another fellow who used to fulfill the requirement of *mehadrin min ha'mehadrin* on Chanukah. He therefore gave his son — his only son — a menorah and candles. The father left the room for a few moments and the son burnt himself to death. Oh, the father was certainly *mekabel be'ahavah*, he accepted Hashem's decree with the utmost of love! "Maybe I spoke *lashon hara*, and therefore deserved this," the father said. "Maybe I didn't daven with the proper *kavanah* ..." But the sin of carelessly leaving his son alone with candles didn't even occur to him! That is a very terrible sin.

The title of the section in which the Rambam enumerates the halachos that pertain to murder is *Hilchos Rotzei'ach U'Shemiras HaNefesh*, the laws of dealing with a murderer and taking care to guard one's life. The two go hand in hand; if a person doesn't take precautions and the necessary steps to insure one's safety, he is a *rotzei'ach*.

Q&A *Should a woman have to suffer from a husband who is a boor?*

Once you are married you must make the best of it! Maybe you are the one to blame for your husband's behavior! In any event, you should look before you leap, but once you do, stay where you are. Live your life in a way that is satisfactory and in the end you'll be rewarded for it. People are so dissatisfied in today's world! The world today is in a motion of disturbance and divorce is often the result. Every divorce is a tragedy; it's a *churban Beis HaMikdash* to destroy a Jewish home. It doesn't matter who you marry; as long as he is *shomer mitzvos* and working to support your family, then you should make it your business to remain loyal to him and stay together. Stick it out, and you will one day marry off your grandchildren together and have much nachas. But whatever you do, don't fuss about your husband and say that you want to leave him. Don't start looking for faults in him; you should have married a better person, you think, a more affectionate lamdan. No, no. The one you married is for you and he is the one that you should stay with.

Q&A *How many times should a yeshivah bachur finish* Mesillas Yesharim *each z'man?*

He doesn't have to finish it many times. Go slowly and don't rush through it, because it is a very deep *sefer*. A great way to learn it is by repeating each line over and over again until it sinks into your head. Reading it quickly is not a waste of time either, but the greatest effect will be achieved when it is read slowly and allowed to penetrate your mind, ultimately becoming a part of your personality. If you learn *Mesillas Yesharim* this way, it will be rather difficult to finish it many times in one *z'man*.

Q&A *Is it a sin if a person deprives himself of sleep and subsequently suffers from exhaustion?*

Each person is responsible for taking care of his body and must therefore make it his business to get enough sleep. It is possible to be well rested even if the little one is up at night; simply ask someone to watch the child for a half-hour each day, and during that time go to sleep. A half-hour of sleep a day is a *yeshuah*! On occasion, a person may need to sleep more than a half-hour during the day. It is up to you to save your life, so preserve your health by getting a sufficient amount of sleep.

Q&A *What should a person think about on his birthday?*

He should think about a great many things. I look back at the years of my life, and I can recall so many people who passed away at young ages, *nebach*. I had a friend who passed away at the age of 14. I had another friend who wasn't much older when he left the world. A person owes a great deal of gratitude to Hakadosh Baruch Hu and must thank him profusely for allowing him to reach another birthday! Don't make a party, just think about how indebted you are to Him. The older a person gets, the more of an obligation he has to thank Hakadosh Baruch Hu and serve him! It's also important to realize that time is passing you by! The wealth of time that was before you when you were young is quickly depleting! The older you get, the less time you have to accomplish in life, and there are so many things to achieve in this world. For example, you could learn one *Ketzos HaChoshen* every week. As the years go by you will become a *baki*, an expert in the *Ketzos*! Do you have any idea what kind of happiness that is? I guarantee you, it's true happiness!

Therefore, as years go by you should take it upon yourself to try to achieve as much as you can. The happiness of life stems from the fact that it is such a wonderful opportunity to achieve.